Helen Holdredge

THE WOMAN

IN BLACK

THE LIFE OF LOLA MONTEZ

G. P. Putnam's Sons

New York

Preface

LOLA MONTEZ has long interested me. This interest, dating from my girlhood, when I read a fascinating article about her in the Portland *Oregon Journal*, gradually grew through the years as I read, one by one, the books and articles which were published about her.

Reading thus, I became aware that succeeding books added little or no new material to those previously published.

My own experiences in research and my success in uncovering new material where none was expected to exist led me to doubt that all new and unpublished material upon the subject of Lola Montez had been exhausted. In this frame of mind I visited Grass Valley, California, for the purpose of collecting material for my books on Mammy Pleasant and her partner, Thomas Bell. When local people, whom I contacted there, directed my attention to the former home of Lola on Mill street, I visited it. While few of Lola's possessions remained, the walls which once housed her and the doors through which she passed and the windows looking out upon the trees which she planted filled me with compassion for the misunderstood woman who had sought here a life of peace and an escape from tragedy.

Thus impelled, I began to make inquiries and to talk of the possibility of writing the life of this mysterious woman, whose unmatched beauty bewitched the leading men of her time, and upon whom the attention of the world was breathlessly fixed as she moved through her capricious career.

I was only mildly surprised by the immediate discovery of abundant new material.

Sacramento, California,

H. H.

*Illustrations will be found
following page 150.*

Acknowledgments

The author is deeply grateful to the following persons:

Mr. Allan Ottley, the head of the California Room of the State Library for unlimited help with research, and to his assistant, Miss Margaret Dennison.

Miss Caroline Wenzel, the retired head of the California Room for the use of her extensive collection of items on Lola Montez. It is due to the search for material on Lola that the truth of Lola's death is revealed.

Mr. Andy Rogers of the town of Rough and Ready for his large collection of research material on Lola Montez.

Mr. James de T. Abajian of the California Historical Society for his generous assistance and interest.

Mrs. Helen Giffin of the Society of California Pioneers of San Francisco for her very able assistance.

Mrs. Grace Taylor Dean and her assistants of the Sacramento City Library for looking up many references.

Miss Nora Evans of Mill Valley, and her brother Perry Evans of Berkeley, for their anecdotes about Lotta Crabtree, who stayed with their grandparents, the Robert T. Ryans of Oroville.

Mrs. William Ely Chambers of New York for material on her grandfather, John Hamilton Still.

Mr. Lew Lengfeld of San Francisco for the books given to me about the San Francisco theatre and especially for the autobiography of Lola Montez.

Mrs. Marilyn De Lano Novack, of Newcastle, for her collection on Lola Montez.

Mr. Lester Clark, publisher of the *Nuggett* of Nevada City, for use of his material on Lola Montez.

Mr. Lewis Ferbraché of San Francisco for the assistance given me in locating letters and pictures.

Mr. William C. Glackin of the *Sacramento Bee* for the use of pictures owned by that newspaper.

Mr. Robert Nesbitt of Washington, D. C., for anecdotes about Queen Victoria, Mr. Nesbitt's ancestor being Thomas Hadley, who had a vested right during the reign of that queen.

Mr. Noel Stevenson of Sacramento for sending me items upon the subject of the biography.

Mr. Walter Pieloch of the New York City Police for his help in locating the site of the house in which Lola died.

THE WOMAN IN BLACK

I

INSIDIOUSLY through the theatre that night there spread a whispered rumor that the notorious Lola Montez was present in one of the boxes. Scarcely anyone credited this, least of all George Sand and Victor Hugo, who were both in the audience and who were close friends of hers. As the performance of the ballet *La Filleule des Fées* continued, from every part of the house men slipped out of their seats to make a tour of the theatre. Pulling back the curtains of each box they peered in at the occupants, seeking through the dimness to discover if Lola was really attending the play. A lady who resembled the celebrated dancer was at last discovered, but she was in a second-tier box, and this settled the question in the minds of many of the curious. Others, still convinced that it might be she, hung about on the staircase; still other gentlemen, some of them joined by their ladies, loitered in the lobby on the chance that they might yet see her if the report proved to be true.

Their reward was slim. Just before the play ended the lady emerged from her box and, without pausing, hurried down the staircase, elbowing her way among the men crowding the steps. The dandies of Paris had only a quick vision of her unceremonious attire, deliciously negligée, the gown cut low to accentuate her voluptuous bosom, the well-formed thighs pushing against the silk of the skirt as she descended lightly on tiny feet. But to everyone's disappointment the lady's face was covered by a black veil, and the question of whether she was really Lola Montez remained unanswered.

As if drawn by a magnet the throng moved toward the portico, only to have their quarry escape. In defiance of the cold rain and muddy streets on this night of November 24th, 1849,

3

the mysterious figure fled down the rue Lepeletier to seek her carriage, not waiting for it to be brought to the entrance of the theatre.

The crowd was now sure that it was indeed La Montez who had soiled her satin slippers in order to elude them, for as they watched they saw her hurl her reticule at the head of her slumbering driver, an action only too characteristic of the noted danseuse.

By next day speculation was rife in the newspapers, and Eugène Guinot of *Le Siècle* published the story that Lola had attended a dinner at Montmorenci, given by a very eccentric and wealthy gentleman who had invited twenty celebrities to his villa to meet her.

She had been the subject of more newspaper copy than had ever been written about any one woman, and her reputation was already legendary. Everyone knew she abhorred convention, obeyed only the dictates of her desires, and followed a road blazoned with triumphs and tragedies.

The more vicious Paris gossips said she had had so many lovers that a centipede could not count them on his appendages. A caustic journalist observed that if she could not ever be quite a lady of quality, she at least achieved notice as a lady of quantity—meaning, he added, that she had four horses to draw her carriage even after successive revolutions in France had made it indiscreet to have more than two.

Whatever the number of her lovers—sometimes she herself admitted to difficulty in remembering them and several times claimed as lovers gentlemen she had never even met—it was said that they had to be either of royal blood, of political importance, or as famous in some way as she was infamous. Two of her scandalous affairs had rocked the Continent, yet she had but to move upon a scene to arouse extraordinary interest. Men and women alike gazed with hypnotized intensity at her beauty, which court painters had sought in vain to capture on canvas. And consciously or not, she dressed in the dramatic style of the doomed heroines of history, in dead black, collared about the

4

throat in white like Mary Queen of Scots on her way to the scaffold, or, again, like a woman whose lover was about to be lowered into his tomb. Her head was draped magnificently with black lace over the raven, copper-tinted curls hanging to her shoulders. A camellia, crimson as the blood of her one true love, whom all Paris knew had been killed in a duel, nestled in her hair. Only black, worn thus plainly, could throw into relief her wasp waist, the magnificent curve of her bosom, the startling and enormous dark blue eyes, black fringed. Her face, white-skinned and perfectly oval, had a straight nose and intelligent brow, with sensuous lips finely chiseled. The eyes were quick and flashing, yet the expression of the face was baffling, noble, proud without disdain.

Lola Montez, then also known as the Countess Landsfeld, was above all a woman of mystery. So little of her past had been exposed that in the cafés and drawing rooms of Paris, wherever people gathered to gossip, there was endless speculation about her parentage, her birthplace, and even arguments about whether her latest lover, George Trafford Heald, was actually her husband or not. At least he was known to have provided her with a seemingly inexhaustible supply of splendid jewels, which she usually wore one at a time, and with the magnificent yet simple gowns that shamed the currently over-dressed fashion.

Rumors about Lola had spread, growing more distorted as they were carried from one gossip to another. Some were sure she had been born in Turkey, others said India. One version insisted that she was the daughter of Montes, the Spanish bullfighter, although when Montes heard the tale he was said to have declared that he was flattered that a woman whose beauty, wit, and reputation were the talk of Europe should be thought to be his issue and only regretted that truth forced him to deny it.

Far more acceptable to the gossips was the story that she was the illegitimate daughter of the British poet Lord Byron and a young Scottish washwoman whom he had enticed into his bed at his ancestral home, Newstead Abbey. Certainly Lola looked like Byron, with his curling hair and sweeping eyelashes over blue eyes, but the more wordly-wise knew that she could not possibly have been born at the early Newstead period in Byron's life. At the time Lola was born Byron had had a mistress, but she was an Italian countess, credited with only one pregnancy which, somewhat to Byron's amazement, ended in a miscarriage two weeks after he had established his initial relationship with her. It was a slight inconvenience and nothing more.

Lola Montez herself had given out vague hints of her noble parentage and sometimes claimed that she had been stolen from her crib by gypsies who taught her to dance and sing but never revealed the identity of her parents until their death. At other times she said she had learned to dance in Spain, where she had gone to visit her relatives, the Montalvos.

Whatever her beginnings, her real story very definitely began in 1844 after she had toured Saxony, Prussia, Russia and Poland as a dancer. When she later wrote an autobiography she described this period as being full of exciting adventures with kings and queens, princes and counts, although there was never a word of confirmation from any of the royal persons she claimed to have known.

She said she had been invited to dance before the King and Queen of Prussia at their summer palace and that she had danced before the Emperor of Russia. She also declared that she had been proposed to by the Russian prince Schulkoski, and later by Count Alexander Owinsky, and that finally she had been invited to become the mistress of Prince Ivan Pashewich of Poland, a sixty-year-old reprobate who was, according to her, "a horrible sight. He looked just like a death's-head."

There were undoubtedly *affaires de coeur* with royal patrons of the many theatres where she had appeared, for such gaiety and beauty as was hers could not have gone undesired, but whatever had happened in this interlude remained unrecorded except in her own vague version.

The most important incident during this period was her meeting with the composer and pianist, Franz Liszt. He was on a concert tour when Lola encountered him in Dresden, and she was playing at the Court Theatre there. She attended his concert and afterwards remained in the hall to meet him.

The burning eyes of the passionate Hungarian studied her for a long moment and it seemed that the decision to possess her was made in that instant.

"As an artist you have no equal," she said tritely, as he held her hand in a fervent and prolonged clasp.

Soon they were able to move away from the others who had waited to greet him. They were observed whispering together, oblivious of the crowds around them, and Lola was heard to say, "I think I am drawn to you more because I feel you are one man who understands women. And I am greatly misunderstood."

He nodded. "I do understand," he said, and again his eyes held hers.

Only a few hours later, her body stripped of the clothes that hid its superb beauty, Lola sought to achieve the heights of passion which Liszt so obviously enjoyed. One of his biographers, Cameron Rogers, said that Liszt was tired of the kind of "tepid" surrender he had experienced with the romantic ladies who sought to ensnare him for their couches. Liszt admitted to a complete satisfaction with Lola, fascinated as much by her intellect as by her body, and never discreet, told other mistresses of his delight in her. But contemporaries who knew both Lola and Liszt were not in agreement as to why the affair was so short-lived. Some said Lola loved Liszt but suffered some disappointment which caused her to leave him, while others claimed Liszt resented the amount of time he spent with her which he felt should have been devoted to his music.

Lola herself gave only an inkling of her own emotions. She later insisted that this was actually only the second time that she had accepted a lover and that she had done so in an effort to experience the passion for which she longed. She remained unsatisfied, however, and attributed this to the fact that at the age of fourteen the first man to enter her life had ravished her. The terror of that night remained with her, returning each time to drive her to final flight.

She had not, of course, had all the lovers she was credited with, nor did she desire sexual experience with every man who sought her favors. In fact, she was apt to grow exceedingly uneasy under the frankly lascivious glances of would-be lovers, as her loyal friend, Mary Ann Crabtree, subsequently affirmed when they met in California.

There were times when she hated the results of her own beauty, when she became despondent and wondered if she suffered from the same mania as the Italian princess who at twenty-six had died of exhaustion due to her sexual excesses. Had she been subjected to religious influence, Lola might have sought retreat in a convent. Since no such determining factor had entered her life, she went her uninhibited way searching frantically for a love that would satisfy her.

In spite of her lack of response to Liszt's passion she managed to capture some happiness, and shared with him an intellectual companionship. When he played she sat near him, spellbound by his brilliant tapestry of tone, full of abandonment at one moment, then slipping into measures subtly derisive and sinister. He told her of his childhood, when he had gone to listen to the gypsies near his home. After they had mended the pots for the women of the city and shod the horses for the men, they danced to the music of violins and cymbals. "Do not fall in love," said one of the gypsies. "Enjoy your passions." He seemed never to have forgotten their advice. He had been intrigued, too, with the story of Dr. Faustus, and from his study of the magician's powers had come the mocking and diabolic quality in his compositions.

Yet Liszt's music, including the sonata written to Lola herself, had far less influence on her life than his attitude toward the times in which he lived and his selection of friends.

While they were in Dresden Liszt wished to hear Wagner's *Rienzi* conducted by Reissiger, whom he had known formerly

8

in Paris. Liszt persuaded the director to give a special performance for him. Nothing like *Rienzi* had been heard before—it was Wagner's own conception, a mammoth opera which lasted for six hours. The leading singers of Germany, Schroeder-Devrient and Tichatschek, had been engaged; to the singers who performed it, it was "heavenly," and to the audience of the opening night spellbinding, despite its fantastic length; not a single person among the brilliant audience who attended failed to remain until the final curtain fell.

It was unlikely that Liszt, whose triumphs had included a torchlight procession in Budapest when twenty thousand of his admirers followed his carriage, allowed himself to be seen. To have shown himself at all would have detracted from the rapt attention of the audience, who had found a new composer of titanic proportions in Richard Wagner.

Somewhere out of sight in the darkness of one of the boxes Liszt, with his classical face, striking profile, and deep-set brilliant eyes, sat with Lola at his side. Together they watched the opera with its Roman setting unfold. Its dramatic sweep and powerful melodies expressed the first rebellious political protests of Wagner and friends of his like Liszt, the plot featuring escape from bondage, the rebellion of the poor against the rich, and, in the mood of the French Revolution, the Republicanism which was now spreading throughout Europe.

When it was over Wagner hurried to greet Liszt, and the two great musicians stood clasping each other's hands in an emotional silence. Liszt, without words, welcomed a new recruit into the company of immortals to which he himself already belonged. Wagner, however, was not yet a complete convert to the overthrow of convention which marked the current revolt of the Parisian intellectuals among whom Liszt moved. When he was introduced to Lola Montez he displayed coldness, even hostility, and later described her as a woman with "bold, bad eyes."

A week after the performance of *Rienzi* Liszt was angered at Lola for taking up too much of his time. She was now occupying his Dresden hotel suite and an impatient remark by Liszt provoked a quarrel. Suddenly remorseful, Lola said that she was tired and would take a nap. "Good," replied Liszt. "I will take a walk."

When Liszt left he locked the door behind him, and as his coachman opened the carriage door for him the composer said, "It is true that I understand women. I have already paid for the furniture she will break when she discovers my absence."

Lola was furious at his desertion, but months later, continuing her dancing tour, she received a message from Liszt asking her forgiveness and inviting her to attend a music festival with him. She agreed to go with him to Paris, and by taking her there at that particular time, Franz Liszt gave her to history.

In Paris they parted, for Liszt had gone to visit Chopin. Lola, who was looking for an engagement to dance, then encountered Vandam, author of the popular book *An Englishman in Paris.*

According to Vandam, Lola told him she had come to the French capital to "hook a prince"—a statement probably as apocryphal as his story that Lola, encountering difficult times, had gone to Belgium in order to attract the attention of King Leopold but had ended by "singing in the streets of Brussels," whence she was rescued by a German who took her to Warsaw.

Be that as it may, Vandam, although he had designs on Lola, foolishly decided that she must meet the playwright, Alexandre Dumas. Vandam had, for the moment, forgotten that Dumas had once bragged that all beautiful women were like fortresses; when besieged they must surrender. With each new conquest he had new and authentic material for a novel. His love affairs were therefore mere tools, while his books, intended for immortality, engaged almost his entire interest. But at that time Lola, too, liked episodic love, and had recently expressed her rebellion by proclaiming, "I am subject to my whims and sensations alone."

Dumas, large, full of humor, still handsome in 1844, had inherited the crisp dark hair and dusky skin of his father, a general under Napoleon who was known as the Black Devil in the French army because of his Negro blood and compelling heroism. Dumas's forthright pride in his background elicited the respect he received.

His affair with Lola was brief and very nearly went unrecorded because he had so many mistresses and because of Lola's capriciousness. Perhaps it was only for a night or two that she shared his bed, listened to his characteristic quotations from the poets, and quaffed wine with him amid the rose petals strewn beneath her on his couch, which he called "my theatre designed for the act of love."

Subsequently she played at the Porte Saint-Martin Theatre and was besieged by a host of noted men who were attracted to her charms. Only the women in the audience were divided against her; their only defense being to urge their husbands to hiss her. Claiming that the men would not disapprove of her "if left to themselves," the tempestuous Lola declared that wives feared her because she "spoiled their trade," and one evening, when the hissing was sufficient to cause a fiasco, danced close to the footlights and gave battle in a daring way against which wives could never hope to compete. She lifted a beautiful leg, and holding it in the air, calmly peeled off her garter and threw it into the audience. The recipient of this trophy held it aloft in triumph amidst the shouts of the gentlemen present.

All Paris heard of this flagrant exhibition and Lola, an indifferent dancer at best, was able to obtain an engagement at the Opéra, where she drew a masculine audience that fully appreciated her animation and her ardor, in spite of her inattention to the precise beat of the music to which she danced.

Even Vandam, who had not seized his opportunity for an intimate relationship with her and was now quite bitter about it, was amazed at the total capitulation of her masculine audience. "Men raved and kept raving about her," was his comment. They threw extravagant bouquets at her feet, sent her costly presents, wrote poetry in her honor, and unsuccessfully tried to enlist her interest in themselves.

For in spite of her interest in Dumas, whom she declared to be "the most brilliant conversationalist I have ever met," she now returned alone to her room at night.

II

LOLA, who needed only the plainest of dresses and a flower in her hair to be the most outstanding beauty in Paris, next moved into the company of Théophile Gautier, who, as drama critic for *La Presse,* had seen her on the stage but hitherto had not made her aquaintance; of Joseph Méry, novelist and poet; of Théodore de Banville, writer of verse comedies; of Victor Hugo, one of the great novelists and poets of the time; of Honoré de Balzac, who had already started his immortal classic *La Comédie Humaine;* of George Sand, the unexcelled woman novelist; of George's lover, Frédéric Chopin; of Ferdinand Delacroix, French painter and the creator of the romantic trend in contemporary painting; of Father Felicité Lamennais, priest and philosopher whose freedom of thought was castigated by the French clergy.

It was in George Sand's drawing room that these people gathered and it was Alexandre Dumas who first took Lola Montez there. Returning many times thereafter, Lola had repeated opportunities to observe not only Sand but all those who surrounded her during the remainder of that winter in Paris. Nowhere else, wrote Lola in her autobiography, could "so many women of wit and genius" be found in the company of literary men; but to the dancer, George Sand was the most remarkable. Lola described her as "a large, masculine, coarse-featured woman, but with fine eyes, and open, easy, frank and hearty" manners toward her friends.

Almost at once Lola observed that George Sand, or Aurore as her friends called her, could not be drawn into an aimless and barren conversation. Let the interchange take a serious turn and Aurore earnestly introduced her theories on politics and economics. She was a champion of the rights and privileges of lesser people; she was against the concentration of wealth in the hands of one group; against the control of government by politicians instead of statesmen; and she was especially disdainful of the enforced continuance of unhappy marriages.

Her passionate conviction that the law of right and not the laws of clerics should prevail in such circumstances may in part have derived from the fact that she was herself the victim of a hateful marriage from which she had withdrawn, to engage in a series of affairs which everyone discussed. Discretion was not one of her virtues, and she advertised her liaisons by such dramatic gestures as cutting off her long and beautiful hair to send to the poet, Alfred de Musset, when her infidelities with his doctor brought about a rupture between them.

Several years later, Aurore had snatched from Countess Marie d'Agoult, a woman of intellectual pretensions, the young, frail, sorrowful-eyed Frédéric Chopin toward whom the countess had begun to display a protective friendship. At Chopin's suggestion they went to Majorca, where they shared a suite converted from deserted cells in a partly ruined Carthusian monastery, and here, in spite of Sand's children and sulky servants, howling winds and intermittent fogs, Chopin worked hard. But by the end of winter, he was wretched for the comforts of civilization and complained bitterly that his sexual pleasures were curtailed.

Concerned for his delicate health, Sand returned with him to Paris, where they occupied separate apartments in the same house in the Cour d'Orléans. It was here, where people of the theatre were free to go uninvited, that Lola Montez found a brilliant and erratic company. Her hostess gave her little or no attention but, amazingly enough, observed and imitated her style of dressing: Sand suddenly appeared in black, a veil over her heavy, dark hair secured on one side by a flower.

In the beige-colored salon of Aurore, with its elegant hangings and rich rugs, Lola set aside her reputation for witty conversation and assimilated the social theories expounded by this company of intellectuals into which a stray dancer had been permitted to wander.

Of all these people, Lamennais undoubtedly had the most important influence on her. Originally a fanatic who had proposed crushing the barriers to any freedom of thought outside of the Church, it had been his contention that such freedom led to atheism and he believed that governments in Catholic countries should be placed under ecclesiastical authority. But although he had been acclaimed by some of the younger members of the laity, the older and more experienced leaders of his church refused to countenance such intolerance, and Lamennais was restrained when he proposed that all basic laws established by royalty be renounced. He was, said the leaders of his church, proposing theocratic government by another approach, and when he established a paper, *L'Avenir*, to promote his ideas, the bishops of the Church retaliated by issuing a condemnation of his ideals. Finally Lamennais had withdrawn from the Church and was now determined to combat the clergy in any governmental control they might try to exercise.

Lola listened to him expound his beliefs with powerful effect, and not too far hence the whole world was to look on in amazement as she put these ideas into practice and caused a king to lose his throne.

But aside from such matters of moment, the wits in George Sand's drawing room enjoyed telling scandalous stories about each other. Sometimes, wrote Lola, even their hostess did not escape if she happened to be out of the room or absent when they took over her salon. Lola learned that Liszt and George Sand had once run away to Switzerland together, leaving his mistress Madame d'Agoult behind to share the company of her aged husband and children, whom she regarded with the boredom a female cat displays toward a litter of half-grown kittens. In a move to regain her lover from Sand's predatory fervor, the Countess d'Agoult challenged the latter to a duel, "the weapons to be finger-nails." Liszt had locked himself up in a closet in Sand's house to get out of the way, and when one of his men friends rescued him from this retreat, emerged shuddering and asked the man to take charge of his body after the victor had finished with him.

Lola afterwards delighted in repeating this story, embellishing it with such details as that the aged Count d'Agoult, who was such a book-worm that he seldom emerged from his library, once searched out his children to introduce them to a guest, and having imagined that there were only two, discovered that there were five and blandly presented them as "my wife's children." Three of them were, of course, hers by Franz Liszt.

So involved with each other's lives were the various members of the group that it was next to impossible to tell who was the mistress of whom at any given moment. Madame Hugo was coveted by the large-headed, blue-eyed, infantile-looking critic, Sainte-Beuve, and according to Lola's account, Hugo's wife did not look at her would-be lover with disdain. But five pregnancies in as many years had made her something of a realist; what advantage was there in exchanging a husband for a lover? Sainte-Beuve lost his head with frustration and distributed among his friends a book of verse called *Le Livre d'Amour* in which he implied that he had enjoyed Adele Hugo's favors, but not even his enemies believed that he had received anything more than a wary smile from her.

For his part the virile Hugo, with his intelligent brow, intense eyes and luxuriant hair, did not lack for other interests. In spite of being in love with his romantic wife, Hugo found time for the dreamy-eyed and passionate actress, Juliette Drouet.

Marriage was taken even less seriously by Alexandre Dumas. As Lola related it, his marriage "was an act of flight from a creditor." The lady was Ida Ferrier, an actress of little talent and devoid of beauty, "but," Lola loved to relate, "her father was a broker to whom poor Dumas owed immense sums of money." In order to avoid going to jail, Dumas had married the broker's daughter, in the presence of such eminent witnesses as Vicomte François Chateaubriand, the French writer, and Roger de Beauvoir, poet and novelist, whose fame in the boudoir brought him more bounty than his writings. Dumas was said to have been astonished when he later surprised his bride in de Beauvoir's embrace. As Lola related it, Dumas silently regarded his friend for some moments before giving vent to the comment, "Good heavens! And he isn't even obliged to!"

De Beauvoir seemed to have had a habit of making use of whatever came his way, for although he had the reputation of being wealthy, and perhaps was, he spent money recklessly. Lola described him as being "always dressed like a Cupid taken out of a band-box," although he was in continual trouble with his creditors, and Lola regarded him as "nothing less than a genius" for the way he got out of his embarrassments. Even the most obnoxious creditor was more anxious to say he had been entertained in George Sand's salon than to collect his account, and de Beauvoir could get almost any of his debts cancelled by taking a pressing creditor to the house in the rue d'Orléans. The socially ignorant creditor imagined that a special invitation had been arranged and felt well repaid for having met the most famous celebrities in Paris.

It is amusing to speculate how Lola's alleged father, Lord Byron, would have reacted to a society "that gathers around such wits and men of genius," as Lola wrote. Byron had confessed that he had "left an assembly filled with all the great names of *haut-ton* in London, and where little but names were to be found, to seek relief from the *ennui* that overpowered me, in a cider cellar." In saving himself from such dullness, and seeking his cellar, Byron, in his own words, had found "more food for speculation than in the vapid circles of glittering dullness I had left."

The only dullness that could assail Lola was George Sand's annual summer departure with Chopin for her family home, the Château de Nohant, on an island off the coast of Brittany. She took with her all the guests that her house there could hold, with the usual sprinkling of people from the theatre.

But Lola was left behind, well saturated with ideas of socialism and democracy, mingled with a growing dislike for the privileges of the wealthy and the clergy, which she felt fully prepared to act upon.

Fortunately for Lola neither Théodore de Banvillé nor Théophile Gautier joined the exodus into the country. And also fortunately, her reputation remained stainless among the remaining company, for no one at the time knew of her affair with Dumas, and Liszt, although he had brought her to Paris, had departed immediately, so that his name had not been connected with hers.

So impressed was Gautier with her appearance upon the stage that he not only gave her space in *La Presse* by describing her beauty, but also wrote that she danced with "abandon and fire." Banvillé attended the theatre only for the pleasure of seeing her. Nor was she merely noticed among the dancers by these two, but another drama critic began to write so extravagantly of her that she won a solo dance for herself, and the young blades of Paris stormed the theatre to view her ravishing beauty, toss bouquets at her feet, and wait at the stage door to see her emerge. It mattered to no one that her dancing was full of deficiencies.

One night Gautier was accompanied to the theatre by M. Alexandre Henri Dujarier, the literary critic of *La Presse*, who was also a half owner of the paper. It was a night when Lola's garter slipped down her beautiful leg—a trick that had gone over well in the days before her career had been endangered by the hissing of hostile ladies. Tonight she had the audience for her own, and Dujarier, during one of her curtain calls, caught a prolonged glance from her enormous eyes and held it. In that instant he fell madly in love with her.

Dujarier was handsome, with straight seal-brown hair untouched by the curling iron, gray-green eyes, a wide intelligent brow, a strong nose, a wide mouth with an impish upturn at the corners, and a fine chin indented with a cleft. He was inclined to impetuosity, sometimes given to irascibility, but was usually uproariously gay. Beneath this mischief he was a man of extraordinary accomplishments, although he was but twenty-nine years old.

In spite of his instantaneous infatuation with Lola, he did not risk a loss of dignity by awaiting her at the stage door. He waited, instead, until circumstances brought about an introduction. It was Claudin who introduced them, one evening when Lola, surrounded by the poet Méry, Gautier, and Sue, the famous French novelist who had recently published his tremendously successful book, *Mystères de Paris*, sat in the Café de Paris, the haunt of the literary world. Her group was joined by François Guizót, Premier of France, that night.

Balzac, after a long session of writing, had also emerged upon the boulevard in search of ideas and had come to the café, but he did not sit down with them when he saw Sue. He scorned the company of the novelist and was credited with the remark that "Sue is all that remains of his grandfather's disgusting skin disease."

Lola had been with these men upon a number of occasions and she was said to hold her own as a wit and intellectual among them. This did not surprise Dujarier, since she would not have otherwise been invited to share this entirely masculine company. As appears from letters written about her a number of years before, Lola was always considered to be brilliant by the women who knew her, but she was also thought to be too giddy to be taken seriously. Now that she had spent a winter among a company of intellectuals, unconcerned with mere social success and amusement, she had developed a more mature mind and an ability to reason as well as to probe thoughtful considerations about politics, the monarchy, Republicanism, and priestly interference in government. Although nothing remains of these discussions at the Café de Paris, much of her idealism is preserved in her letters.

Dujarier had heard of Lola's gaiety, seen her beauty, and was curious about her much-admired intelligence. He sought her friendship first without seeking her love. To ladies of the stage he was given to bold and outrageous statements, predicated upon the reputations of those whom he singled out. These allusions were designed to give the impression that he was enjoying sin in the fashion of the moment, a period when those who were Paris-born were supposed to show no enthusiasm for spending their nights in their beds alone, and were not expected to hide their amatory experiences behind a mist of discretion. Actually Dujarier shrank from such behavior. Extremely restrained for that day and age, he was naturally incited to anticipation when he saw a beautiful woman whom he knew he could have for the taking, but he did not hurry. Instead, he often wavered and withdrew from the definite approach expected of him. The Bohemians among whom he lived appalled him with their whirlwind of emotion and advertised virility and led him, as came out later in a court trial, not to imitation, but to an analysis of his own emotions and to discrimination and independence. In spite of his speculative glances he was actually censorious, and this in turn kept him abstinent. In the end, although with some reluctance, he had acquired a mistress who complained that she saw little of him.

In this wary man, so conscious of the defects of the women about him, Lola Montez's uneasiness when men hungrily looked at her must have aroused interest. Never before had a man seen her as she really was, her defense of intellectualism oddly at variance with her smooth white skin set off by rich silk or velvet gowns and lace headdresses. Later she told of carrying a fan as a defense against men who took it for granted that all actresses were immoral. Dujarier is supposed to have noticed that when men pressed too close to her, she took umbrage and imperturbably pushed masculine hands aside before they touched her. The lace headdress, too, Lola later described to intimate friends as a defense. Men were in the habit of kissing actresses on the shoulders, close to the sides of the throat. The entanglement of lace and curls about Lola's shoulders kept them from indulging this custom with her, just as her close-fitting dresses with their Byronic collars vanquished the more intimate investigations which some men found amusing when paying court to her fellow performers.

Dujarier detected that her coquetry and lively conversation, her concern to please everyone, and the magnificent taste and refinement of her dress were also for the purpose of insuring herself theatrical engagements in spite of her mediocre talents, of which she was fully aware.

He told her he was amazed at the brilliance of her mind. When he learned that she had for months been in the company of the intellectuals who crowded George Sand's salon, he said that she had not wasted her time while there.

So Lola settled down into friendship with Dujarier. She delighted in discussing politics with him, assimilating much of his magnificent command of the whole field of political science, which was to have a great deal to do with her future.

His love for her developed steadily and surely. It was not a wild storm, with the impatience of a conquest quickly sought. It was something that Lola had never before had in her life and it began with sentimentality; not with elegant bouquets thrown onto the stage under her dancing feet, but with a nosegay of dewy violets, which she loved, purchased from a flower vendor; or a pause to watch a puppet show on a Sunday afternoon spent strolling in some park—the whole subordination of passion to a succession of harmonious and conventional occupations designed to prove that nothing would ever be the same for them again were they separated.

Gentle breezes stirred the newly formed leaves upon the trees, the sunset brought colors never seen before, and Lola, reveling in the charms of nature of which until now she had scarcely been aware, reluctantly parted from Dujarier at the door of the theatre. There he removed her glove to press a chaste kiss in her warm palm, which she carried there like a precious gem until they could be together again. This memory stirred her throughout her life.

"Dujarier," wrote Lola, "spent almost every hour he could spare from his editorial duties with Lola Montez," for it amused her to write of herself in the third person.

Every day was memorable, enhanced by tenderness, by avowals of love. This was what Lola had wanted all her life and had never had. To her past she closed her mind because it had been cruel and hard.

She wished to be adored and idolized, to be the object of attention which she had never received. The theatre had been her answer. That it was only the attention that is given the notorious and scandalous she preferred to ignore. Any attention was better than none, better certainly than being continually hurt by a world in which she had searched in vain for love.

She, who on the threshold of life had been unprotected, had early employed defiance, as the forlorn must, to protect her heart and set aside her dreams. She ended in rebellion against convention, as George Sand had done, against the smugness of a society that arranged marriages, not with any looked-for compatibility between the young people involved, but solely for financial or material advantages. For these marriages "of the purse," as she called them, Lola had the utmost contempt and delighted in telling "laughable stories" to ridicule them. She often related the story of a peasant "who was about to lead to the altar a young bride, all blushes and muslin, when her father observed: 'Now I think of it, I must remind you that the great cherry tree in the orchard remains mine.' 'No,' said the bridegroom, 'it must be mine.' 'No,' said the father, 'it remains mine.' 'Well, then,' said the bridegroom, 'I will not marry your daughter.' And so the ceremony stopped."

Dujarier had found Lola, not in the company of courtesans, but surrounded by women who dared to espouse emancipation for their sex by taking lovers at will, and who refused financial support in order to maintain their hard-won independence and self-assertion. Marriage to them was a loss of privileges; alliance to a man exercising his prerogatives under the bonds of matrimony was regarded as the most undesirable existence imaginable.

It was this situation that now faced Lola Montez: Dujarier wanted to marry her. She became engaged to him, but although she postponed the marriage itself, a tremendous change came over her. The wild twistings and strainings against the circumstances of her unhappy life ceased, just as the corkscrew ceases winding when it has spiraled its way to the bottom of the cork. The unforseen circumstance of a happy marriage made her wish to abandon her past. She now wished to hold herself in check, to weigh every word she spoke and not give way to the ribald wit in which she had once delighted. Her behavior must be suited to her newly acquired dignity, every effort must be directed toward pleasing Alexandre so that he might be proud of her.

She had no desire to deceive him, yet she found he did not wish her past delivered up to him. Perhaps he knew about and was guided by the situation that had existed between Alfred de Musset and George Sand. De Musset had tortured Sand for every detail of her past, which, when at last she confessed it in its entirety, had served only to destroy their relationship permanently, leaving them with wounds whose scars they still felt.

Contentment was a new sensation and respectability had an enchantment that Lola had never imagined. She moved somewhat away from the authors she had known while George Sand's salon had provided her social life. Although Dujarier was a close friend of Honoré de Balzac, the latter was apt to be shut up with his writing for months at a time. Dumas, too, who was extremely fond of the literary critic of *La Presse*, went out but little and expected people to come to his quarters, where they made themselves quite at home whether Dumas found time to see them or not. Closer still to Dujarier in daily companionship was Joseph Méry who, because he wrote plays, liked to spend his time with people of the theatre, and even closer was Emile de Girardin, the editor of *La Presse*, who had always been very generous in giving space to Lola, although he had not always praised her dancing.

The company, according to Lola's account, consisted also of Mlle. Anne Mars, a comic actress without beauty but with great charm, who had been renowned in the plays of Molière but was now retired from the stage. In later years Lola described Mlle. Mars as having had, at this period, a lover less than half her age, the Count de Morny. Lola had seen him "hang over her chair,

23

as though he were about to dissolve into sighs: it was spring madly laying its head of flowers in the lap of winter." With them there was often Pauline Dejazet, another comedienne who, although she had a kind heart, would sacrifice any current lover for a witticism. A young nobleman delivered a present to her every evening and finally remarked that he would bring her a present every other day from now on. "Then," said Mlle. Dejazet, "come only every other day."

Also in the company was the famous Rachel who, said Lola, "loved nothing but money. She had no talent for conversation. She had indeed but one gift, that of delivery, of concentrated mimicry, in which she surpassed."

Rachel was most famous for her role as Camille, heroine of *La Dame aux Camélias*, which had been written by Alexandre Dumas fils and was based on the life of Marie Duplessis, the fascinating demimondaine who kept seven bureau drawers in her bedroom to hold the nightshirts of her seven lovers, but was finally deserted by them all and died of consumption. Her possessions, when sold at auction, were bought by prominent Parisian women who displayed a sentimental envy of her amorous career. Lola aptly commented that "vice had an ugly fashion of going naked in Paris."

Lastly there was Joseph Samson, head of the Comédie Française and Rachel's teacher. He was good-natured and full of jests but not enough impressed with Lola Montez's dancing to engage her for that celebrated theatre, although he always paid her court at social gatherings.

It was inevitable that in this easy-going company Lola, having so long postponed her marriage to Dujarier, should be suspected of merely trying to conceal their true relationship and of playing some game the nature of which was not immediately apparent. She had in fact become his mistress, but Dujarier still insisted that she should marry him. Lola was brimming over with a happiness she had never before enjoyed, for Dujarier gave her the tender affection she had looked for throughout her whole life. He was her idealized lover and she no longer wished to postpone the marriage, for she now knew that their sexual relationship was harmonious.

It was March, 1845, and they would be married in the spring after she had finished her contract at the Théatre de la Porte-Saint Martin. Dujarier demanded circumspection of her; they spent nearly all their nights together, since procrastination could not be borne, but Dujarier had developed a jealously protective attitude and would allow no other man to escort her anywhere. Neither would he allow her to associate with the lower class of actresses among whom she was thrown at the theatre.

One of these rowdy actresses, Anais Liévènne, gave a party at her home to which both Lola and Dujarier were invited, together with a number of authors, newspapermen and actresses. When Lola begged to go Dujarier refused to allow her to associate with such women, although it was really the celebrated writers that Lola was interested in meeting. Dujarier did not himself wish to go. As a journalist he was at the very top of his profession; Anais and her theatrical associates would scarcely have been invited to his apartments and he was extremely reluctant to accept an invitation from them. It had been Dujarier's intention to send his regrets close to the date of the affair, for it was generally known that he would renouce any social activity which might conflict with his newspaper work. But he delayed too long in sending the actress a note, and in the end felt obliged to attend the party.

It was the usual party of the Bohemian set, champagne toasts drunk from ladies' slippers, ribald jokes, almost naked bosoms, furtive hands slipped under petticoats, dainty fingers straying where they ought not to be, and eventually a cross-fire of aroused passions and jealousies. Dujarier, seated next to the hostess, made a vulgar remark to which Roger de Beauvoir took offense. The hostess was merely amused that de Beauvoir should show any instinct for decorum. Was there not that delicious story going the rounds at this time, that Dumas had come home unexpectedly to find Roger hiding in his dressing room and shivering so much with the cold that Dumas had invited him to crawl into bed with his wife to get warm?

During the party de Beauvoir in turn irritated Dujarier with his discussion of a story he had sent to *La Presse.* Dujarier's reply was cutting and conspicuously put de Beauvoir in his place: "There are more important writers than yourself."

When a great deal of champagne had been consumed, the party left Anais's residence for the Provençaux restaurant for dinner. As soon as this was over, the dinner table was removed and a table set up for a game of lansquenet, while the ladies retired to an adjoining room to dance with other gentlemen just arriving.

Jean de Beauvallon, a journalist from the rival paper *Le Globe,* moved forward to join Dujarier. He well knew that Dujarier did not like him and would eventually quarrel with him if given provocation. Dujarier's attitude toward de Beauvallon was predicated upon his knowledge that the rival newspaperman, a Creole from Guadeloupe in the West Indies, had been involved in a disgraceful affair of stealing. He did not now suspect, however, that de Beauvallon, motivated by a curious reason, was trying to antagonize him into fighting a duel.

De Beauvallon's sister was married to Granier de Cassagnac, who had once worked for *La Presse* and had borrowed heavily from the former owner of the paper, who had advanced him funds from the capital of the newspaper. When de Girardin and Dujarier had bought the paper in 1840, de Cassagnac's debt to the paper was somehow overlooked and it was not until later that Dujarier discovered it. When asked to pay, de Cassagnac ignored the demand and Dujarier and his partner secured a judgment against him. De Cassagnac was enraged and his wife furious at the damage to her social standing. Jean de Beavallon had promised his sister to get even with Dujarier.

De Cassagnac sought his own revenge by launching vindictive attacks on *La Presse* through *Le Globe,* which he now owned. He was at a disadvantage in this campaign because the journalistic talent of the staff of *La Presse* was far superior to that of

Le Globe. Lola later wrote that people dreaded "the scorching and terrible power" of Dujarier's pen.

Thus no advantage was to be gained by Dujarier's enemies unless de Beauvallon could provoke him into fighting a duel, as it was well known that Lola's beloved could handle neither sword nor pistol.

This was the situation that night when de Beauvallon moved forward to play lansquenet.

Both Dujarier and de Beauvallon, at the beginning of the game, had insisted upon raising the limit set by the banker by making a deposit of funds, Dujarier contributing twenty times more than de Beauvallon. When both men won more than the bank contained, de Beauvallon suggested that they take a loss so that the banker would not have to make it good. Dujarier refused and his position was upheld by the other players. At the end of the game Dujarier had lost to de Beauvallon and the latter asked for an immediate payment. De Beauvallon knew that Dujarier would be insulted, for he was practically accusing the editor of being a poor credit risk. Dujarier, as de Beauvallon had hoped, returned the insult; he borrowed the necessary sum from the owner of the restaurant, a circumstance that was noticed by everyone present.

De Beauvallon had now achieved just what he had been striving for. He had placed Dujarier in a position where he could be accused of having dealt out an unforgivable affront. De Beauvallon had made the most of the journalist's deteriorating temper and stated in measured tones that he would see him the next day.

Dujarier had no illusions about what was meant, and he awaited the outcome at the newspaper office the following morning. During the course of the day two callers made their appearance. The vicomte d'Ecquevillez and the comte de Fleurs were there, they announced, to serve as the seconds of de Beauvallon, who "demanded satisfaction."

Within a matter of hours the salons of Paris rocked with the news and everyone in the Bohemian world who spent his leisure time in the cafés had heard of the challenge. Everyone, in fact, heard of it but the person most concerned; people who knew Lola Montez refrained from telling her.

Dujarier named his friends Arthur Berrand and Charles de Boigne to act for him. He then left the newspaper office and went straight to Alexandre Dumas. All the impulsiveness, the irritability, and especially the effects of last night's liquor, had worn off, and the editor knew he had been fool-hardy, that he had been pushed into his present position by *force majeure*, and that in having allowed himself to show his dislike for de Beauvallon he had done exactly what the owner of *Le Globe* and his brother-in-law had hoped he would do.

In seeking out Dumas for help, Dujarier had selected a man who had the greatest loyalty to his friends; Dujarier wished to retreat from having to fight a duel and to Dumas he could admit it without the loss of his self-respect. But after listening to the account of the offense and reflecting upon what courses were open, Dumas told him that the matter could only be settled with his antagonist on the dueling ground.

"But I don't know what I am fighting about. It's a duel between *Le Globe* and *La Presse*, not between Monsieur Dujarier and Monsieur de Beauvallon."

Dumas told him that he had at least the choice of weapons, since he was the challenged person.

"I am not a swordsman and am a very poor marksman besides," Dumas was to quote Dujarier in the later trial over the matter. To Dumas's horror, Dujarier confessed that he had never even handled a dueling pistol.

Later Dumas went to Dujarier's apartments in an attempt to persuade Dujarier to select swords as the least dangerous weapons, but Dujarier, who had never handled a rapier, believed his chances were better with a pistol. Upon leaving, Dumas encountered Lola on the stairway, and was so overcome with emotion that he could only nod a greeting.

Dumas's visit had left Dujarier depressed. He had hoped that the author would say that an amicable settlement could be arranged, but Dumas had dashed all his hopes. He therefore received Lola in a spirit of melancholy, an attitude he sought to conceal, but the sight of her whom he so loved was agonizing. His inexperience with either swords or pistols made his cause seem hopeless, and his air of detachment and inaccessibility immediately alarmed Lola, for she had not the slightest idea of what caused it. Convulsively he drew her to him, winding his fingers in her curls and holding her against him so that she could not read the deep distress in his face, a memory which was to haunt her afterwards when she understood it. At the time she only sensed that some misfortune had overtaken him. This he was willing to acknowledge and he told her that he was to fight a duel with de Beauvoir, not daring to mention the name of such a formidable antagonist as de Beauvallon. Lola was satisfied and even amused. Well, then, why should he be upset? That silly band-box cupid! He could only fight a duel with love darts in some lady's boudoir. The matter was not worth a second thought, she decided. Relieved at the ease with which he had allayed her fears, he continued to conceal his agitation by talking of trivial matters, such as a press notice in which she had been praised for her dancing.

According to Dumas, Dujarier saw Lola home to her apartment in the rue Lafitte. In the carriage, with his arm about her, she soon forgot all else.

He promised to come to her in the morning, and Lola remained trusting and incurious. She was on the crest of a wave of calmness and peace, ready to submit to convention and to be done with the whirlwind of life of transient lovers. She needed no absolution from society once she was married to Alexandre Dujarier; he belonged, if not to the aristocracy, to that society of the cafés and theatres which was all that men of literature desired, except Balzac, who tortured himself by wanting more. As Madame Dujarier, Lola would have a salon where authors and newspapermen would gather and where the better class of actresses would be welcomed. She would be able to wear the most fashionable clothes and to have a carriage and jewels, for

Dujarier was a wealthy young man, not only with the investment in *La Presse*, but with capital invested in one of the leading theatres and in other equally profitable holdings. Only because she was bound by her theatrical contract, and therefore unable to leave Paris on a honeymoon until it was completed, did she delay the marriage.

March 11th, the day of the duel, was piercingly cold and dark. A howling wind swept across the snow-covered ground in the secluded portion of the Bois de Boulogne which had been selected for the settlement of this quarrel. Since Dujarier had chosen to use pistols, de Beauvallon's second, the vicomte d'Ecquevillez, had agreed to provide the weapons.

While Dujarier was trying to eat his breakfast, which his valet urged upon him, Lola's maid arrived with a message and he sent back word that he would be along very soon.

It was only seven, and Alexandre, being restless, went to the home of his second, de Boigne, to thank him for a review of Lola Montez's performance he had written. There he found not only his other second but de Beauvallon's seconds in consultation and drafting the agreement for the duel, one clause of which provided that one of the contestants should fire first. A coin was tossed to decide and the initial shot fell to de Beauvallon. Dujarier, having signed the agreement, returned home to find the doctor who was to accompany him awaiting his arrival.

In the company of his seconds and the doctor, Dujarier arrived at the appointed place and, dismounting from the carriage, stood about in the cold awaiting his antagonist. A half hour went by, then an hour. His seconds grew restless, then impatient, and finally demanded that he wait no longer, since his opponent had neglected to keep the engagement. Dujarier wrapped his cape more firmly about him and refused to abandon the field, although he would have been within his rights to reject a duel in which the challenger refused to put in an appearance. Doctor de Guise also protested that the period of waiting in the cold had given Alexandre a chill and he should not be made to continue, for he was now in no fit condition to fight. The challenged man refused to leave because he did not wish to be accused of cowardice.

An hour went by and a second hour of waiting had begun when the pale gleam of carriage lamps appeared in the distance and a few moments later sweating horses delivered the challenger and his seconds.

This tardiness should have aroused suspicion and Dujarier's seconds should have questioned the feeble explanation that de Beauvallon's seconds had been unable to procure ammunition. Alexandre's other second, Arthur Berrand, actually put his finger tip into the barrels of the weapons and found them to be blackened, yet accepted without question the flimsy excuse that one of de Beauvallon's seconds had fired several caps to see if the pistols were in working order. The prolonged interlude during which the challenger was occupying himself elsewhere should have suggested the reason but it was allowed to pass.

De Boigne made a final effort to bring about an amicable settlement of the quarrel.

"The position is the same as yesterday, when it was settled that we should fight," was de Beauvallon's adamant reply.

Even though Dujarier's other second discovered that the pistols had very likely been used just before the meeting, the vicomte d'Ecquevillez "on his honor" declared that they had never been in the hands of de Beauvallon.

Dujarier, in accepting his pistol, was so nervous that when he touched the trigger the weapon fired so close to de Boigne's head that had it been any closer it would have killed him. De Beauvallon must have been delighted at this show of nervousness and awkwardness, and he took his place with an expression of proud scorn and cold revenge on his face. Having been placed thirty feet from his opponent, Dujarier faced him. They both advanced the required six paces and the signal for de Beauvallon to fire was given. Dujarier lost his head, fired first and without aim, and the bullet whistled through the air at a safe distance from his challenger. Undisturbed, de Beauvallon took careful aim while Dujarier stiffened, hypnotized and stupefied. So deliberate was de Beauvallon that de Boigne, in fury, cried out, "Fire, damn you, fire!"

With a sure finger he pulled the trigger and Dujarier sank to the ground while the doctor rushed forward. He remained conscious for a time.

When he did not come to take her to the theatre as he had promised, Lola had begun to wonder if the duel was scheduled for that day. Then a messenger arrived with a note that Dujarier had written during the night.

> My dear Lola:
> I am going out to fight with pistols. This explains why I did not come to see you this morning. I have need of all my calmness. At two o'clock all, all will be over. A thousand embraces, my dear Lola, my good little wife, whom I love so much, and the thoughts of whom will never leave me.
>
> D.

Dazed with the shock of its contents, she sent for a carriage to take her to Dujarier's apartments a few blocks away on the same street. Alexandre's valet, Gabriel, was scarcely less nervous than herself. "My master will never return," was his gloomy prediction.

From there Lola went to Dumas's place to learn from him that the duel was at that moment taking place and that her lover was meeting de Beauvallon, not de Beauvoir.

"My God," she exclaimed in despair, "then he is a dead man!"

Dumas disclaimed any knowledge of where the duel was being fought, for he knew how impetuous Lola was. Besides, he had once seen her skill as a marksman at a shooting gallery to which he had taken her, and he knew that she was easily the equal of de Beauvallon. She declared that if she had known the true state of affairs she would have "prevented the duel," and Dumas knew her well enough to feel certain that she would either have thrown herself in front of Dujarier or seized the pistol from his hand and shot de Beauvallon exactly in the heart.

Should Dujarier be wounded or killed, he knew she would accuse de Beauvallon and his brother-in-law of carrying out a plot together to murder Alexandre Dujarier, nor would she rest until de Beauvallon was punished.

Since Lola could not learn the location of the dueling ground she returned to the apartments of her lover, where she alternately paced the floor of the reception room and ran down the stairs to look up the street. Of little help was Dujarier's valet, whose whole attitude was one of resignation; he was certain that his master was by now dead. Lola, in absolute despair, could not cease her trembling and shivered as if with a chill.

The trees prevented her from having a clear view of the street. Finally hoofbeats sounding below suddenly ceased and a carriage was brought to a stop. Lola dashed out of the room and down the stairs, sobbing uncontrollably as she unlatched and flung open the entry door. One of the seconds was opening the carriage and Dujarier fell forward, for the moment giving Lola the impression that he was uninjured and merely getting out of the vehicle. Then she saw the wound and the blood, already dried, on his forehead, and the fixed expression of his face. Before the seconds could bring the body into the house, Lola, with a cry of wild grief, threw her arms about her dead lover's shoulders and repeatedly rained kisses upon his fast chilling lips. Dujarier had died in the arms of the doctor a few minutes after being shot.

Lola herself wrote that she "received the corpse from the carriage, and made such preparations, with the help of his friends, for the funeral," as she was able to "under the crushing load of sorrow and despair" which weighed upon her.

III

When calmness finally came to Lola a terrible change took place. The only person in the world who had been genuinely devoted to her had been snatched away. She again returned to her solitary world, for the moment stupefied but finally convinced that it was her unhappy destiny to be forever a wanderer, to be set aside from the world of favorable circumstances, of stability and of self-respect. She must now return to the life where public attention was all important, where a woman's reputation, the moment she looked at a man, would be bandied about, where experience in love on her part would be taken for granted. She had been ready for regeneration, willing not to consort with the disreputable actresses Dujarier disliked. What an irony it was that if she had gone with Alexandre to the party, as she had begged to do, the duel might never have taken place! Accompanied by her, he would not have allowed himself to give way to irritations and she would have been able to prevent the crushing sarcasms he had delivered to de Beauvallon, who had deliberately taunted him.

All her restlessness returned and soon she was drawn back to her old life. She could not keep to the recently found path of propriety. Her lover could no longer help her. He lay in his coffin, destroyed at the age of twenty-nine by the vanity of a rival writer. She had given her heart to Alexandre Dujarier, the only man she had ever completely loved, and she did not want it back to give to someone else.

She turned once more to his letter in which he spoke to her from the silence of eternity. This was the love given to her forever. A legend of the ancient Greeks declared that every man had his own star which received his astral spirit when he died.

The still body lying in the coffin on draped trestles and surrounded by magnificent floral tributes, whose overpowering scents robbed the room of air, had no longer any meaning for her.

Years later in California, she tried to describe her belief in this idea to the small circle of friends who later surrounded her in Grass Valley—to Mrs. Mary Ann Crabtree, mother of the famous actress Lotta Crabtree; to her neighbor Mrs. Robinson; to her colored maid, Hyacinth Fhlerey, whom Lola called Periwinkle.

Dujarier, she said, had been received into a constellation in the sky, where his spirit awaited hers. He still existed for her, real as he had ever been. Her friends only vaguely understood what she meant. Over and over, she claimed, she was able to capture Dujarier's nearness to her at unexpected moments, and not always through the same medium. Sometimes, said Lola, he would be with her suddenly when she was listening to music; often, when the rains of spring showered the earth. Many times she captured his fleeting presence after a rainstorm in successive Aprils. She once found a clump of violets in the woods, hiding under the curling umbrellas of their foliage, and Dujarier seemed to be with her as if in memory of all the bouquets of violets he had given her in Paris. Once, just once, he came to her, she said, when she sat in the forest alone looking at some ferns, as yet uncurled as if they were testing the weather.

She did not want those she told to think that she was a believer in spiritualism. She insisted that the power to join with Dujarier in a divine moment when life and death were fused was a power within herself.

To her joy, when she met Periwinkle, the girl did not talk of trances, mediums, and their practices, or say that Lola was psychic when she mentioned being with Dujarier. Periwinkle alone in those later years knew why Lola wanted to walk in the woods alone, why music sometimes laid a spell upon her.

At the time of Dujarier's death, Balzac may have influenced Lola in her thinking. Certainly he tried to console her with one of his oft-repeated observations: "Heaven was not meant to be found on earth." Allegedly Lola replied to him: "Heaven I have just left and I must now return to Purgatory."

Lola now found herself an alien in Dujarier's quarters. Dujarier had a mother and two nephews who clung together in their sorrow, and who could not be expected to share this shocking misfortune with a woman who, although the affianced of Alexandre, was a stranger to them.

The funeral was held three days after Dujarier's death and the burial took place at the Montmarte cemetery. Balzac, Méry, and Dumas were among the pallbearers and the impressive funeral procession included some of the most famous men of Paris. So overpowering was the emotion shown by the mourners and so spent and weary the despairing figure of Lola Montez as, shadowed in veils, she leaned on the arm of one of Dujarier's close friends, that the story of the scene was repeated throughout the city and even penetrated the domestic circle of the "Citizen-King," Louis Philippe.

Three weeks later Lola returned to the theatre to continue playing *La Biche au Bois*. The gaiety and abandon with which she had previously danced seemed to be gone and during her solo dance there were again hisses at her inadequate performance. Lola turned in anger on the women in the audience and spoke abusively to them. The theatre manager did not condemn her. The men in the audience were solidly in her favor and they had a certain sentimentality toward her because of her bereavement. But Lola was unequal to the struggle against the criticism of her dancing, and for the time being she discontinued her career.

Dujarier had left her a considerable estate, she did not need to work, and she turned her attention toward de Beauvallon, hoping to bring him to account for his deed by legal means. A rumor was current in Paris that the pistols which de Beauvallon's second, d'Ecquevillez, had furnished had been warm when brought to the dueling ground, and this lent support to one man's story that he had seen de Beauvallon in the act of practicing just before the duel. Everyone was shocked, for this circumstance, if true, was not in accordance with established procedure in the code of duels. D'Ecquevillez denied any irregularity, saying that he had borrowed the pistols from a friend. The friend declared that his guns had been in the possession of his gunsmith until shortly before the combat, when they were taken directly to the dueling grounds. Here again there were denials. The gunsmith, a man of sound reputation, flatly denied having had possession of the pistols at any time. Both de Beauvallon and d'Ecquevillez got wind of the rumors and knew that charges would be brought against them. Precipitously they absented themselves, allegedly to Spain.

Then the police inquiry into the affair of the duel was, for some reason, dropped, and de Beauvallon and d'Ecquevillez, feeling safe, returned to Paris. They were immediately arrested and charged with murder, charges against them having been properly filed by Dujarier's widowed mother and her two nephews.

While de Beauvallon had been absent with his second, Lola, with Dujarier's friends, had been gathering the necessary evidence for the opening of the case against them. De Boigne, the second who had told Dumas that the dueling pistols were blackened, had fortunately shown the powder stains to the doctor before the duel. Authorities who were consulted on this point regarded it as absolute evidence that the pistols had been fired before the duel. In the light of this circumstance de Beauvallon's tardiness assumed a sinister aspect: he must have been practicing to assure his success in the duel. The irregularities in the procedure of the duel were nailed down so that the charge of willful murder could be brought against him.

Although a year had passed since the duel, the emotional state of the citizens of Paris over the incident was such that the French government decided to hold the trial at Rouen, where a more impartial jury might be obtained. When the trial opened, however, Parisians overflowed the packed courtroom like hot lava pouring over the sides of a volcano. Among them was Dumas, an expert on the dueling code, who would testify that it was an absolute rule that the contestants must use pistols unfamiliar to either of them.

This trial, which was to establish legal procedure for dueling trials, was to become famous in jurisprudence.

The case opened on Thursday, March 26, 1846, and was tried in the enormous Lawyer's Hall of the Palais de Justice. Inside the tightly packed room, with its fifty-foot ceiling and its great length of one hundred and sixty feet, the air was stuffy and the vast Gothic building was in danger of having some of its outside ornamentation knocked off by the spectators from Rouen who clung to every window. For their benefit the windows were opened, although this did little to alleviate the stifling interior.

Lola Montez, dressed in black, her face covered with a heavy veil which concealed her features from the gaze of the curious, presented a strong contrast to the judges in their robes of crimson.

In testifying, de Beauvallon now offered a new story of where the dueling pistols had been: the concierge of his apartment house had them in his keeping. The concierge, when called upon to substantiate this, was so taken by surprise that he could not rise to the occasion by affirming the lie, as he was expected to do in loyalty to a tenant. Embarrassed but truthful, he said he could not remember having had charge of the pistols at any time. De Beauvallon then tried to counteract the damage done by this fiasco, saying that he remembered having given the pistols to his second, d'Ecquevillez, and then, with a touch of hauteur, declared that the detail of where the pistols had been was unimportant.

When brought to the stand, d'Ecquevillez further confused matters by claiming he had never had charge of the pistols. No coherent facts could be wrung from him. He had finally to admit, however, that he was not a man of title but of peasant stock, masquerading as nobility.

All the people who had attended the party which brought

about the duel were put on the witness stand, but little was gained except entertainment for the spectators, who enjoyed seeing so many actresses from Paris so far away from the footlights.

Toward the beginning of the trial Dumas had been called. "When asked what his profession was," Lola wrote, "he made this remarkable and characteristic reply: 'I should call myself a dramatic poet, if I was not in the birthplace of Corneille.' This answer," recorded Lola, "touched the hearts of the audience."

From Dumas it was learned that Dujarier had made a pitiful effort to learn to shoot the evening before the duel, an effort which had occupied him so long that he had not called at the theatre for Lola. Dumas had asked his son to take Dujarier to a shooting-gallery where, as Lola afterwards related the story, "he was able to hit a mark as large as a man only twice in fourteen times, while his antagonist was one of the best shots in Paris."

Dumas was interested in the affair from the aspect of honor and chivalry. When he had given his testimony he hurried back to Paris, where one of his dramas was being performed for the first time.

The issue at stake then became more clearly seen by those attending the trial. The law was brief and to the point: "All voluntary homicide is murder." The duel was therefore actually forbidden by law, but there was a point so French in feeling that it was quite outside the law itself. This point was whether or not the duel could be charged to extenuating circumstances; and though to kill a man in a duel was murder, the jury had the right to declare the survivor not guilty if there was proof or even reason to suspect that the duel had been brought about by his having been subjected to mental distress. The actual circumstances of the duel were ignored; the questions of whether the duel was fairly fought and of de Beauvallon's "*loyalty of honor*" never arose.

When the matter of the party was brought up, the participants were spoken of as being respectable, modest, and fashionable, and the spectators laughed so freely that they had to be admonished and reminded by the judge that they were in a courtroom and not at the theatre.

Lola Montez took the witness stand with a rustling of lace-trimmed black silk. When she was seated she lifted the veil from her face, and the entire courtroom gasped at her beauty. From then on, she became the emotional focus of the trial as the gentlemen lost their hearts to her and the ladies, both of Paris and Rouen, who had managed to squeeze into the room envied her breath-taking loveliness.

Her testimony was necessarily limited, since she had no personal knowledge of the circumstances which had led to the encounter. She was aware only of the ill feeling between de Beauvallon and Dujarier and the former's reason for taunting the journalist.

She described Dujarier's return from the supper party in a state of excitement and apprehension, but since she had believed the duel was to be with de Beauvoir she had not been too troubled. When at last she discovered that her lover—and she did not hesitate to call him her lover—had gone to fight de Beauvallon, she expected never to see him alive again. "Had I known who the antagonist was, I would have been prepared to fight him myself," was her convincing reply.

When recalled to the stand, de Beauvallon accused Dujarier of having snubbed him. The attorney for the dead man's mother exclaimed in amazement at this statement. Was that not the privilege of an individual when he found the company of another man distasteful? Again and again the course of the trial swung away from the points that Madame Dujarier's attorney was trying to make, to return to the question of de Beauvallon's provocation in challenging the dead man.

The trial lasted four days, during which everyone in Rouen tried to catch a glimpse of the bereaved beauty on her way to and from court, or at the noon hour when she took lunch at her hotel, or upon her return there in the evening.

As she gave evidence, Lola was often racked with sobs, and

when Dujarier's last letter was read to the court she cried as though her heart would break, leaving no doubt in anyone's mind that she had loved him with a consuming passion. At times, while listening to testimony regarding the horrible death of her beloved, she turned pale, closed her eyes, and looked as if she might faint. Sometimes she drew her black shawl closely about her, as if she were in the throes of a chill in spite of the airless warmth of the packed courtroom.

That there had been a plot to kill Alexandre Dujarier became all too evident, but de Beauvallon had engaged the most renowned lawyer of the time, Pierre Berryer, to defend him. This great lawyer, who had defended—though unsuccessfully—both Marshal Ney and Louis Napoleon, persuaded the jury that Jean de Beauvallon, a vindictive murderer, was innocent because he was justified in challenging his rival to a duel.

When the jury filed in, the foreman was asked, "Is the accusation true?"

Replied the foreman: "The declaration of the jurors is that the accused is not guilty."

The trial was over and the Court ruled that de Beauvallon be required only to pay a sum of twenty thousand francs to Madame Dujarier as damages.

Lola claimed to be so outraged that she turned over to Dujarier's mother the four hundred thousand francs she said she had inherited from Dujarier, keeping only the eighteen shares of theatre stock and his share in *La Presse*, which he had left her.

Yet de Beauvallon was not in the end to escape. Due to the persistence of Lola's friends in collecting additional evidence, he was again tried more than a year later and at last sent to prison.

An interesting sidelight on the trial was the presence of a young man, blond and blue-eyed, who was somewhat of a recluse. He could not take his eyes off Lola Montez during the course of the trial, and asked endless questions about her. His name was Gustave Flaubert, the future author of *Madame Bovary*, that searching, pitiless picture of a woman betrayed by love. In court he made an observation about Lola Montez which was to be often repeated in after years. "She looks," he said, "like the heroine of a novel, but as no heroine in life really looks."

For some time after the trial Lola remained in Paris, but her social life was almost completely changed. She was dependent almost entirely upon the company of Théophile Gautier, who had been responsible for raising the mystery of her past when he had written: "Which is her country? That is the question!" As a critic he had damned her, but by the time she became engaged to Dujarier she and Gautier were fast friends. Now he tried to ease her grief and to renew her interest in Republicanism, the burning issue of the day. She and Gautier were often joined by Méry, who was always gay and amusing and who felt a special sentimentality toward Lola as the survivor of a tragic love affair; for Méry, too, had once fought a duel and had come off badly, although with his life.

Lola recorded that Gautier and Méry were alarmed when they discovered that she had found temporary solace with an unhappy man who was anti-social, somewhat of a hermit, and the victim of a tragedy which obsessed him: the loss of his only child, a beautiful girl of fifteen who had died of consumption. The man was Alphonse de Lamartine, the poet and historian.

His English wife, who claimed to understand him, did not approve of French society and cared not in the least that her husband had isolated her from its follies, never recognizing the fact that he needed gay company as an antidote to his overwhelming depressions. Lola wrote that she met him often, but it could not have been a very happy association.

Her other, and even more alarming, interest was the scientist Pierre Tissot of the French Academy, described by Lola in her writings as the gloomiest man in France. He was a friend of Lamartine and was at that very time furnishing the author with the material for his *Histoire des Girondins*. Lola called Tissot a "remnant of dead France; a guide book through all the labyrinths of its revolutions and scenes of blood." Tissot had watched the Reign of Terror, and Lola, in her mood of preoccupation with death, became an interested listener to a man whom most contemporary Parisians avoided. She herself said of him, "He wanders about Paris, pointing out all the places of the past." It was probably Tissot who pointed out to her the house of Jean Marat into which Charlotte Corday forced her way to stab the Revolutionary leader to death in his bathtub. The scene made such an impression upon Lola that when she later played the part of Charlotte Corday, she was said to be impressively authentic in the role.

About the period following her association with Tissot little is known. It seems to have been one of those blank spaces in Lola's life of which she neither wrote nor talked. Then suddenly she quit Paris for Bavaria to play in the theatre in Munich. It was one of those peculiar paradoxes which marked her whole life that she wrote of her pre-Paris period as filled with associations with royalty which would never be confirmed, yet in the post-Paris cycle there are innumerable records and verifications of her friendships with personages of royal birth although she made no mention of them. At Baden-Baden she encountered the Prince of Orange, who was attracted to her phenomenal beauty; and she met Henry, Prince of Reuss, who had seen her dance on a theatrical tour she made through his miniature principality. He was supposed to have fallen madly in love with her, paid court to her wit and beauty, and invited her to visit him— which she did. Then one day she offended him by walking over and not around a bed of flowers in which he took exceptional pride. For this affront she was asked to leave.

Lola's decision to go to Bavaria marked a turning point in her life. It was to bring the attention of the entire world upon her.

IV

With her mysterious background and the endless legends of her origin, Lola Montez now entered the Kingdom of Ludwig I of Bavaria, a man whose sole aim was to adore beauty.

In his youth Ludwig was accredited with masculine good looks, but his face, in spite of some flattering accounts, was on the whole very much that of the rustic, far better suited to a rural setting. He had a blunt nose, wide-set eyes, and healthy, florid coloring, and there was nothing of the delicate aristocrat in his appearance. At sixty his countenance had taken on a weather-beaten look as if he had spent his life—as indeed he had —outdoors. Even his parsimonious ways were those of the German farmer.

As a child he had been morose and unsociable but with good reason, for he had been subjected constantly to the terrorized whisperings of his elders, who had continually talked revolution in France and of heads falling beneath the blade of the guillotine. The horrible death of Marie Antoinette particularly concerned him, for she had been his godmother. Royal refugees, each with a shocking experience to relate, took shelter with his parents.

Ludwig's father, on the death of his older brother, became Prince of Zweibrücken, and had to flee from his seat in Lorraine to Mannheim until, in 1799, by forming an alliance with Napoleon, he became Elector of Bavaria and his thirteen-year-old son was sent to look upon his future kingdom. Five years later Ludwig discovered Roman architecture on a trip to Italy, and returned to Bavaria determined to turn Munich into a city of magnificent classic revival. To this project he was to devote his life.

When Ludwig succeeded to the throne he had already accomplished some of his building and once king, he continued with his plans, living a frugal existence to pay for the widened streets and classical buildings being erected in Munich. He had already married the beautiful Theresa of Saxe-Hildburghausen, by whom he had seven children, but she all too soon disappointed him by becoming as ordinary as any housewife, and he turned to a succession of beautiful actresses whom he took as mistresses.

Toward the government of his country Ludwig displayed complete indifference. He was content to let the Jesuits dictate the policies of the government, although he was himself irreligious. But he refused priestly guidance only as it concerned his personal life, aware that his mind had not been molded by ecclesiastical hands, that dogmas did not have the authority for him that they should have for the upholder of the faith. The whole purpose of the state religion of Bavaria was lost on Ludwig. Had he practiced the allegiance he owed to his church, he would have been concerned for its great tenet, that man is on earth solely to secure his passage into heaven. Ludwig's interest was in temporal things, in works of art and beautiful women, although at the moment Lola appeared on the scene he had not had a mistress for some years.

Thus by chance Lola moved onto a stage exactly designed for her. For the first time in his life Ludwig was about to acquire a work of art not made by the hand of man, but transcending in beauty anything his craftsmen had created. People were to say that Lola was the mistress of Ludwig and as such she would go down in history, but Ludwig denied this, even to the head of the Church in Munich, and it is to be noted that he had never attempted to deny any other previous connection of the sort. Lola, too, always emphatically denied it and her statement could hardly have been other than the truth. Much later, in 1858, in a London court where she was called as witness in a debt case, she was asked by an attorney if she had not been the mistress of Ludwig. "What?" she replied. "No, sir! You are a villain, sir! I take my oath on that book which I read every night that I had no intrigue with the old man. I knew the King, molded the mind

45

of the King to the love of freedom. I was engaged in political business." Since this statement was made after she had turned to religion, the denial merits attention.

The incident by which Lola met Ludwig was not any credit to her, but was brought about partly by frustration and partly by hysteria. She had come to Munich to perform at the Court Theatre but the director, upon seeing her dance, had refused to allow her to appear. This blow, following close on an incident in Paris when she had been hissed off the stage, was too much for her.

Unable to obtain the engagement promised her, she decided to appeal to Ludwig himself as the only person who could, if he chose, see that she got it.

When he received the message that a dancer wished an audience, Ludwig was both amused and annoyed with his aide-de-camp, who, overwhelmed by Lola with her shining black curls and her enormous blue eyes under their curling lashes, insisted upon interceding for her. Meanwhile Lola was convinced that she had been left in the ante-chamber to cool her heels until in sheer discouragement she should decide to leave. She could not conceive that an aide-de-camp would dare take up so much of the King's time in her behalf, and deciding that he had merely escaped from her through an adjacent chamber, she rose with her usual impetuosity, meaning to make a brash entrance on her own account. Just as she opened the door a guard rushed forward to intercept her, and in his attempts to pull her away from the door and at the same time close it, he grabbed at the material of her bodice. She jerked away from him before he could capture her and, running through the entry, slammed the door and locked it.

There are countless legends about what happened then. The mildest version was that Ludwig asked her to dance for him; another version was that he stared at her bosom with such ill-concealed curiosity that she seized a pair of shears from his desk and cut her bodice open; another account credits her with having used a knife to carry the opening even further. The official version—for there was a written report of her having managed to penetrate the private apartment of the King—stated that the dancer had boldly invited Ludwig to investigate what remained unexposed inside her torn dress.

But all accounts are in agreement that Ludwig dismissed his aide-de-camp from the room and seemed stunned to find Lola's beauty even greater than had been reported to him.

Later, Lola wrote: "I received from an aide of the old King Ludwig an invitation to a royal audience on the next day."

Through Ludwig, Lola obtained her theatrical engagement and the next evening, October 10th, she danced twice between the acts of *Der Verwünschene Prinz*. It was not an enchanted prince who watched her, as the name of the play suggested, but an enchanted king.

Their overwhelming curiosity mixed with feelings of resentment, the director of the theatre and the première-danseuse, Fraülein Frenzal, as well as the audience, watched Lola Montez perform. Dressed in a full-skirted Spanish costume she was bewitching; not only was the King enchanted but also the audience.

Yet in this short time between her visit to the royal Residenz and her appearance in the theatre, rumors had been launched which had probably been sent out by the jealous Frenzal, who told the director of the theatre that it would be imprudent to let the Spanish dancer appear. This Lola Montez was an adventuress, the gossips whispered—hadn't she freely admitted that she had been the mistress of a French newspaperman? But the most vicious rumor accused her of being an agent sent by the Freemasons of England to invade Bavaria, that stronghold of a priestly power which dictated to the King's ministers with his firm support.

A peculiar aspect of this situation was that Lola had not shown any disposition to criticize anyone in Bavaria, let alone the Church. Yet mere rumor was apparently all that was needed to touch off a debate on the clergy's right of ascendency, and once having been called into question, it became for the first time a matter for debate and violent dispute. Insidiously, those who were not devout and who either lacked loyalty to their church or were not members now expressed discontent and began to speak of it as a tyranny. The majority of the populace did not seek to oust their Jesuit masters, but having once criticized them, they then began to blame the King, saying he had let power slip from his hands while giving all his attention to turning Munich into a second Rome. So far they had not questioned the King's right to construct arches, erect statues, and keep a court painter constantly busy; but now they saw these masterpieces as a mere whim of their ruler, acquired at the expense of government pensions and funds for education and the poor. It was also charged that the tremendous number of churches, several of them built by Ludwig, had been erected at the cost of privation to the citizens, since they had to support an overwhelming influx of *religieux* who had come into Bavaria after being driven out of France and Switzerland.

Four nights after her first appearance Lola danced again, and since she faced an audience that was doubtful of her intentions, Ludwig had packed the pit to insure an ovation for her. The precaution was probably unnecessary, because the audience was entranced with her undeniable beauty and charm. The King's own estimate of the effect she had upon him was encompassed in one very adequate sentence, often quoted, which the enchanted ruler of a kingdom might well have used. "I am bewitched," he said in surprise, as if Lola had waved a fairy wand over him and thereby brought him all he had ever wished for.

Ludwig's overwhelming infatuation with Lola transcended anything he had ever found with which to occupy himself. She was the perfection he strove for in making Munich an art center, more beautiful than any statue he had mounted upon pediments about the city, surpassing every one of the six-foot paintings in his collection of the most beautiful women in his realm. Social prestige was not a criterion for inclusion in this remarkable collection. The daughter of the town crier, the daughter of the court butcher, and a dancer, all met on equal terms with royalty in his gallery, called *Die Schönheitengalerie*. Outstanding beauty was the only common denominator, a recognition of the common people which touched them and made them love their king, just as his habit of walking on the streets among his subjects made each one he encountered feel that he personally knew his monarch well.

The people had always been inclined toward indulgence when the King acquired a favorite. It was years since he had had a mistress, but if he now chose to acquire the beautiful dancer, there was no need to show alarm. The countless priests, monks, and nuns who filled the churches, monasteries and nunneries might, like sharp-eyed eagles, have their wings outspread ready to clutch upon his latest fancy if she showed the slightest inclination to snipe at them, but they would not fly at her in blind animosity.

For the moment, the rumor that Lola was anti-clerical seemed to subside, but gossip about the supposed liaison travelled across Europe to be recorded in unexpected places. The young Disraeli, ill in England with an attack of influenza, wrote to his sister about Lola. And as far away as California, a man writing to a friend recalled Ludwig's habit of stopping veiled ladies on the streets of Munich to lift their veils and behold the concealed face. He told how Ludwig had raised one veil only to drop it when he beheld the ugly woman hidden beneath, exclaiming, "Madame, you are right." This expatriate in California seems to have unwittingly revealed just how much of a fanatic Ludwig was in his worship of beauty. No other contemporary appears to have understood that Lola, often declared to be one of the most beautiful women of all time, was for the King of Bavaria another art object to be added to his collection—the greatest masterpiece he had yet acquired.

It was only incidental that her charm was as great as her beauty, an idiosyncrasy that she was politically minded; and before long he was to regard her as an oracle. He had never been given to making decisions, but soon the theories she expounded on government were to be received by him as if they were a revelation which must be acted upon at once.

Ludwig's infatuation with her beauty and her mind led him to a new occupation: he wrote impassioned poetry which he imagined to be immortal, those about him assuring him it was written for posterity, and during those hours when he and Lola were apart he kept messengers in a steady stream delivering notes to her.

Lola had by now moved from her hotel to a small villa on Theresienstrasse, where Ludwig sent her a poem each morning, to be read when she awakened, and later in the day eagerly followed up his subsequent messages with a visit to his chatelaine. They spent hours together. Often he read to her, or she played the piano or the guitar and sang to him. Sometimes they sat together on a sofa while she occupied herself with embroidery. And gradually they achieved a unity of thought and a coalescence of ideals which should have worried the Jesuits far more than the rumors of their alleged sexual excesses.

Lola has left a record of why she stayed on in Munich and what these political conversations were based on. She was in reality repeating all she had heard from Lamennais, the French priest and philosopher who had saturated her with his ideals, his knowledge of the causes of revolution, and his conviction that the clergy had no right to interfere with governmental administration.

"The King," wrote Lola, "manifested great surprise at some of the information I gave him [about France] and was so deeply interested as to ask me to stay in Munich as his guest for a few days. I at first declined, and finally observed, 'Will it not give cause for scandal against your Majesty?' [He replied] 'No, I have no fear of that.' I consented to stay a few days and renewed my conversation with the King several times on visits to him at his instance. These visits were ceremonious. I talked to the King as I always do to everyone—truthfully, frankly and without concealment."

Lola had certainly been listening to her philosopher friend in Paris on the subject of the government in Bavaria. There was a reasonable explanation for Lamennais's particular preoccupation with this country, since it was at Munich that he had received his chastisement from his church and it was here that he was sent the copy of the papal letter, written to the bishops, which condemned his proposal to place governments under ecclesiastical control. At that time he had himself met Ludwig, and, suddenly a crushed and disillusioned man, had gone to opposite extremes and tried to use Ludwig as a means of retaliation against the Church. He had attempted to induce Ludwig to think for himself and to persuade him that it was weakness on the part of a monarch to be controlled by the clergy.

Interested only in his classical revival, Ludwig could not overcome his boredom with government enough to care whether the Jesuits dictated to his statesmen or not. He had also stubbornly insisted that governmental change was ruinous to kings, and Lamennais had accomplished nothing with his new anticlerical theories.

It was ironical that Lola brought these principles back to Ludwig second-hand. Point by point, everything Lola believed in was identical to the principles of fraternity Lamennais had promoted after breaking with the Church, and it was from him that Lola had learned to detest what he called priestly suppression. Bavaria was controlled by priests and priestly sympathizers; having developed a hatred of this form of government, Lola was now bent on destroying it.

Of these talks with Ludwig, she was to write: "I told him of errors and abuses in his government, I told him of the perfidy of his ministers. Honest and unsuspecting, he did not believe it, but I proved it to him. I exposed to him especially the art, duplicity and villainy of his prime minister, Baron Abel, a Jesuit who had wormed himself into his confidence."

If anyone was making for the ruin of Ludwig's empire it was Lola herself, but the King was too spellbound by his sorceress to listen to anyone but her.

Alarm spread as the King put his new-found theories into practice. Prince Metternich of Austria, a diplomat and statesman who was an expert at putting down liberal ideas, was induced by Baron Abel to come to Munich to help him get rid of Lola. She consented to meet Metternich, knowing that he had some scheme afoot, because she had heard of his reputation for suppression. The Prince offered her four million francs and the title of Princess in return for her promise merely to persuade the King to do as his government advised. But as this scheme was being discussed, Ludwig was concealed behind a curtain in Lola's room, and could hear every word of this plot to make him the tool of his ministers.

"King Ludwig," wrote Lola, "was convinced, in spite of all the scandalous fabrications that were circulated, that I was his friend, as I was most truly. For a long time his profligate and faithless counselors could not imagine from whence their betrayed and abused master learned the facts as to their conduct. When they did, what a torrent of scandal and falsehood was opened upon me! I was everything that was bad and vile. But they could not injure me with the good King."

The King himself revealed how he had learned the truth of the machinations to keep him subservient. To Prime Minister Abel he said, "She told me the truth. I will do as she told me." The furious Abel said insultingly, "She is the King, then!" To which Ludwig replied, "Yes, she is King."

The international scandal attached to Lola's name was born with that incident, and Abel spread stories of her among people of royal birth who were bound to carry malicious reports of her reputation throughout the courts of Europe. "Abel," wrote Lola, "was determined to drive me away and he plotted against me, raised all kinds of scandal about me, sent to France, England, the East Indies and Spain."

The Jesuits were actually concerned more with Ludwig's morals than with his political theory, and a bishop of the Church dared to ask Ludwig how a man who committed adultery could be expected to receive absolution for his sins. Ludwig was shocked, and assured the bishop that his relations with Lola Montez were *sans reproche*, their connection being one entirely based on friendship and mutual interests.

V

IN HER AUTOBIOGRAPHY Lola wrote that Ludwig was "the most learned, enlightened, and intellectual" monarch that Europe had had in a hundred years. She believed that he could be persuaded into making changes because of the many projects he had introduced for the betterment of his country. She observed that he had built a canal "which united the Main with the Danube" and that he had established "an uninterrupted line of water communication from Rotterdam to the Black Sea." He had also introduced national railways and established the company which ran steamboats on the Danube.

That he had scarcely given the government a thought until Lola's advent was all too evident. Historians have ever been amazed at the remarkable feat she accomplished in taking over power from the Jesuits within a period of eight weeks.

She described the government of Bavaria as having "degenerated into a petty tyranny, where priestly influence was sucking out the lifeblood of the people. There was a rigid censorship upon the press, and the cloven foot of Jesuitism was everywhere apparent, until the King had grown sick of the government which necessity seemed to force upon him."

As she herself said, she laid "bold and novel political views" before him and "induced him to form his new ministry from the ranks of the people, without respect to the rank of nobility." She was teaching a king to be a Republican, a feat which had never quite been accomplished even in France, where Louis Philippe had been elected by deputies. It was an impossible transition for a monarch.

Fresh from the salon of George Sand where the ideals of Republicanism were constantly discussed, and "familiar with the state of politics throughout Europe" from her association with Dujarier, Lola actually intended to bring about a miracle by ousting not only the Jesuits but also royalty from political power in Bavaria.

When she had first arrived in Munich, she wrote: "The nobility had such power that a tradesman could not possibly collect a debt from one of them by law, for they could only be tried by their peers. And the poor people, alas! had no chance when they came under the ban of the laws, for the nobility were alone their judges."

She had forgotten Balzac's warning that the common people turned upon and destroyed those who championed them.

A Royal Decree turning the control of the Department of Education over to a new Minister of the Interior served as the first inkling that someone had been modifying the King's ideas. Carl Abel, who had held this position undisputed for years, and whose loyalty was to the ascendancy of royalty and the Church, protested to the King against his dismissal, and when that availed him nothing he blamed Lola Montez. With Abel there went the control of the Jesuits over education, and when the Hauptmann der Polizei of Munich had the audacity to declare to the King that it was Lola who had instigated the dismissal, the King retaliated against the chief of the police by banishing him from the kingdom.

Over their beer and white radishes the Bavarians discussed Lola's ability to dominate their king. Jesuit sympathizers were outraged, as they had good reason to be, and since they still had control of the press, they vented their wrath upon Lola in the form of satire. They even dared to make the King a laughing-stock in his capital city, hinting that he was rejuvenated but suffering from excessive sentimentality.

Ludwig paid little attention either to the Jesuits or to the neglect shown Lola by the ladies of the nobility. At the time, she was having her portrait painted for the Gallery of Beauties by Josef Steiler. This was to be the picture which most nearly captured her beauty as, dressed in black velvet, with a white lace collar at her throat and a red carnation in her hair, the intelligence of her face was fully revealed. Ludwig was present during these sittings, his face aglow with happiness.

The new Cabinet which had followed the dismissal of Abel was headed by a man who had been ordered to deny to the clergy any right to mix in the affairs of state. To secure an even firmer control, the remaining members of the Cabinet were Liberals, calculated to keep the Jesuits out of politics. Word of the changes taking place in Munich spread through Bavaria and attention was focused on Lola Montez; she was declared to be the champion of liberty throughout the country, although this view was confined mainly to the Protestants, who represented only thirty per cent of the Bavarians, and to those who hoped for political positions.

The platonic lovers next set themselves a new project, the building of a small palace which was to become Lola's residence. The architect Metzger was summoned to draw up plans for this dwelling, to be built on the aristocratic and fashionable Barerstrasse. Lola and Ludwig pored over the plans, the happiest of companions, as the Italian-styled palace emerged on paper with its simple, balanced design, decorated only by a bronze balcony at the second-story level.

The drawing room was to be painted with scenes from Pompeii—and certainly the hand of Ludwig was to be seen here. The winter parlor adjoining it, however, was to be comfortably English in character, proof that the mansion represented the wedding of both their ideas. The King promised her statues from the Glyptothek, which he had built to house the sculptures he had collected in Rome, and from the Alte Pinakothek he selected some of the most important paintings for her, one of them being a Raphael.

Once the house was built, the library was stocked with volumes from the King's own collection of books, and if the nobility was outraged to have the national buildings robbed for the King's favorite, the selection but served to confirm her interest in politics, thereby increasing the storm.

Its strength was measured by an incident which now occurred at the little palace. According to a story published years later in California in the *Placerville Herald*, the decorator had fitted up Lola's boudoir with its satin bed curtains and window draperies, its gold leaf cabinet and table, and a sofa "as hard as his heart," and presented a bill that was nothing less than fantastic. At first dismayed, Lola then became furious, showing a temper which until now had never been fully aroused. She suddenly realized that she was in a position to assert herself.

In the midst of the argument the King arrived to discover Lola resisting the decorator's insults with flashing determination. Ludwig was indignant that the tradesman should assume Lola knew nothing of the true values of the fittings and should attempt to rob her. The decorator was being paid by Lola and he knew she could not, like the nobility, get the debt scaled down by court action. But the King called his bluff by announcing that he would take the bill over and then refuse to pay it. The decorator answered with a vulgar aside to Lola, which escaped the King because he was somewhat deaf. But the remark, designed to put Lola in her place as "the King's whore," which she was now often called, failed to do so, for Lola seized a vase and threw it at the man's head.

Amidst the shattered remains the decorator, red as a cranberry, maintained an air of superiority and delivered his threat: "Very well, Madam, but these rooms will cost you far more than I have asked."

The decorator had lost some money but not his tongue. For weeks on end he poured into willing ears the story of how the King had almost wept over Lola Montez's extravagance, accusing her of misusing the taxes paid by his hard-working subjects. The tradesman was believed, and although Lola eventually paid the bill, he continued to circulate the story among the citizens of Munich.

After the palace was finished Lola decided to add two wings of white marble, gilded inside, one of which housed an amazing staircase of heavy glass. At the windows, overlooking the courtyard between the wings, were jalousies of iron and in the center of the enclosure a marble fountain which sprayed perfumed water, a conceit of the King's own planning.

Ludwig spent every possible moment with Lola, utterly fascinated by her company. Her conversation was brilliant, her ideas absorbing. Life at her palace fell into a pattern. In the morning she sat with her secretary answering the many letters written to her by the common people, who urged her to appeal to the King for social reforms. During her breakfast hour she was available for consultation with men looking for governmental berths, with university professors, or with visitors from other countries, and intently listened to whatever information they imparted on politics. At eleven the King usually arrived to spend one or two hours with her. Sometimes, however, it was she who visited him at the royal palace, where she met with his new ministers. It was no longer to his Jesuit counselors but to Lola that he turned for advice. The new ministers, far from resenting her presence, seemed to feel that she was a genuine aid in considerations of state policy, for they were, of course, all Liberals like herself. They knew she had acquired her knowledge of political science from the writers she had known in Paris and from Dujarier, who had been singularly well informed in this respect, but did not yet suspect that as a disciple of Lamennais, Lola intended to crush the Jesuits. There would be no revival of the old government as long as Lola's influence lasted.

She drove to the palace in the magnificent carriage which the King had given her and which was trimmed with gold and lined in ermine with cushions of a rich crimson. Sometimes the King joined her at his Residenz and they drove together out into the countryside. Often they walked in the Hofgarten, strolling along the shaded paths and through the arcades in which were painted scenes portraying events in Bavarian history. Historians would speculate endlessly upon what Ludwig and his "mistress" discussed on these walks; Lola herself said in letters that they talked of government, especially as it had to do with Ultramontanism (a term meaning "beyond the mountains"), which referred not only to a school of logic but to the party which backed the Jesuits. The philosophy of this group and their supporters was that the Church had the sole right of political power and jurisdiction over education, literature and science.

Until the advent of Lola the King had had no thought of opposing the concept that the Church had the right to political power and that he must therefore carry out its policies, which had been carefully considered at Rome by the Pontiff and his nuncios. That Lola should have interfered with the performance of this accepted policy in Bavaria was a matter for deep concern. The Jesuit party believed that the whole Christian world belonged under one head and that the other religons of the world would eventually capitulate.

However brief her period of association in Paris with philosophers and political theorists, she had acquired a powerful ability to see the world as she herself thought it to be. She had arrived at the conclusion that Christianity was a delusion, that it was only a recreated form of the religious doctrines of the Hebrews and that practically all of its symbols were merely interpretations of age-old doctrines of the Far East.

In robbing Ludwig of his political beliefs, Lola robbed him also of what remained of his religious beliefs and gave him in return the theory that no one power would ever control mankind. Let the poor be downtrodden by the rich; then the poor would turn upon their masters and destroy them. Let a country rise to become too powerful; then the lesser countries would join together to destroy that power. Let the representatives of one religion attempt to obliterate other religions; then those representatives would in turn be driven out.

The King was persuaded to these theories of Lola's, possibly because as a child he had been an actual witness to the revolt of the poor against the rich in France. In addition, the Jesuits had been driven out of France once in 1830 and again in the year just past.

It is ironic that so much of what Ludwig built and what the clergy, who had fled there from France, had constructed as places of worship was to disappear in the rubble of World War II, all because a house painter named Adolph Hitler had to conquer the world. Yet the painting of Lola survived the war, to be hung again in the summer palace, the Schloss, where the Gallery of Beauties was re-established for the pleasure of future generations.

VI

THE JESUITS were having trouble in Austria and in Switzerland at that time, as well as in France and England, so it was not unnatural for them to believe that Lola had been posted in their Bavarian refuge as part of a scheme hatched in England by Benjamin Disraeli, then a Member of Parliament.

The population of Munich was largely conservative. They had not hesitated to appeal to Lola Montez for favors, but when she started to disrupt their way of life, feeling toward her began to change. She was the enemy of the Church and of royalty; it only needed rumors of scandal about her, a report that she was a British agent, for the worthy, substantial element to be solidly against her.

There was little similarity between the people of Paris and the people of Munich. Here the nobility lived in castles, drove about the city in their carriages, attended the theatre, and gave very proper balls and dinners. The bourgeoisie attended to their trades and walked in the parks on holidays. It was the officers of the army and the students and visitors who swarmed to the cafés.

Twin rulers, the Jesuits and Ludwig were masters of this amiable, religious, and utterly respectable kingdom. The single complaint of the common people was that they were bled white to support the Church and the nobility, but their resentment was not translated into action as it had been in France.

Although the King had had mistresses, they had always been kept discreetly in the background and maintained on a rather stingy budget. The people refrained from discussing their ruler's affairs and certainly never made sport of them, for unlike the French, they did not regard sex as something natural, amusing and free from shame.

Stories of Bohemianism among the intellectuals in Paris were common in Munich, and Lola's former acceptance by that group was considered proof that she was as immoral and promiscuous as George Sand and her friends.

Lola herself did not help matters, for when she was censured she usually allowed her temper to rule her. Often she had heard Victor Hugo's warning, "Meet attack with silence," but she had never been able to discipline herself in this regard, and when criticism put her on the defensive she fell into such a rage that people soon enjoyed baiting her.

Once, in retaliation, she set her English bulldog on Professor von Lassaulx, whom she duly hated because he was a Jesuit. The dog had grown to recognize any man of the cloth, and when he uttered a few growls Lola urged him on until he had acquired a reputation for misbehavior equal to that of his mistress.

Again, she was out walking with the dog one day when a nervous tradesman slapped at him with a whip. The animal did not defend itself, but Lola pulled the driver off his beer cart and slapped him with the whip she carried to control the dog. Immediately a menacing crowd gathered, shaking their fists at her. Although Lola was not frightened and would have stood her ground, a sympathetic tradesman pulled her into his shop to protect her and berated the pedestrians for unseemly behavior. This was the beginning of her chronic troubles with the citizens of Munich.

Soon after this incident Professor von Lassaulx was relieved of his duties at the University because he had angered Ludwig by protesting the dismissal of Carl Abel. Lola interceded for him because she was ashamed of having set her bulldog on him, but Ludwig was adamant. He insisted that the Professor had implied that the Jesuits were more important than their king, and having long been content to admit that they were, Ludwig had suddenly begun to want his power as a sovereign to be recognized —an idea that could easily be traced to Lola, and added to her unpopularity.

A group of impulsive students from the University, slightly

intoxicated on beer, gathered before von Lassaulx's residence to show their support of him against the King. The clergy, however, was far from pleased with the Professor's interference in a situation which they felt he should have accepted. They preferred to believe that Ludwig would soon tire of Lola and that they would then be reinstated without making an issue of the Professor's dismissal.

In the belief that Lola had had the Professor dismissed, the students next went to her palace to demonstrate against her and cry vengeance. Lola was at home and with nonchalance and admirable, if foolhardy, bravery walked out on her balcony overlooking the street, alternately nibbling a marzipan and drinking champagne. When she lifted her glass in a toast, she was greeted with a hail of bricks through her windows.

Suddenly Ludwig appeared, and in the dead silence which fell upon the would-be rioters he entered Lola's house. When he emerged several hours later the crowd had not left, but had been swelled by citizens who had turned out to watch the curious contest. Voices were raised from the crowd to cry insults at the ruler of Bavaria, and before he could return to his Residenz it was necessary to call a military escort. It was the first time the King had had to be protected from the people over whom he ruled.

But although Ludwig proceeded to dismiss more of the university professors who had been outspoken in their support of von Lassaulx, he had the wisdom to win the students back to him by giving them privileges which they had not had before.

Lola decided that she might also win ascendancy over the students if she encouraged them to come to her salon. But her initial success in this gave rise to an unfortunate chain of events. Two of her youthful champions, Fritz Peissner and his friend Count Hirschberg, suggested that they should form a guard for her in the guise of a new university corps—a fraternity devoted to her service.

The corps became known as the Alemannia and was joined by about twenty out of the thousand students who attended the

University. Out of the funds given her from Bavarian taxes—or so the taxpayers said—Lola provided the group with uniforms and red caps. And no sooner did these champions of Lola appear on the campus among the more traditional student corps than minor riots occurred.

Ludwig, who had built the University to take the place of the smaller one at Landshut, declared that he wished to God he had never established the college in Munich.

At last the Jesuits, outraged that Lola flaunted her authority, demanded that all good church members unite to drive her out, and under this pressure, the good citizenry of Munich abandoned their natural discretion. Once thrown into a mood of true resentment, they began to talk scandalously of her, as they had never done about the King's previous favorites. The more the stories were repeated, the more scandalous they became.

They could not see the real Lola Montez as she no doubt was, a happy escape for their King after years of lonely preoccupation with art and buildings and many hours of boredom. Yet neither the aristocracy nor the bourgeoisie blamed the King for his infatuation. Lola was the witch who had cast him under a spell. The most unspeakable orgies took place in Lola's boudoir, said the burghers over their beer, and she was killing the King with her demands on him, physical and financial.

In vain the servants and the guards at Lola's door protested that Ludwig had never entered her boudoir since her home had been completed. True, he had been there while the decorators were engaged in installing the Louis XV furniture and the Sèvres porcelain mantelpiece, but nothing untoward had taken place between them.

Those who paid court to Lola in her salon defended her by saying that when the King visited her, he could always be found in the drawing room or library in full sight at all times. Scores of the visitors were men whose word was not to be taken lightly, for they included the most famous scholars, painters and musicians.

But their defense was useless. The people did not want to believe it. The bourgeoisie, as Balzac could have told Lola, had turned on the very person who had secured so many privileges for them.

Visitors to Bavaria gathered delectable samples of the salacious rumors of the day. Stories of the affair began to interest the outside world and soon Londoners and Parisians were excitedly reading accounts of the old King, charmed by a dancer whose background was a mystery. The London *Times*, which concerned itself mostly with either Parliamentary proceedings or gruesome murders, even went so far as to devote an editorial to the situation in Munich. The newspaper came into Lola's hands and she made the mistake of writing a letter to the *Times* in which she said that the Jesuits had "long made Bavaria their stronghold and Munich their headquarters." To this she added, "They have not left a stone unturned to get rid of me."

This unhappy situation finally affected Ludwig's health, and he took to his bed for a month, to emerge in May still ailing, only to attend the theatre where Lola already awaited him in the royal box. The audience arose when he entered, but to the indignation of the King's subjects Lola remained seated. The King, however, had eyes only for her whom he called "the star of my life," and he sat down beside her in the box apparently without even noticing her lapse in manners. To the audience, her behavior clearly indicated that she was now serving public notice of her equality with the monarch. The Queen evaded this implication by holding her court elsewhere, but she offered no objection to Lola and was even said to admire her intelligence.

With the coming of summer the King departed for the castle of Brückenau, a full military guard accompanying him in the royal train. Traveling incognito Lola followed him, also by train, but was recognized at Nuremberg. Although this was in Franconia, where more than two thirds of the population were Protestants, Jesuit sympathizers had been informed of her passage through the city, and were on hand to shout insults at her. At Bamberg she fared even worse. This city, situated in a fertile

65

valley on the river Pegnitz, had good reason to be indebted to Ludwig, for it was here that he had built the canal which united the Danube with the Main. But in spite of the Protestant population, there were many cathedrals and churches under the control of the Jesuit clergy now so unpopular with Ludwig. Forewarned of Lola's pending arrival, their sympathizers, and not the powerful episcopal forces who controlled the town, met the train. People were on hand at the station to hurl verbal threats at her, and when she entered a carriage to be taken to her hotel she was followed out of the depot by a crowd throwing pebbles at her. Never one to submit to such an attack, Lola calmly reached into her bag and drawing a pistol forth, dared her persecutors to throw more stones.

By the time she resumed her journey she was protected by a strong contingent of Protestant admirers, including the town officials and a number of wealthy tradesmen, who went to the railway station with her to show their regret for the discourtesy to which she had been subjected.

Her trip ended in the Fulda forest out of which the castle of Brückenau rose in breath-taking beauty, where she was to spend the summer with the King. Here she was under the eyes of the officers who accompanied him, and they paid her court with a boldness meant to test her virtue. One evening she struck one of the officers with her fan for making a sly remark about her status. She was quick to apologize for her loss of temper, but no officer thereafter took such a liberty. Soon they were willing to declare, to a man, that the King and his companion shared only an intellectual companionship and that Lola Montez was a woman of principle, not a wanton.

In the evenings, one of the officers would play his Mittenwald violin for dancing, and sometimes Lola, according to an account sent to France, danced with the other officers under the doting eye of Ludwig. He could not himself dance, since he was taking the baths for his health at the Brückenau Spa, but he enjoyed watching Lola's graceful figure moving lightly through the intricate steps and turns, and for him alone there was always the flash of perfect white teeth, revealed in a quick smile, that told him she was dancing just for his entertainment. The King retired early, and often Lola sang and danced the night away, but she always retired to her own quarters alone. The gallant officers could not resist flirting with her in this forest-girdled castle, but they all feared her displeasure, knowing that whenever a man proved disloyal he was all too quickly banished.

In after years in California, Lola was wont to explain that her terrible unhappiness after the death of Dujarier had been assuaged by the kindly sovereign who had become her adoring protector and champion but who was, above all, her friend, and asked no compensation except that of her company.

Lola maintained, and probably truthfully, that it was August Papon, a servant of hers who had worked for her in Paris and was engaged by her for a short time in Munich, who had later published a thoroughly ugly memoir, allegedly written by herself, which told of her affairs at that time with a variety of men, including sailors and physical culture instructors.

It was apparent from the sale of this lurid record of Lola's supposed debased relations with men that people wanted to believe the worst of her. The impression was broadcast and registered for history that Lola would stoop to any alliance to satisfy her uncontrollable desire. But Lola had no redress, since the law of libel did not then exist.

In her long hours with the King, Lola did not, of course, always talk politics. She afterwards related that Ludwig told her of the days he had spent in Rome and in Greece as a young man and that he longed to show her these places. Being the clever woman she was, and regardless of their relations, Lola understood quite well that it was her perfection of beauty which Ludwig worshiped. She did not like to think of the future when that beauty might fade, and prayed she might die young for Ludwig's sake. Meanwhile, "I want to live before I die," she said.

While the King dreamed of taking her to Rome's Seven Hills and to Pompeii, where Vesuvius had cast her angry ashes over a living city to preserve it for posterity, Lola returned to take

67

up her life in Munich above a rumbling volcano of another kind.

The King had ended the summer by going to Bad Kissingen and finally to the court at Aschaffenburg in the north, where Lola, as an enemy of the Jesuits, had been looked upon by the preponderantly Protestant population as a liberator.

Once more, she took up residence in her petite palace on the Barerstrasse. Once more she bathed in the room lit by the *couleur de rose* window; and once more she sat before her mirror combing and brushing her midnight curls for all the world like a Lorelei luring her helpless lover to destruction.

During her absence the windows of her residence had been filled with iron grillwork so they could not be broken with bricks, and Lola was constantly reminded of her destiny. A woman without fear and determined to separate the Church from the state, she slept serenely in her Louis XV bed, only half aware of the unrest that seethed beyond her guarded doors.

VII

Upon her return to Munich, Lola was made a countess. She demanded a title from Ludwig to flaunt in the faces of the aristocrats who had almost from the beginning gone to great lengths to ignore or snub her. Ludwig had little trouble in persuading his new ministers that Lola was eligible, for she produced a connection with the titled Montalvos of Spain which was deemed sufficient evidence of *noblesse*, although remote, for the granting of a coronet. While at Aschaffenberg, Ludwig had selected Landshut and Feldberg as the domain for the proposed countess, and combined the first syllable of each to make the title—Countess of Landsfeld. He also gave her the title of Baroness Rosenthal and she thereby became the mistress of lands inhabited by two thousand people. As a final insult to the Jesuits, in order to make them look as foolish as possible, Lola became a canoness of the order of St. Theresa, headed by the Queen, who still took a very lenient view of the newest favorite.

Several months earlier, when Lola had been given Bavarian citizenship, one of the cabinet members, whom she had influenced Ludwig to appoint, had indiscreetly said that the naturalization was a "calamity." He now remained silent about this latest honor given Lola, but the newspapers did not. Those in sympathy with the clergy were loud in their criticism of the cabinet for approving Lola's admission into the Bavarian peerage. The cabinet could have stopped all public criticism by placing a censorship upon the press, but they were loath to do so because the newspapers had only recently been released from the clerical bondage in which they had been for years and it was indiscreet to muzzle them again so soon.

Meantime Lola found supporters among the students of the

University. Several students of one of the older corps frequented her salon in order to mingle with her other admirers of notable attainments and to listen to her brilliant conversation. For this they were dropped from their society, so they then went over to Alemannia, the corps which had taken up quarters in a house just behind Lola's enclosed rear garden. This was immediately blown up into a scandal: Lola, gossip had it, was ravenously engaging in marathon intimacies with these poor defenseless young men. The King, of course, was still suffering from fatigue and his inability ever to satisfy her. Lola's lovely, fairyland palace was thus transformed into a den of debauchery. But in all this buzz of scandal not a word was spoken in criticism of the King's equal responsibility in sharing a supposed life of sin. He was a married man, yet with that incongruity of the self-righteous, the burden of the alleged affair fell entirely upon the woman.

The crisis was exaggerated to even greater proportions when Lola, dressed in a feminine version of the Alemannia uniform, departed with the corps for a celebration at Nymphenburg. She stayed at the baroque palace outside Munich, where the members of the Alemannia were invited to a banquet. There, in the Great Hall, with ceiling three stories high and galleries from which hung priceless tapestries portraying scenes from Bavarian history, the youths sang and toasted their honorary member with steins full of the best Bavarian beer. Naturally the account of this gay and innocent affair was twisted when it was relayed to Munich.

During January of 1848 the death of a prominent member of the Ultramontane party produced another antagonistic display of public feelings toward the new policy of the King and toward Lola. Confident of her own strength and incapable of fear, she faced a mob which gathered outside her house, believing herself equal to any opposition. Three of her student admirers, Peissner, Hertheim, and Laibinger, were in the house and entreated her "not to present herself before the infuriated mob." Her appearance on the steps "must have seemed," wrote Lola, "like an act of insanity." Mostly the rabble consisted of university students who belonged to the older corps, but many hoodlums and idlers had joined them. This time Lola did not even seek the safety of her balcony, but emerged from the front door to stand facing the crowd only a few feet away from her. When they affronted her with insults she heard them out, and then in a voice as coldly certain in its attack as a well-handled rapier, she replied, "I will have the University closed down."

This monstrous threat, spoken with flashing eyes by a woman considered a disreputable light o' love, could not have been better calculated to arouse people who had unprotestingly accepted repression from the clergy, and who were moralists by practice as well as inclination. The forfeit which this courtesan so calmly demanded made it seem as if she could deprive them of anything she chose. They had been betrayed by a mere dancer who had usurped the throne.

Without plan, but only with a desire to destroy, the infuriated students surged forward to get at the defiant woman who taunted them. Immediately the members of the Alemannia corps, hovering nearby in anticipation of a mob attack, surrounded Lola with a protective wall. With her loyal students about her, she retreated through her garden and headed for the Church of the Theatines, while the crowds behind her, for the moment diverted from their prey, smashed the windows of her palace and tried to batter down her front door. In the battle between the Alemannia and the other corps, young Count Hirschberg was stabbed, although not seriously hurt. The rowdy toughs, who had been moving about at the edge of the crowd, took up the cry to burn the palace, but the majority of the rabble were more intent on breaking in to loot and secure some of its treasures for themselves.

When Lola disappeared into the church, most of the mob lost sight of her and joined in the riot in which those wearing the red caps of Lola's corps became the center of the fighting. Then suddenly the mob was surrounded by troops called out from the nearby barracks. With them appeared the King, his face white with anger. Without addressing the mob he rescued Lola from the church, and in a hush which indicated surprise rather than the usual respect for the sovereign, the people allowed their intended victim to be escorted to the Residenz.

But this unlooked-for escape of their prey only momentarily checked the disorder. The streets of Munich seethed all night with restless, ill-tempered students and hirelings of the Ultramontane party, who had been paid to keep the uproar at fever pitch. The King foolishly took the attitude that nothing more would happen and took no further precaution than to order a patrol set up in the streets, while crowds of students and their supporters retreated into nearby beer gardens.

Ludwig had miscalculated the feelings of his people to such an extent that Lola, with only an escort of Alemannia boys, was soon returned to her own residence. But the minute the door closed behind her the protective corps was attacked by another university society while the troops looked on indifferently. Eventually the city police had to interfere.

It was Lola who had voiced the threat to close down the University, although it was not originally her idea but the King's. She had merely unwittingly revealed what was being planned and now Ludwig followed her announcement by actually doing so. It was his contention that he had built it and endowed it and he had the right to punish those who did not appreciate the gift by showing their loyalty to him. It would have been far wiser if he had temporarily suspended the students embroiled in the riots and used his army to place them on trains bound for home. The majority of them lived out of the city and Ludwig could have terminated the trouble by fining the students and turning them over to their parents, who, being almost without exception thrifty and careful of every penny, would have seen to it that their sons did not repeat the offense.

Instead the students were allowed twenty-four hours to depart for their homes—a day in which to do just as they pleased. While the rest of the rabble roamed the streets after they had consumed all the beer they could hold, the prospect of losing the trade of a thousand or more students brought about another crisis in the shape of a petition prepared by the tradespeople of Munich, asking that the order for the closure of the University be rescinded.

Having once made the ruling, Ludwig had to enforce it, if only to prove to his subjects that he was still their king in more than name only, but the students, unrestrained, marched in formation about the streets singing farewell songs, while merchants and bystanders watched them and bemoaned the loss of trade. All was confusion.

Had Ludwig been as strong as was his beloved Lola he would have met the situation with determination to enforce discipline. But when he looked out of his Residenz at the sea of angry faces in the streets of Munich he grew hesitant, and instead of setting up martial law immediately, compromised with the students by agreeing to reopen the University in May and treating the current term as having been completed.

This failure to enforce his original order left Ludwig in the position of being intimidated by mere striplings, who were quick to realize that the King was in their power. By next morning Ludwig found his Residenz surrounded by a crowd of citizens and students, who had not hesitated to arm themselves. They demanded that the University be immediately reopened and that Lola Montez be deported.

Already two members of the police force had been wounded, but the King, looking out of the palace window at the students gathered below, was torn by his desire to keep Lola regardless of what happened to him or his kingdom. Ludwig had never been able to arrive at a decision independently, and now he listened to those who surrounded him. Prince von Leiningen, a member of the court, urged him on behalf of the nobility to send Lola Montez out of the country at once. But not until the Duchess of Leuchtenberg, who was a relative and a power at court, pointed out the possibility that Lola might be killed, did Ludwig face the situation. Even Captain Baurer, an admirer of Lola's, believed that control of the soldiers in Munich was uncertain because they were too much in sympathy with the students.

Still of uncertain mind, Ludwig called a meeting of his cabinet. Although its members were not in sympathy with the Ultramontanes, they were sure of the power of the money being distributed among the Munich mobs by Count Arco Valley. It had been furnished by the party and was at the bottom of the whole affair. The Jesuits had even bought off the troops in Munich. Carts had been tipped over in the streets to be used as barricades. Many of the people, like the troops, had gone over to the side of the students. All were armed. The feeling of the Cabinet was that in order to avoid bloodshed, the King would have to accede to the demands made upon him or fight a revolution.

While newspapers in Europe, the British Isles and America reported the contest with wonder, Lola was barricaded in her palace. Her Alemannia boys were in retreat, having taken refuge in a restaurant. With that impetuous courage which marked her character, Lola, hearing from her servants that the corps was about to be arrested by the police, decided to go to the restaurant where her champions had fortified themselves. Few people were in the street and she did not know that nearly everyone had gone to the Residenz to await a reply from the King to the demand for her eviction.

Before she had gone any distance she was recognized by some stray students. She fled to the entrance of the Austrian Legation, whose officials were too cowardly either to open the door or to escort her back to her house. Once more she retreated into the Theatiner church, confident that an edifice which housed the Eucharist would be considered too sacred to be invaded by the mob. Soon members of the guard which had protected her when she had once before taken refuge in this asylum came, although all too unwillingly, to escort her to their guard room.

At the same moment a decree for the banishment of Lola Montez was put before Ludwig and he signed it.

The students who had followed Lola moved away from the

guard room where she was being held under protection once they heard the King had left the Residenz. This brief respite in vigilance enabled Lola to return to her palace. When she arrived, however, people were at her back door, trying to break in, and she was obliged to hide in the garden. Soon the crowd, unable to effect an entrance because of the steel shutters closed over the back windows, went to the front. Lola then hurried through the garden to the back entry where her servants were waiting. There her coachman, Georg, told her he had her carriage ready. Lola had already hidden her jewels where only Ludwig could find them. News came that a great crowd of people were bearing down upon her shuttered house from the Barerstrasse, and in the end she acceded to the tearful entreaties of her devoted servants to depart before she was killed.

Soon after she had left in her carriage in the direction of Blüthenberg, Ludwig appeared at the entrance of the barricaded palace he had built for Lola. Wearing neither hat nor coat, his hair blown by the breeze and his face showing tremendous strain, the ruler of Bavaria faced the people who had defied him. They were armed with battering rams and instruments for breaking down the doors.

"Scoundrels!" he called out to them, adding, as if the triumph was his and not theirs, "The house is empty."

Ludwig had sent instructions to Lola's coachman to have her carriage take her down the road past the Nymphenburg Park and along the high road by the river Würm. Here, four miles from Munich, was a junction from which branched several roads, and it would be confusing for any pursuers to attempt to follow her. Just beyond the junction lay Blüthenburg, the royal hunting lodge with its magnificent chapel.

Ludwig believed that no one would look for her so close to Munich, but if pursuers unfortunately anticipated this ruse she could then take asylum in the chapel of the lodge. There she might remain in safety.

After Lola had arrived at the four-hundred-year-old hunting

lodge, she was put in charge of the gamekeeper and the carriage was returned to the junction to be driven back to Munich by another road.

Less than an hour later a group of army officers, who had orders to arrest and imprison her, arrived at the lodge and pounded on the door, demanding to know if the woman they sought was in hiding there. Before the gamekeeper could reply, his daughters, standing beside him in the doorway, attested with sweet and convincing innocence that they had seen the lady in a carriage which had passed by earlier.

As soon as the riders had left, Lola took advantage of the respite before they could return, and with the help of the gamekeeper's wife donned a peasant costume belonging to one of the daughters. She had already decided that she would be safer in returning to Munich than in attempting to go in some other direction and she was determined to hear from Ludwig's own lips confirmation of his wish that she should leave Bavaria. As soon as it was dark she hurried out of the lodge, "across fields, ditches and forests," as she wrote, and over the snow-covered ground.

From a distance she finally saw the Residenz surrounded by blockades, but the grounds were deserted. It was all too evident that the King had actually capitulated to the demand to banish her.

Certainly there was no member of the Alemannia, so bitterly referred to by the townspeople as her "male harem," to whom she could turn, for it was manifest that they would have had to remain under cover once the mob learned that she had left. These stupid, bovine people, she believed, had undoubtedly celebrated her departure, but, tired from their merrymaking, had retired to their homes.

Afraid to remain near the Residenz alone, Lola hurried to the home of one of the King's ministers, Berks, head of the Department of the Interior. He was devoted to his sovereign and in sympathy with Ludwig's love for Lola. He agreed to help her.

At midnight, dressed in men's clothing, she was, according to her own account, escorted into the apartments of the King. When she entered the suite she found the King in a state of extreme depression, his head sunk in his hands, and it was a moment before he awakened to the full impact of Lola's presence. Then even her composure broke down as the King held her against him, trembling with joy.

If her account is true, they talked of politics. Ludwig told her that he intended to abdicate to his Jesuit-hating son, "for the good of the people and the honor of Bavaria."

Lola bade the King a sad farewell. There is no record of what was said. There was nothing left for Ludwig but his Gallery of Beauties, the little palace on the Barerstrasse, which he had locked and whose keys he carried, and his memories of one of the most sensationally beautiful women he had ever known.

But dilatory as he was, Ludwig took no further action to enforce his anti-Ultramontane policy. Instead he sat down and with tears in his eyes wrote a poem to Lola entitled *Lamentation*.

Rumors of Lola's presence in Munich had spread from the household of Berks and before even the two hours she had spent in the city were up the news was abroad. Lola attempted to communicate with Fritz Peissner by sending a message through the owner of the café where the Alemannia corps had retreated during the rioting. This indiscretion made it imperative for her to quit Munich at once, and with the help of Berks she left by way of the valley of the Mindel. By what means she travelled through the factory town of Mendelheim and reached the ancient town of Lindau on Lake Constance, she did not record. Protestant sympathizers may have aided her, but once in Lindau she was joined by Peissner, who had received her message. With him were Count Hirschberg and Lieutenant Nussbaum, determined to protect her.

Several days later Prince Wallenstein, who had been watching Ludwig in Munich, ascertained that he was receiving messages from Lola, who had no thought of relinquishing her opposition to the return of the Ultramontane party in Bavaria. Lola's letters revealed her fear that the King was far less concerned than she in crushing opposition, and that by procrastination he would again become subservient to those supporting the return of the clericals. She was dumbfounded to receive in reply to her messages only poems written in her honor. She expressed the opinion to her companions that it was a shameless way for a king to amuse himself while the future of his kingdom was at stake.

Lola urged Ludwig to take a firm stand, but the vacillating monarch decided to try out his popularity by appearing at the theatre. He was greeted in the usual manner and his personal fears were set at rest.

When Prince Wallenstein discovered that Lola was in Lindau, he hurried there and escorted her over the border into Switzerland. The temper of the Bavarian people was uncertain, and it was thought better to get her out of the country than to have her adherents pity her should she be put in prison.

With all the hauteur of which she was capable, Lola turned to the Prince after she was escorted over the border and made a prediction for the future. "The King will follow me out of Bavaria," she declared.

By February 24th the newspapers of Europe, until then so interested in the affair, had another political situation to engross them. Louis Philippe, the "Citizen King" of France, had fled after abortive efforts to re-establish the absolute monarchy.

Emotions and not statecraft ruled the mood of 1848 and the common people in more than one country found they could dictate to their masters. Their power was felt in Munich when they demanded that Ludwig dismiss his ministers. He refused, only to be again confronted by barricades set up by the citizens in the streets around the Residenz. He found, too, that his soldiers were reluctant even to raise their muskets. Ludwig hurriedly agreed to call a council.

A report was circulated that Lola was again in Munich and it was probably true, for later she wrote of seeing the Residenz blockaded and "buildings plundered and anarchy in all directions." The public must have had some knowledge of her

78

presence, else the King would not have posted a new decree forbidding Lola Montez to come into Bavaria. At this time she received, it was said, a large check from the King drawn on the Rothschild bank, and a guarantee of an annuity if she would promise not to risk her life with another visit. She probably did not see the King, but she did receive the check, for she later cashed it in Frankfort.

For the last time Lola left the city of Munich, with its cobbled streets, its houses with their crow-stepped gables, its Gothic towers, and its classic structures built by King Ludwig.

A month later he abdicated in favor of his son and was free to travel, to meet Lola elsewhere, or to finish the buildings he had begun in Munich. Lola was in Switzerland—in her own words, "the nearest shelter from the storm that was beating about my head."

Even before the abdication she had persuaded her three Alemannia protectors to return to Bavaria and she was now alone except for her servant, August Papon, who was secretly writing the scandalous *Private History and Memoirs of Lola Montez.*

Lola was not, however, engaged in infidelities, although her notorious reputation was being maintained by the thousands of newspaper accounts of her, no two in agreement except to blame her for the abdication of Ludwig I. She stayed quietly in Switzerland, hopefully awaiting the arrival of her King, who, deprived of his jewel, spent hours alone in her little palace recapturing his memories, or seated in the Gallery of Beauties looking at her portrait.

Between the separated friends letters passed almost daily. Often Ludwig had to communicate with her through his friends, not even daring to write to her directly because of the hostility of his people. Lola's passionate letters, written in that balanced, determined and yet impatient hand, were brought to Ludwig by an intermediary. They were carefully preserved and placed where they were not likely to be discovered; each time he finished another building in Munich a bundle of Lola's letters was placed in the cornerstone. Some were not found until nearly a hundred years later, when British bombs reduced the buildings to rubble during World War II.

In the Swiss capital, Lola was naturally not without admirers, and for the moment she chose for her companion Viscount Arthur Wellesley Peel, whose father, Sir Robert Peel, had been Prime Minister of Great Britain. Later to show his worth as a statesman, the young Peel was now Chargé d'Affaires at the British embassy at Berne. A few years ago Peel's excessive adoration and sentimentality would have entertained Lola and held her interest. Yet, though he was brilliant, somehow his company and his conversation were tedious after the endlessly interesting interchange of views and opinions with her beloved monarch of Bavaria. But it was still impossible for them to meet anywhere, and as she rode over mountain paths on horseback with Peel, walked in the park, or dined with him, her restlessness increased. She had changed from a frivolous and frolicsome girl into a maturing woman. Until she had met George Sand, her head was filled only with giddy concern for her attire and her social amusements, but having gone from Sand's salon to Dujarier's company and thence to that of Ludwig, her whole outlook had gradually changed to one of serious concern with the affairs of the world. The age and its cycle of adjustments was all that seemed to concern her, and she had just come through a storm of experiences which were to leave their stamp on history.

Yet in spite of her hatred of the Jesuits, she had a reluctant admiration for their wisdom in letting the contest in Bavaria find its own level without active interference. The belief of the clergy in their divine right evoked Lola's grudging regard for these men who worked for the glory of God without regard to immediate personal gain.

As her outlook changed she developed a defensive arrogance which she did nothing to check. When people in Bavaria had first realized the extent of her power they had besieged her with requests, and she had never turned a deaf ear to a worthy petition. Yet as soon as the people had presumed to criticize her for her political activities, she had begun to treat their petitions with a high-handedness which had incensed the Bavarians. To her they were simply ungrateful, for she entirely failed to perceive that their reaction was a direct result of her own behavior. This only confirmed her in her belief that she could not gain the affection she craved from anyone save Ludwig, and in revenge against those who since her childhood had wounded her feelings, she would henceforth treat all people with contemptuous scorn. To anyone who dared to insult her she would be quick in retaliation. As a dancer she had taken all the criticism she could accept; if she should return to the stage she would no longer worry about ingratiating herself with critics, who would probably only laugh at her attempts to achieve artistic stature.

For Lola the world no longer held enchantment. Why was it that everything must be taken from her? She had heard that Dumas had prophesied that happiness would never be hers. "She is fatal," he had said, "to any man who dares to love her."

This mood of despair was lightened by a brief period of happiness at Pregny. Here, on the north shore of Lake Geneva, she leased the Château de l'Imperatrice, where Empress Josephine had once lived. During her stay there she spent a great deal of time on the lake in her yacht *Le Corsaire*. It was later said that she acquired the château and the yacht because she was expecting Ludwig to join her. Only the London *News* attempted to trace his whereabouts and could only report that he had disappeared. If he had actually joined Lola no one knew he was there.

VIII

ALL ENGLAND had been kept fully informed of Lola Montez's startling career in Bavaria. They had read of how a king had been reconciled to the principles of Republicanism by a woman whose past was a riddle and whose beauty was a legend. Even more bewildering had been his meek acceptance of her dictum that the national religion was oppressive.

It was scarcely credible that a dancer of more beauty than talent should be possessed of novel concepts of political philosophy. The Bavarians, who had thrown up barricades about Ludwig's palace while alternately yelling "Long live the Republic" and "Down with the whore," had no realization that Lola Montez had triumphed in what she had set out to do. The helm of state in the hands of Ludwig's successor was ill directed, but it soon became apparent that Lola had laid the groundwork for the trend toward Republicanism.

Yielding to the demands of the common people had become almost universal. The abdication of Ludwig was quickly followed by that of the Emperor of Austria and the resignation of Prince Metternich, who fled to England, narrowly missing the ship that later carried Lola there. He "thanked heaven" he had not been forced into "contact" with her, and it amused Lola that her "dangerous presence" could so easily upset a man who had been forced to learn that men of plebeian backgrounds were not necessarily born to remain underlings.

Louis Philippe, the "Citizen-King" of France, had also learned that the Republican trend was stronger than his royal pretentions. The exiled leader of the French slipped into England with his family, stripped of everything but what they wore.

In Italy the people of Lombardy, supported by the Tuscans

and the Romans, had revolted against the rule of the Austrians. Pledged to stand aloof from aspirations for conquest, the Pope declared his neutrality and was forced to flee from Rome, accused of being a traitor by Italians who were intent on unity.

Ironically, it was in Bavaria that revolutionary tendencies ceased to exist, and Queen Victoria was reported as saying that the contest had been between the Jesuits and Lola Montez and not between royalty and Republicanism.

Unlike Ludwig, the British sovereign and her consort were not given to vacillation and Victoria knew how to assert herself with finesse. She did not speak of the Divine Right of Kings, but depended upon the intelligence of her country's leaders. When Republicanism raised its head in England, with a riot in London in which the discontented bore down on the Queen's residence with cries of "Vive la Republique," in imitation of the French, the rebellion was firmly and quickly subdued. British leaders knew a country could not flourish in the hands of untutored and unskillful rebels, obscure in their intentions, unruly in their agitation, and totally ignorant of the values of moderation.

Yet even the sovereign of England submitted to ancient vested rights. Amusingly, Albert and Victoria could seldom look out of clean windows in Buckingham Palace: one of their household was vested with the right to wash the windows on the outside, while another had the right to wash them inside, but the two concessionaires rarely appeared the same day. Similarly, one servant laid the fuel in the dining room fireplace, while another was charged with lighting the fire, but it was seldom that the two services were performed simultaneously and Victoria and Albert were often obliged to shiver through their meals. And in parallel with the case of Lola Montez, the moment Prince Albert decided to coordinate these activities he was called an interfering foreigner.

For Lola, England was the worst sort of refuge. She was a notorious and exiled countess who would be viewed by everyone as an upstart who might attempt to gain political influence. Her sudden appearance provoked a storm of speculation, and from the time she arrived in December of 1848 the newspapers attacked her unceasingly because of her audacity in unseating a king.

She left England just as suddenly, however, and for a long time thereafter the newspapers could only report on her whereabouts by unconfirmed rumors gleaned from other newspapers in out-of-the-way places.

Passionate and discontented, Lola may have been merely dramatizing herself when she claimed that during this period she was hidden away with Ludwig in Italy, although French newspapers reported that the King had come to France to meet her. Certainly the condition of Italy at that moment made it a peculiar choice of refuge, for it had united in a war against Austria, whose armies were blockading Rome.

If Lola was indeed with Ludwig it is more likely that they were in Greece, for the despotic King of Greece, Otho, was Ludwig's son. At eighteen he had been elected under an international agreement to rule Greece, but had proved an unhappy choice. Openly contemptuous of Greek culture, he had further antagonized his subjects by levying higher taxes and by importing Germans to fill many official positions.

But Ludwig was known to the Greeks as a worshiper of their antiquities. He had first visited them as a king, to be received with wild enthusiasm, and he had returned many times since. It seems natural that as an abdicated monarch he should now return, and it is reported that in his wanderings among the ruins he often stopped to talk with some other lover of Ancient Greece, never revealing his identity to these chance acquaintances but using his family name of Wittelsbach.

It is quite probable that Lola did in fact join Ludwig at this time. In later years she unwittingly revealed that she had seen the wonders of Athens, and at least once she lectured on the ancient culture, betraying a knowledge of Greek architecture.

Then, according to the New York *Herald*, in the early part of 1849 Lola again arrived in London to take up residence in

Half Moon Street. According to another account, Ludwig had returned to Bavaria. Years later, she said she had gone to London on Ludwig's advice to find a respectable husband. Ludwig had told her of a princess whose reputation had been ruined by scandal but who, once she had made an advantageous marriage, had been accepted by society again. And the princess had achieved this feat in staid, Victorian England. Since Ludwig himself could not marry her, he wanted her to find security and happiness with someone else. He begged only that they might continue to correspond and meet when they could. Her income from his personal fortune, regardless of what she decided to do, was to continue.

This was the situation as she was to relate it afterwards, and subsequent events were to testify to this remarkable arrangement between these two friends whose relationship would never be understood by others, but whose attachment was to last to the end of his life.

In a matter of days after Lola's arrival, London was agog. In defiance of Victorian stuffiness, Lola's first move was calculated to shock. She made her initial appearance in public accompanied by no less a person than Lord Brougham, the Scottish political leader who was engaged in hearing appeals in judicial cases before the House of Lords. Tireless in his efforts to correct abuses in the law, he was endeavoring to introduce vigorous innovations, and it was no surprise that he should champion a woman who believed in reform.

Lola Montez was dressed in her customary black when he escorted her into the Peeresses' Gallery of the House of Lords. There, with a bow, he left her in a front seat from which she could watch as he presided over the night session, which was considering a change in divorce laws. The session dismissed, Brougham reclaimed his companion and they departed in his carriage, of the type that had been named after him, and returned to Half Moon Street.

Soon everyone in London was talking of Lola Montez and trying to get a glimpse of her. Women copied her hair dress, her clothes, and her graceful carriage. Tradespeople put her picture on snuff boxes, fans and souvenirs.

Rumor flew from tongue to tongue: Lord Brougham had asked Lola to marry him and had been refused; the middle-aged Lord Normandy, former Lord Lieutenant of Ireland and now Ambassador to France, was madly in love with her. Lola held soirées which drew the most desirable young bloods of the kingdom, such as Richard Greville, son of the Duke of Buckingham.

But in spite of the brilliance of the company, she remained uncommitted to anyone. No one got to know her well enough to gain her confidence, though newspapermen invaded the house in Half Moon Street and were welcomed into the laughing, talking, music-making company, whose hostess had a facility for making her guests feel welcome and gay. But they learned nothing of her private life or of her hopes and aspirations. Men praised her wit and her beauty, but in the flickering topaz candlelight of her elegant drawing room, it was in better taste to ignore the reports of her affairs in Bavaria.

London became engrossed in Lola's every activity, her every whim. Every day when she walked by herself in the park, a carriage followed her slowly, keeping far enough behind her to escape attention. One of her admirers finally asked her if she had noticed it. Lola said that she remembered only seeing a beautiful dog in a carriage upon a number of occasions, and that if her admirer knew the owner, she would like to inquire whether the animal might be purchased.

The next day the owner, accompanied by a large black New-foundland, made his appearance to present her with the animal as a gift, and she invited him into her house for tea.

The young man who had followed her about the park every day was George Trafford Heald, commissioned as a cornet in the cavalry. Heald was just twenty-one and had come into an inheritance. Blond, with blue eyes, he was exceptionally tall, very juvenile in aspect and figure, had a turned-up nose which did not dignify his appearance, and sported a mustache. An uncomplicated youth, he was eager to find a woman who could return his fervor, and was quite distracted by Lola. But he yearned for her in vain, received no encouragement, and fell violently in love with her. Besieged, she refused to become his mistress, and he had no alternative but to marry her.

Oddly enough this hasty union proved to be supremely satisfying for both of them—to such an extent that they were inpatient of the society of others. Ambitious mamas who had marriageable daughters fumed with disappointment that this most eligible bachelor had been snatched from under their noses. The young man had eight aunts and uncles, all of them bachelors and old maids, and he was the sole heir to their collective and extensive fortunes. Orphaned at an early age, an old maiden aunt, Miss Suzanna Heald, had brought him up, and on his twenty-first birthday, in addition to a lavish income, he had inherited Berrymead Priory, a handsome pile with round tower, battlemented wings and Gothic windows, an epidemic of tall chimneys, and a park commensurate with the size of the former monastery. It was to this splendid retreat that Heald took Lola immediately after their marriage.

Lost in their new-found delight in each other, they received neither the local gentry nor Heald's four bachelor uncles and four maiden aunts. It was July and the nights were warm. By moonlight they walked through the park, enchanted by the perfume of the flowers, and dreamed of a life together that nothing could disturb.

But at that very moment Miss Suzanna Heald was looking for some way to get the marriage between her nephew and his bride set aside so that she could once more dominate the young man who had so long been her charge. This pinch-faced lady, whose virtue had never been tried, was determined to break up this union between a déclassée, immoral woman and the innocent young man whom she had decoyed into her house in Half Moon Street.

Immediately following the marriage Miss Heald had begun to search for damaging secrets in Lola's past, and discovered that Lola had lived in India. Further research along this line revealed exactly the evidence she needed to rid the Heald family of its heir's unthinkable bride. Miss Heald thereupon sought an attorney.

Lola and Heald had been married on July 19th. Nineteen days later Lola returned to London to close down her house in Half Moon Street. She had just unlocked her door when a constable arrived and asked her to accompany him to Marlborough Street Police Station to answer a charge of bigamy.

At the hearing which followed, the police court was so thronged with people that it had to be cleared to make room for the necessary witnesses. At one thirty in the afternoon Lola appeared. Apparently unperturbed, she entered the courtroom with an air of great propriety, wearing a plain dress of black silk and a black straw bonnet trimmed with a ribbon of faïence blue which made her eyes seem the same color; the London *Times* took the trouble to describe her costume in detail. Accompanied by Heald, she took her place in the witness box, with Heald seated close beside her. Her eyes, under their long, black eyelashes, turned almost incessantly toward her husband, and he, sitting near enough to hold her hand, lifted it frequently and pressed it to his lips. Seemingly oblivious to the excitement around them, they talked together in intimate whispers.

Some distance away sat Miss Heald and her attorney, Mr. Clarkson, who presented his case to the magistrate, Mr. Bingham, with an air of being slightly ashamed at finding himself in such a position. Referring to Miss Heald, he began: "Sir, however painful the circumstances under which the lady who sits at my left is placed, she has felt it to be a duty she owes to her deceased brother to lay before you the evidence of her young nephew's marriage with the lady at the bar."

Then, pausing for effect, he continued: "Mr. Heald, the son of the late, well-known Mr. George Heald of the Chancery Bar, has gone through the ceremony of marriage with the lady by his side, Eliza Rosa or Rosanna James."

This first revelation of the real name of the mysterious Lola Montez so startled the courtroom that speculative whispers nearly drowned Mr. Clarkson's next remarks: "I shall further prove to you that the lady is the wife of Thomas James, now captain of the 21st Regiment of Bengal Native Foot, who is at this time with his regiment in India."

The attorney went on to picture Heald as an inexperienced youth of twenty-one, and by implication Lola emerged as a scheming and rapacious female, Clarkson employing the skillful approach of trial lawyers by means of which a subject which is declared to be too scandalous to be discussed becomes by its bare mention the focus of greatest attention.

With the merest glance at Lola, as if it pained him to even look at her, he said: "Whatever may be her distinction or notoriety, I shall refrain from making any allusion to it on such an occasion."

He then told the court that Lola had been married twelve years earlier to Captain James in Ireland, that he had taken her to India, and that she had returned alone five years later. Records in London showed that James had applied for a divorce from "bed and board."

Lola's own account of this marriage is not to be disregarded. She wrote later that her husband, Thomas James, had a mistress with whom he had run away.

"I was obliged to part from him," Lola explained in court. "No one ever accused me of falsehood to my vows of fidelity to him. We were divorced. In that separation I was thrown upon the world friendless, without resources, or any means of support, except my own industry and humble abilities. I was in the East Indies. I went to England and from thence to the Continent and became, as the only resource for an honorable and virtuous livelihood, an artiste, a danseuse. I encountered all those terrible trials incident to a resolution to take care of myself without dependence upon anyone."

When she was asked if she had ever been married before marrying Heald she replied, "I don't deny it."

It was revealed at the hearing that the decree of separation from Captain James was dated December 15th, 1842, but it was not a divorce and neither person could remarry during his or her lifetime.

To this Lola replied that Lord Brougham had later obtained for her a divorce by an Act of Parliament and that he had been present when the divorce had been finally granted. In this she was entirely, though apparently honestly, mistaken.

Clarkson and Lola's attorney, Mr. Bodkin, so far had engaged only in polite tilting, but now Clarkson gave way to the acid retort: "If such an Act of Parliament is in existence, no one knows how to avail himself of it more than my learned friend who appears for the defense."

The existence of the nebulous Captain James was then confirmed by a document showing that he had been alive a month before the Heald marriage.

At this, Lola showed some irritation: "I don't know whether Captain James is alive or not, and I don't care. It was not a legal marriage." To this she added a seeming *non sequitur*: "What will the King say?" Although it was undoubtedly addressed to Heald, who knew and approved of her friendship with Ludwig, the remark appeared reprehensible to those in court.

A few minutes later Lola was startled to see coming forward as a witness Captain Charles Ingram, commander of the East India trader, *Larkin*, the ship upon which she had been a passenger from India.

Her attorney managed to keep the captain at bay for a while by raising a dispute over procedure, for he sensed that Lola was far from popular with the captain. "Never," he objected, "have I seen a case of bigamy in which neither the first nor the second husband came forward as the complaining party."

Then the day's proceedings were brought to an end by the posting of five hundred pounds' bail. Lola and Heald could not even move from their seats for the crowds of spectators waiting in the hall who pressed inward into the room. The police had to clear the court before the Countess could emerge, and even then the street outside was thronged with people, curious to see the woman who had for so long been the subject of constant sensational publicity.

Lola and Heald were scarcely out of the courtroom when she said to him, "We must leave England. There is no tolerance here."

IX

WHEN THE HEARING was resumed Lola did not appear in court, nor could her attorney explain her absence. Neither was Lola's snub-nosed husband to be seen, which was just as well, for the self-righteous, vengeful Miss Heald had been unearthing the Countess's past.

Captain Ingram seemed eager to get at the business of wrecking Lola's currently respectable life, and another surprise witness had been produced by the plaintiff who was the brother of Lola's first husband. He was the Reverend John James of the Parish of Rathbiggen in Meath County, Ireland, a condescending country clergyman who had come to do his part towards nullifying Lola's present marriage. He had performed the ceremony, he said, when his brother had married Lola, and it had been attended by a nephew and sister-in-law of the groom. Captain James and his young bride had gone to live in Dublin and had taken up "lodgings in Westmorland Street."

According to the London *Times*, Miss Heald, with a wintry smile, watched with satisfaction while Captain Ingram traced in minute detail Lola's departure from India and her arrival in England without a husband. Then the Captain's wife, Mrs. Ann Ingram, elaborated the scandal with almost spiteful glee. She had been aboard the *Larkin* at the time Mrs. James embarked at Calcutta, accompanied by both her step-father and her husband. Mr. James, she said, did not leave the ship but stayed on for some time after they had left port, and had talked to his wife earnestly. It seemed that something had happened between the couple and that it was irremediable on the part of the wife.

After asking Captain and Mrs. Ingram to look after his wife, Mr. James had left the ship at Madras. Mrs. James had, however, scorned surveillance and was even more opposed to the concern which Mr. and Mrs. Sturgis, also passengers and said to be friends of Lola's husband, displayed toward her. It was unconventional enough for a young wife to travel alone, but disastrous for her not to submit to the guardianship of her husband's friends. Mrs. James appeared to despise authority and betrayed her scorn whenever her husband's name was mentioned, but Mr. and Mrs. Sturgis seemed to have known the reason for her attitude for even Mrs. Ingram testified that the young lady evidently had their affection and sympathy.

"The *Larkin*," related the captain's wife, "touched at Madras and there received Lieutenant Lennox of the Madras Cavalry as a passenger. Within a few days after, I observed that the conduct of Mrs. James toward him was very unguarded and flighty. Their intimacy soon allowed him to visit her in her cabin. As she was not placed under *our* care," added Mrs. Ingram, with an audible sniff, "we did not think ourselves entitled to expostulate with her. I have," she continued, "repeatedly seen Mr. Lennox and Mrs. James sitting on the sofa, his arm being around her waist. Upon being remonstrated with, she replied that she was her own mistress. I found it necessary to discontinue associating with her and to exclude her visiting my cabin."

Collateral testimony was then offered by the impatient captain: "I have heard Mrs. James address Mr. Lennox as 'dear Lennox' whom she used to receive alone in her cabin," he stated. "He used to be there at very unwarrantable hours; they were alone together while the rest of the passengers were attending divine service on deck."

"I have seen him," he continued, "with his arm around her waist while they were sitting far aft or on the bow late at night. I more than once spoke to her; she answered in a very cool manner that she should do as she liked and would not be under the control of anybody. I saw no more than violent flirting, which in a married woman I considered as very improper. Mrs. James and Mr. Lennox landed from the *Larkin* at Portsmouth on the 20th of February, 1841. Mr. James had not been on board the vessel after Madras."

The maid of the captain's wife testified that she had been able to satisfy her curiosity at first hand. By offering to lace up Mrs. James' stays, she gained access to the cabin, and what went on was apparently enough to make her twitter for days. "I have, more than once, seen Mr. Lennox lace Mrs. James' stays. I have also seen him kiss her. I have also seen Mrs. James in the act of putting on her stockings while Mr. Lennox was in her cabin. It was a general remark on board that they were too intimate."

The next witness was a Mr. Browne Roberts, who had been in the employ of the East India Company. He had been introduced to James and his bride in Dublin, and could therefore testify that such a marriage had existed.

The sister of Captain James then gave her testimony. Lola, she said, had come back from India alone, after having gone out there with her husband. The Captain had written his sister a letter explaining that Lola had had a fall from her horse and was forced to return to England for medical attention. The Captain had also written to his aunt, Mrs. Rae of Edinburgh, asking her to assume charge of Lola upon her arrival.

A Major McMullen next appeared before the bar to say that he too had been asked to take charge of Mrs. James upon her arrival from India. An aged retired major of the East India army, he had invited Lola to stay at his home, but she had "declined to avail herself of the hospitality."

Roberts, recalled to the stand, related that he also had been charged with protecting Lola and had met her upon her arrival. She had, however, disrupted all plans by going alone to the Imperial Hotel. Roberts had visited the hotel the next day in another attempt to place Lola under his protection, but it was evident that she did not intend to be tethered to anyone.

Mrs. Elizabeth Walters, the proprietor of the Imperial Hotel, made it apparent by her testimony that while she was an upholder of British convention, she was even more concerned about collecting her room rent, regardless of its source. She began by describing "a gentleman and lady who arrived in a hackney coach," at her hotel. They had a great deal of luggage and

94

it was obvious that Mrs. Walters was intrigued, if not perplexed, by the fact that some of the manteaus were marked T. Lennox, while the hat boxes and small trunks bore the name of Mrs. T. James.

"I inquired of the lady," recalled Mrs. Walters, "whether one or two bedrooms would be wanted, to which the gentleman answered, 'One bedroom,' and the lady added, 'We want only one bedroom.' The same lady and gentleman supped together. I cannot depose that I actually saw the said lady and gentleman undressed or in bed," she added almost as if in apology for being unable to elaborate on the activities in the "four-poster." "On the following morning," concluded Mrs. Walters, "Mr. Lennox paid the bill and went away."

The next witness was Mrs. Ann Martin, mistress of a lodging house on Great Rider Street. Here Lola had taken the maid into her confidence, saying she did not wish any men callers to be shown in except Mr. Lennox, who came every day, arriving at 9 A.M. but never staying beyond midnight.

Had she so chosen, Lola could have told a quite different story of her departure from India. Her husband, inadequate lover and paramour of another woman, had tried to preserve appearances by feigning remorse over her departure from India, and by accompanying her as far as Madras. He spread the story among his friends that she was returning to England for medical treatment. Lola had no desire to bolster her husband's flagging reputation by such a ruse. He had deserted her, had left her without support, and she had had to bear the humiliation of being placed under the protection of people antagonistic to her.

Outraged by her husband's behavior, she was determined to retaliate, and Lieutenant Lennox, who had boarded the ship at Madras, was a convenient target. Lennox was sincerely in love with her and intended to marry her, but by the time her divorce had been granted in 1842 the Lennox family had come between them and forced the lieutenant to return to India.

But Lola did not wait to tell her story in court. When this excoriation was at last complete it was discovered that she and

Heald had fled England. Miss Heald, therefore, while she had succeeded in denigrating Lola's character, had failed to extricate her nephew from his bogus marriage and had in fact merely insured that the couple would be hounded by newspapers everywhere, thereby dragging her family name into the limelight.

But although the bigamy case ended with the flight of the principals, it was certain that Captain James had divorced his wife "on the usual terms," which meant that neither husband nor wife could again remarry. Lola therefore was not legally married to Heald, in spite of her insistence that Lord Brougham had somehow made arrangements to obtain her absolute freedom.

British propriety was outraged. The Marquis of Londonderry, who was the Colonel of the Second Life Guards, sent a recommendation to Queen Victoria that George Heald's commission be resigned. The Queen apparently agreed, and Heald, who obviously thought life with Lola more colorful than bearing the standard in his regiment, was relieved of his commission in absentia.

X

LOLA WAS DETERMINED not to give up Heald, although the trial seems to have seriously affected their relationship, for she wrote later that she had entered at this time "upon another marriage experiment, of which nothing but sorrow and mortification came."

Just a month after the flight from England, news of the exiles reached London through a letter sent to the editor of the London *Times*, proving that there was to be little privacy for the lovers.

"A youthful bridegroom and a fair lady, answering the description of the enamoured couple," went the letter, "who lately figured at the Marlborough Street police-office, appeared and disappeared yesterday from Naples with all the circumstances of eccentricity which have ever distinguished la belle dame Mrs. James, otherwise known as Lola Montez, the Countess, or Mrs. Heald."

The correspondent reported the rash pair as wishing to avoid the curiosity of the public but displaying great devotion to each other. In Capua they took the train for Naples, but in order to escape from the curious left it en route and engaged a carriage. In Naples the rooms which had been reserved for them were indignantly rejected by Heald as being unfit for his love, and a magnificent apartment on the first floor was given to them instead.

Soon the news of their arrival was spread over the city and the excitement over these nonconformists became so widespread that the indignant hotel-keeper found his public rooms jammed with people waiting patiently but noisily for Lola to make an appearance. Instead, the far less interesting Heald, looking much too unsophisticated to be the lover of such a notorious woman, emerged to visit the bank. There he picked up a letter, the contents of which evidently piqued the curiosity of the crowds, for Heald dashed back to his hotel in evident distress. Within the course of an hour he and Lola, who had locked her door against even the prying hotel help, unexpectedly emerged, taking everyone off guard. Without their servants and with the bulk of their baggage left behind, they attempted to find a boat going to Marseille. They finally gave up the search and engaged a special steamer for the unheard of sum of four hundred pounds and embarked for an unknown destination.

Even the special correspondent for the *Times* had been unable to learn the reason for the sudden flight. Rumor, however, had it that they had gone to Egypt because there one could have more than one wife. This did not explain very clearly what one did about having two husbands.

Lola and her companion had actually gone back to England, for the letter which had been handed to Heald at the bank demanded that they come to London immediately to clear up the misunderstanding about their marriage.

They reached London nearly two weeks later at midnight. Early the next morning Lola sent a message to her solicitor, but word was brought back that he had left for his country place. She wondered at this odd behavior, for the letter she had received in Naples had come from Mr. Bodkin and it seemed peculiar that he should leave London at the very time his letter said he would be awaiting her. She decided to follow him to his country place, but on her arrival she was distracted to learn that Mr. Bodkin was not there, nor was he expected until the next day, having left for Ramsgate on a legal matter. The weary traveller was more and more mystified at her attorney's behavior, for his manservant volunteered that he was certain Mr. Bodkin had not been expecting her in England since he had left no message for her.

Lola returned to the railroad station and took the train for

Ramsgate, determined to track down her solicitor. When she emerged from the train she was delighted to see Mr. Bodkin, but the shock of seeing her stupefied him for the moment. When she spoke of the letter he had written her he hurriedly told her they must get away from the station. In a nearby tea shop she was stunned to learn that he had not written her any such letter.

Bodkin told her that he could only conclude that she had been made the victim of a hoax. He refrained from stating that he believed it was a scheme on the part of Miss Heald to have the bigamy case revived, but he did, however, urge Lola to leave England at once before she was recognized.

The next morning Lola and Heald hurried away, and through their bank made arrangements for their servants to join them with their luggage. Heald was angry at his aunt and indignant at the legal procedure which had been used to besmirch the woman he loved.

In order to make it difficult for anyone to follow them they declared they were on their way to Italy, but Lola went ahead on the Folkstone packet and took up her residence at the Hotel de Londres in Boulogne. Here, with insouciance, she registered as Mrs. Trafford and was gratified that neither Madame Boutoir, who owned the hotel, nor any of her servants recognized her.

Several days later her maid joined her and they walked about town together. Lola seemed to be sure that no one would discover who she was. With her characteristic heedlessness, she called on Duchochois, the jeweler, and left a superb diamond ring to be repaired. She gave her name as Mrs. Trafford and calmly went back to the hotel. The jeweler discovered that engraved on the inside of the ring was a crown and the name "Grafin von Landsfeld." He was mildly curious but not being particularly conversant with the story of Lola Montez, for the moment he thought no more of the inscription.

Later that same day a postman arrived at the Hotel de Londres with a letter addressed to the Countess of Landsfeld. Madame Boutoir said that no one of that name was registered and Lola was obliged to go to the post-office for the letter and identify herself to the postmaster.

Only then did the town become aware of the beautiful visitor's identity. The citizens were frantic to see her and the next time she appeared on the street, news of her presence quickly spread from one person to another. Lola wore a gray dress and a gray bonnet trimmed with orange that day, and everyone remarked upon the size of her lustrous blue eyes and the paleness of her skin. The men especially observed what they called her "negligée figure."

Four days later the gentlemen of the town, who had been eyeing Lola Montez speculatively and evidently wondering if she was ripe for a new attachment, were disappointed to find that she had been joined by Heald.

A newspaperman who dared to talk to Heald learned that he believed implicitly in Lola's statement that Lord Brougham had changed the English divorce law in order to free her from James. Although Lord Brougham bedazzled his opponents in court with his proud dignity, he was eccentric to a degree. Bitterly opposed to his Aunt Suzanna's proceedings against Lola, Heald had fled with his inamorata, believing that a proposition to change the divorce law, introduced by Brougham at the time he had surprised all London by being seen in public with Lola, had actually been passed. Brougham was forever engaged in the betterment of the law and Heald had no knowledge that the amendment had not been passed, nor had Lola. Bodkin, having found no recent changes in the law, had been trying unsuccessfully to see Brougham at the time that Heald and Lola decided to outwit Miss Heald by disappearing.

Heald had not seen Bodkin since their flight. He did not, therefore, yet know that his marriage was void, since Lola had kept from him the details of her conversation with Bodkin in the tea shop at Ramsgate. Without regard to the legal aspects of the situation she saw no reason to be deprived of the physical satisfaction she had found with Heald or the pleasures she was deriving from an indolent life of complete financial security.

To a group of companions in later years she told of her decision to flout the law and convention: "I would do what I pleased and doing what I pleased I should have my will, and having my will I should be contented and when we are contented there is no more to be desired."

Yet though Heald considered the world well lost for Lola, a lifetime of training, of judgments, of reserves, of natural reactions was not easily dismissed. Basically he was the true disciple of British convention, only temporarily absorbed by his passion and rejecting any interference from his relatives with what he still believed was a perfect marriage. It was not improbable that he might tire of gratification and come to regard himself as too much guided by passion. But for the moment he stood as the bulwark against what he called the "persecution of Lola" by those who had no understanding of love, whose practice of continence had warped their natures. "I will protect Lola from them," Heald once said, "if it takes my whole fortune."

Scarcely a week after Heald and Lola met in Boulogne they had their first quarrel, apparently over her acceptance of a ring from Ludwig. At the time of her marriage to the guardsman, she had agreed to relinquish the large pension from Ludwig, but the matter of the jewelry he had given her remained unsettled. Heald himself had given her a diamond engagement ring worth more than five hundred pounds, as well as his family jewels, and when he suggested that she return at least the crown jewels Ludwig had given her, Lola so frightened him by a violent burst of temper that he had not referred to the matter again. He had been lenient in regard to the daily letters from Ludwig and had even been willing to meet the ex-King in France for a brief visit. Lola shared Ludwig's letters with her husband and let him read her replies. She had therefore assumed that Heald would regard with equal complacency the gift of a new ring from Ludwig. Instead Heald held that her action in accepting anything more was unpardonable, and all her wiles had failed to change his point of view.

A month later when Lola and her lover in their incessant travels reached Barcelona she was approached by a correspondent of the New York *Herald* who asked her to tell him of her romance. Lola was not averse to the interview, although the reporter caught her rather by surprise. He was much taken with her and was impressed with her sincerity and frankness in explaining her friendship and great regard for Ludwig. Quite openly she told of the pension and of the daily letters, saying that the King had been a benefactor and that she looked upon him as if he were her father.

"Nothing can be more romantic than the manner in which she relates the circumstances attendant on her marriage with Mr. Heald," wrote the enthusiastic newsgatherer. Lola told him how Heald had followed her in a carriage about the park, of his first visit to her house in Half Moon Street, and of their engagement when he had placed upon her finger the valuable diamond which she showed to her interviewer. Growing still more confidential, she revealed that Heald had arranged to pay her a life annuity and had provided for their possible children.

Once again Heald and Lola were at variance. Heald was more than a little put out at having his private affairs discussed with a newspaperman and he made it clear that he was gravely offended by her unconventional behavior. Lola should have been forewarned by the use of the term unconventional, for these increasingly frequent displays of wrath over her conduct indicated that gradually he was reverting to his British conservatism.

In Barcelona, matters reached a climax. From an Englishman and his wife he learned the story of the results of the investigation into the charge of bigamy which had been brought against Lola. Heald now knew that he was not actually married to her. For some time he had been uneasy but, still under her spell, had listened only to Lola's version of her status. Having now learned that he had been deceived, and urged by the Englishman and his wife to terminate his relationship with Lola Montez, he was torn between desire to break with her and an unaccountable dread of her being possessed by another man. His new knowledge, which at first he kept from her, beat at him like the slapping of water against a pier. Finally, loathing for his anomalous situation drove him to face her with her duplicity; she had, he said accusingly, seen his solicitor, Bodkin, and she must have learned from him the true status of her second marriage. Lola did not deny it. There was no display of that uncertain temper of hers. Instead she appeared merely depressed and withdrawn from him. He finally drew from her the admission that she was convinced the world was against her, that it was her inevitable fate always to have happiness snatched from her.

Just what the situation was between them thenceforth can only be gathered indistinctly from a few rather incomplete records.

People in Barcelona who knew Heald noted that he grew increasingly pale and thin. When someone remarked on his pallid appearance he made an attempt to hide it by rouging his cheeks. To his intense embarrassment this device was detected by a newspaper correspondent.

The New York *Herald* correspondent, still covering the news in Barcelona, commented on the unexplained rift between Heald and Lola. They no longer appeared in public together and Heald was provoked when anyone asked him about Lola.

From the office of the British Consul the *Herald* correspondent learned a strange story. Heald appeared at the Consul's office one day and announced: "I am come to ask your advice. I have some friends here who recommend me to abandon my wife. What ought I to do? I am afraid of being assassinated or poisoned. At Perpignan she stabbed me."

Heald thereupon unwrapped a waistcoat stained with blood which he offered as proof of the incident.

The Consul was annoyed. "I am astonished," he replied, "that after the attack you speak of, you have not laid a complaint before the police at Perpignan, and that you have since lived on such intimate terms. But if you wish to abandon your wife, I have no advice to give you." He did, however, offer to viser Heald's passport to any place he wished to go.

Since the Consul repeated the story of Heald's visit to his friends, it was not surprising that Lola herself finally heard it from someone.

Strange to say, Lola was not angry that an accident Heald had suffered should have been twisted by him into this melodramatic version. She was angry, however, that having criticized her for making innocent enough disclosures to a newspaper reporter, he should have proceeded to invent a tale which was utterly fantastic and which had now been broadcast throughout the world. In a bitter quarrel, she accused him of being unstable, which was apparently more than the over-wrought man could endure. The result was that Heald sent his passport to the British Consul and later that day he vanished from Barcelona. The Consul refused to reveal where he had gone.

Oddly enough Heald's friends had by now swung over to Lola's defense. Feeling that they must remedy the damage they had done by telling him of the illegality of his marriage, the Englishman and his wife (whose names have not been preserved) decided that they would make amends by writing her a letter. The letter was unsigned but it read: "Use discretion or you are lost," and went on to reveal Heald's destination. Lola was advised to join him, and was told that Heald could be reasoned with if she would ask his forgiveness.

Not knowing the source of the letter at that time, Lola was frightened that it might be some sort of scheme to get her to enter France, where Heald was reported to have gone. If she now entered France she could be extradited to England, where the charge of bigamy could still be brought against her. She decided to remain where she was, and although she seemed to be friendless, she showed signs of neither restlessness nor anxiety. She daily rode horseback, dressed with her usual care and went to the post-office to mail letters as if nothing had occurred.

Lola knew Heald better than those who had attempted to advise her. In a matter of weeks he returned to her. Her behavior during his absence was exemplary, for she anticipated that inevitably some gossip would keep tabs on her whereabouts and activities. Being above reproach, she could afford to receive him in a truculent mood when he returned. If he wanted to work his way back into her good graces, he would have to woo her with every attention.

When Heald and Lola emerged from seclusion after his return, it was to visit a gambling casino, and an indefatigable collector of gossip, a certain Baroness des Marguerites, was on hand to describe the occasion, later to be published in a book she wrote. The Baroness either knew nothing of the dissolved marriage or did not recognize Heald, because she referred to him merely as a *cavaliere servente* and described him as being upper middle class.

To the Baroness, Lola seemed listless, dispiritedly hanging onto her gentleman companion. Nor did the Baroness judge Lola's character correctly. She described her as being disinterested in her surroundings but growing immediately excited when she drew close to the gaming table. Lola, said the misinformed chronicler, was a "desperate gambler" who found the bright lights and the crowded room exciting.

Lola left the room for several moments and when she returned without shawl or bonnet, the attention of the room was riveted upon her. Both men and women forgot the piles of gold on the table and even the cold-eyed, utterly remote croupier allowed his eyes to focus upon her.

She was dressed in a velvet gown of ruby red, with tight fitting waist and draped skirt. Her head was crowned with thick braids which ended in shining black curls at the back of her neck. The Baroness enthusiastically compared her beauty to a painting by Titian.

When she moved toward the gaming table people followed her and shortly nearly everyone in the room had moved up behind her to watch her white hand, heavy with an enormous ruby, engaged in pushing piles of gold to the stake. Pile after pile disappeared, but her face showed no expression except a slight tightening of the lips as if she were determined to win at least one stake. Heald stood behind her and she kept putting her hand over her shoulder for more gold pieces. Finally, when Heald ran out of funds, Lola turned her head with annoyance.

Relentlessly the croupier called his song-song, "Faites vos jeux."

Lola turned to her lover, saying impatiently, "Come. Money, quick the money!"

Heald flushed, replying, "You have played enough. Come away."

Lola stamped her foot and hit the table with clenched fist in a sudden temper. When Heald remonstrated that he had no more money with him, Lola arose from her seat and hit him on the head. "Learn," she said, "that he who has the honor to accompany Lola must always have money at his command."

That evening they quarreled again and again he ran away. But he could not bear to be parted from her, intolerable as he found his situation as merely her lover. Over and over they separated, only to come together again, he sacrificing his pride, she glorying in her power over him.

XI

A LONG STAY in Madrid, marked by violent quarrels and reconciliations, was followed by a gap of one month in which there were no rumors or stories of her whereabouts.

Then in Paris in November of 1849 she was seen one evening at the ballet *La Filleule des Fées*. It was here that people gathered on the staircase to see her emerge only to discover that they could not positively identify her because her face was veiled.

Her appearance at the theatre, her flight to her carriage where she had ruined her slippers in the mud in order to escape from the people trying to identify her, threw Paris in an uproar. Everyone had supposed that she was afraid to come to Paris for fear of being extradited to England to face the charge of bigamy, which had never been withdrawn.

But several nights after her veiled appearance at the theatre she arrived at the Opéra in a calèche, drawn by four white horses and manned by a footman and coachman with powdered hair, both dressed in startling crimson. From the carriage she emerged unveiled. Heald was with her, but no one bothered to notice him. Men and women alike looked upon Lola's beauty in amazement, the women not a little envious, the men openly admiring.

Within a matter of days Lola left again for Madrid with Heald. She had told friends in Paris that Heald was ill and that his doctor had advised him to return to Spain. But it was neither her lover's health nor her capriciousness which had caused their departure but fear of extradition. The newspaperman Eugène Guinot had got the truth from her in a hurried interview. Once more Heald's relentless relatives were trying to disrupt their romance, but Lola declared that she was competent to deal with the struggle. "The sentence is not yet ready to be pronounced. I am rich enough, and the English lawyers have plenty of skill to prolong the duration of the trial for ten years to come. Ten years are as long as eternity."

Heald was on Lola's side, and he had made no move to terminate the marriage that had been proved illegal. She was well aware of his relatives' attitude toward her; they did not wish her to share in the money they would leave Heald as their only heir. Suzanna had inflamed her sisters and brothers against Lola and all of them, without exception, joined her in exhorting their nephew to leave her. Heald's friends were solidly on his side and urged him to stay away from England. The relatives' only hope was that they might have Lola brought to England and there disgrace her so completely that George would be compelled to leave her.

Their expectations that he would abandon Lola for good were not fulfilled, though they labored in a delirium of plots and counterplots, hoping to bring their mad nephew to his senses. One of the silliest schemes of all was conceived by one of the bachelor uncles, an epicurean in principle, who offered a reward of three hundred thousand francs to any girl who could bring George back to England by winning him away from Lola.

Lola, enraged by this final insult, made up her mind that she and Heald would move from place to place so rapidly that any woman who believed she could divide them would be left behind, unable to follow their rapid course. They went from Paris to Madrid, to Palermo, to Naples, to Nice, where they visited Ludwig, and to Geneva. Even the newspapers could scarcely keep up with their course.

In spite of this frantic travelling to escape Heald's relatives, an agent of the family caught up with them and advertised to the young ladies of Nice the spoils in store for anyone who could wrench Heald away from his fascinating companion. In this conspiracy the agent found an abundance of candidates.

Little did Heald's relatives suspect that Lola delighted in the game they forced her to play. Any attempt to separate her from the young man who loved her so madly quickened her pride in the possession of a lover who could give her so much intimate pleasure, in spite of his recurrent periods of pulling away from her because of his basic belief in conventional behavior. While he was actually unhappy to be considered a man of easy morals, the thought of foregoing this magnificent passion only strengthened his determination to continue to possess a woman as beautiful, as witty, and as intelligent as Lola. How he held her interest was an enigma to him. She had given up her income from Ludwig and a far more glamorous life to be alone with Heald, when she might have selected a title, wealth as great as his, or any one of a dozen clever men who would have paid obsequious court to her. Heald annoyed her with his changeable humors and she was quick to take offense at his bluntness, but she was the first to compromise, to ask forgiveness, to forget that anything had happened between them. He never had to reassure himself about her love. She never mentioned their social ostracism or dissatisfaction with their isolated life. When she became restless, as she often did, whatever pleasure she sought was always set aside if it did not amuse him. Surely no man could ask for more than to have such a gay and charming woman desire to be with him constantly.

They went back to Barcelona and from there to Cadiz on their endless peregrinations. Here Lola had one of her outbursts of rage at Heald's bondage to British convention. She failed to realize that, torn between his relatives' constant hostility to his present mode of life and her smoldering temper at his family's harassment of her, Heald had grown unstable and had developed a dread of trouble from any source whatever.

With his English servant, Heald made an unexplained departure on Christmas Day. From the Hotel Ismenez he went straight to Gibraltar. Lola was in a frenzy of outraged feelings. With her usual talent for quick action, she pressed into service the owner of the hotel and a willing guest and went with them in a French steamer to Algeçiras in an attempt to persuade Heald to return. This chaotic trip was in vain; to her dismay Heald had already embarked for England on the steam packet *Pacha*.

Lola was now a friendless and lonely woman sacrificed by a weak man who had given way to the pressure of his relatives. However, she brooded for but a short time on rash schemes to get Heald to return, and regaining her tranquillity, decided that she would remain where she was since he was bound to return of his own accord.

She curbed her passion for activity, refusing to accept the attentions of other men who were only too eager to console her. Her heart had been ruthlessly injured; she was cynical, yet she waited.

Then one day the French newspaper, *Le Siècle*, had news of Lola for its readers. "Paris is in a great uproar. The excitement is terrible. Lola Montez is back again in Paris!"

Lola, attended by a steward and her maid, had arrived to take up residence in an elegant mansion, the Hotel Beaujon, located at the end of the rue de Pouthieu. The gentlemen of Paris were delighted to see her alone because they assumed that she had tired of Heald and left him. She was gay, she was charming, and she was vulnerable. And here in Paris a man might be a libertine without criticism.

All the great beaux of Paris—the Prince of Como, Count Blum, Michel de Coral—began to calculate upon how soon they might call and still preserve social decorum.

They could scarcely contain their chagrin when five carriages rolled up in front of the house on the rue de Pouthieu a number of days later to disgorge, in addition to a staff of servants, the snub-nosed, blond Englishman, ubiquitous pseudo-husband of the great beauty.

Word of Heald's arrival was spread about Paris. Lola could not have planned a more successful stratagem than to bring him to the French capital, for in spite of herself she was the object of rivalry among the fashionable men of the town and the advent of Heald was timely.

The French press kept track of what Lola was doing, even learning of some of the activities in her household. The owner of the house which Lola had rented had left stored in the wine cellar an abundant supply of vintage wines. The landlady, without warning, decended upon the house with a cart to haul away the wine, and was assisted by a group of chattering relatives of the owner who dispersed themselves throughout the household, peering curiously into everything owned by the Countess. Lola, at breakfast with Heald, flew into a violent temper at this commotion. Antagonistic toward the owner, who was a woman of avaricious nature and little manners, Lola had already forbidden her to come into the house as long as she was in possession. Now when Lola attempted to push her out of the door, the owner resisted. She was a huge Irishwoman with a temper worse than Lola's, and in the struggle she hurled the insulting phrase "your ex-Grace," which infuriated Lola, whose Bavarian title had been recognized by Ludwig's son. Lola emerged from the contest considerably scratched and presented a formal complaint before the police court.

In England the London *Globe* was not exactly keeping trace of Lola, but in its columns was a record of the latest attempts to prove her marriage illegal. The final proceedings were begun in the case through the written order of the Marlborough Street magistrate either to produce Lola in person and complete the charge against her or to forfeit the bail put up for her appearance.

To the amazement of everyone Heald, who was probably tired of Lola's tempers, suddenly left for England, went over completely to the side of his relatives, and brought the lawsuit to a sudden end by allowing the marriage to be declared void. He was free and Lola no longer had any claim on his money or his inheritances.

XII

A MONTH LATER Lola appeared in the Champ de Mars, on a Sunday afternoon when the stands were packed and the avenue to the racetrack crowded.

She entered the stand shortly after the second race began. As soon as one horse pulled into a safe lead, the attention of the crowd was turned to Lola Montez, the most exciting, the most distracting, the most notorious and independent woman in Paris. She was not afraid to appear alone, this legendary woman, who was emerging seemingly unscathed from a tempestuous love affair that had been the talk of the Continent.

Her choice of costume betrayed her dark frame of mind; her black dress, copied from the last garment worn by Mary Stuart, and the red carnations in her hair indicated that she had again returned to her Dujarier period. The preceding day she had slipped out of her house and visited the grave of her lover. Here she felt the full depth of her bitter frustrations and disillusionment. For some reason inexplicable to her she was unable to summon up the presence of Dujarier and from then on no calamity was as great to her as the loss of her power of "feeling" the spirit of her dead lover.

Seven years later, after another lover was to die tragically, she was to tell of her experiences in bringing Dujarier's presence back to her, but she confused those about her in her attempts to explain this peculiar awareness of the nearness of a person no longer alive. Such people as Laura Keene and Edwin Booth and the mother of Lotta Crabtree listened to her sympathetically, but only Mrs. Crabtree understood her well enough to capture her meaning. A California newspaper, the *Golden Era*, speculated about her odd claim and came to the conclusion that she had taken up spiritualism.

In Paris that day at the races she did not want the company of the living except at a distance. She was breaking her heart with a wild grief because she believed that she would never find Dujarier again. Those who beheld her saw, or so the Paris newspapers said, only a beautiful woman with a proud and remote air.

A day or two later an American banker, Mr. Green, was told that a lady wished to see him. A beautiful woman was ushered in whose walk was firm and graceful and who was dressed with perfect restraint. Her expression was vexed and her voice betrayed a cold fury which she sought to conceal.

"You are Mr. Green, the banker?" she asked.

"Yes, madam, at your service," he replied.

"Well, sir," she declared, "I wish you to keep this for me."

She threw on his desk with an air of disdain a bundle tied up in a large embroidered handkerchief.

"What is it, madam?" asked the banker.

"Four hundred thousand francs," was the scornful reply.

"Eighty thousand dollars. Well!" exclaimed Mr. Green. "To whom have I the honor of speaking?"

"To Lola Montez," she answered. "I have no confidence in French funds and think it more proper to invest my money in American stocks."

Mr. Green tried in vain to conceal his astonishment. Lola unbent with a little smile. "My intention," she said, "is to buy a house in the Champs Élysées. No matter about the price. I have more funds, which I will soon put in your hands."

The banker opened the bundle to find stocks and bonds, all of them sound investments.

"Now," said Lola, "I have many things to buy, and I must have bank bills to pay my milliners, dressmakers, and other people."

"How much do you wish to have, madam?" asked Mr. Green.

"About 50,000 francs," she replied.

The American banker immediately put this sum at her disposal and Lola, without even asking for a receipt for her securities, swept out of the office after a bow of thanks.

The following Sunday, at a grand soirée given by Mr. Green at his house in the Place St. Georges, the banker talked of his visit from Lola Montez. Since Mr. Green had already spread the story of her interest in American investments, speculation was rife as to whether or not La Montez was going to America. The ladies present had another theory. One of them recalled the report that Lola had once said she would "hook a prince." Perhaps Lola was planning on capturing Prince Louis Napoleon, then President of the French Republic?

Napoleon was not popular with the people, and although he tried to meet them on common ground by driving through the streets in an American buggy, his efforts were received more with contempt than warmth. Few people along the boulevards gave him a cheer. His horsemanship was remarkably expert, but even this brought only sarcasm from a noted wit: "It would be well if he knew how to drive the chariot of our government as well as he does that American buggy."

When Mr. Green's guests suggested that Lola might be trying to attract Louis Napoleon, one man called forth a general laugh by saying, "Louis Napoleon is small change beside Lola Montez."

Lola took up her residence on the Champs Élysées in an elegant private hotel from which she emerged each day to enter a shining carriage drawn by four white horses. She dressed often in an amazing gown of faïence blue, which, even at a distance, matched the color of her eyes under their heavy, curling lashes, and which threw into relief her delicate complexion, the pomegranate red of her lips. Over her glossy black curls she wore a high hat with a broad brim, trimmed with purple clematis, a rather peculiar choice since that flower was known as "Virgin's Bower" in Paris.

Inclement spring weather with a high wind kept fashionable Paris at home. May brought even more miserable weather and

Lola stayed beside the fire which was kept going day and night against the bitterness of the cold. Gossips about Paris said she was writing her autobiography, but she was in fact occupied mostly in keeping up a copious correspondence with Ludwig, who was at Nice.

Not until May 24th was Lola seen out again, when she went to the Opéra. While Lola watched the performance from a box, her servants were in difficulties with a mob of men who had gathered about her expensive carriage, shouting that it was an insult to the common people for anyone to drive about in a carriage so lavishly equipped. Only through her driver's quick-wittedness was it rescued from the same fate as her carriage in Bavaria, which had been destroyed by a mob. When the angry men asked who owned the carriage, the driver said it belonged to Eugene Sue, the French novelist, at the moment a candidate for a public office, nominated by the common people. In embarrassment the would-be rioters desisted.

After this fracas Lola kept to her house. Outside the wind howled and there were incessant showers. Wearing a *robe de chambre* over her dress in order to keep warm, she sat for hours beside her fireplace. From her window she could look out upon the all but deserted street. She did not venture forth from home until June, when she went to see the opening of Alexandre Dumas's play *Pauline*.

Since Lola made only a few appearances at the theatre and lived quietly, taking an occasional drive in the afternoon along the boulevards, she was thought to be capricious and people criticized her extravagance in keeping a coachman, a footman and four horses to drive her calèche. She indulged in no flirtations, in spite of the gentlemen who repeatedly called on her. She was uncommunicative, estranged from everyone, scarcely talked to her servants, and was remote and formally polite to the milliners and dressmakers who served her. Her greatest interest seemed to be in books, and she bought the latest writings of her friends Dumas, Hugo, Gautier, the close friend of Dujarier, and George Sand. A bookseller told a newspaperman of seeing Lola buy a bunch of violets which she then pressed against her cheek while tears welled from her eyes. She was, perhaps, remembering the times that Dujarier had purchased violets for her.

Toward the latter part of June, Victor Hugo held a soirée in his residence on the rue Rochechouart for twenty-four guests, most of them men. The day proved to be unbearably hot and the men dressed in silk jackets, while the few ladies came in linen. Hugo had invited Lola but, because she had withdrawn almost entirely from society, he did not expect her to appear. He was therefore filled with delighted surprise when her calèche drew up before his entry. Moments later Lola entered, ethereal in a deceptively simple Grecian gown of white crêpe. Her long hair was wound about her head in two braids, and here and there from its black depths were peeking the tiny blossoms of forget-me-nots. In their excitement at seeing her Alexandre Dumas and Théophile Gautier embraced her and kissed her on both cheeks.

The dinner which followed was in honor of Manin, the ex-president of the revolutionary Republic of Venice. To have captured Lola for the occasion was a decided triumph for Victor Hugo, for she had the reputation of being a recluse whom no one could entice out.

This evening seemed to mark the end of Lola's period of depression. She even went to public ceremonies where, as the newspapers reported, she was the center of everyone's attention, being the most beautiful and the best dressed woman there. Since the President also attended, gossip was revived that she intended to capture the interest of Louis Napoleon, despite the fact that everyone knew he was enamored of Mrs. H—— at the time, identified only as a lady from Baltimore.

On that same day the Parisians found advertisements in the bookstores of Lola Montez's memoirs, and those of George Sand, both of which were soon to appear. Parisians wondered how many of their sins the two famous women would confess. Booksellers promised they would tell all; good and bad and in detail.

But Lola's memoirs did not appear and a month later an upholsterer, who had furnished the house which Heald had rented for Lola when they had been in Paris together, appeared at her door to say that he was to have been paid this month. Lola told the tradesman that Mr. Heald had returned to England without leaving her the money promised.

The following day the upholsterer returned to press his claim. To his shocked surprise he saw the very furniture he had sold Heald being loaded into a cart. He applied to the Commissioner of Police for an order to prevent the removal, but learned to his dismay that Lola had left hurriedly for Compiègne to meet no less a person than George Trafford Heald. The upholsterer discovered that some nervous creditor had already seized the furniture in an attempt to secure money due him.

Also nervous over her hurried departure was M. Jacquand, the artist who had painted a portrait of Lola and Heald which was to be shown at the forthcoming exhibition at the Louvre. At Lola's house, with its red silk wall coverings and velvet hangings, he managed to quiet his fellow creditors by assuring them that Mr. Heald was very wealthy.

Lola, through her banker, Mr. Green, eventually paid her bills, but she did not return. It was said she had departed for Brussels with Heald and from there had gone to some unknown place.

XIII

LOLA HAD NOT JOINED Heald, as had been reported, nor had she gone to Compiègne. For a time her trail was lost, although the newspapers eventually learned her movements.

She had gone to England in pursuit of her lover, but despite her boldness, when she arrived at Berrymead Priory, she could not elbow her way past a whole household of blunt servants, bristling with propriety. Heald, like some tender fledgling, she believed to be nestled among the miserable maiden aunts and bachelor uncles, all standing with compressed lips awaiting the battle. Lola's passionate manner, her wearisome arguments, accomplished nothing with them. Perfume and elegance and flashing eyes made no impression upon these adamant people. But in the course of the unproductive interview, she gained the distinct impression that Heald was not at Berrymead Priory and that they did not know where he was. He was mysteriously hidden not from her but from them. She caught this tiny thread and looked for its end. The problem of finding Heald occupied her mind to the exclusion of everything else, and her imagination led her to untangle and put together the broken skein.

The truth was worse than anything she could have supposed. It was only fourteen months since that first meeting with Heald in Half Moon Street and she had lived a century of episodes, not all of them pleasant. She thought suddenly of the man who had introduced them, and going off to London at once by post-chaise on this fall evening, she eventually arrived at the door of Heald's friend. The man, whom Lola identified later only as John, showed bitterness toward her. Yet he was also critical of Heald's family. He blamed Lola for her caprice and Heald's relatives for their tyranny. John admitted he knew Heald's whereabouts, but he was determined that Suzanna Heald would not learn where her nephew was hidden and he was equally disinterested in helping Lola. She had succeeded only in making herself ridiculous in the opinion of a disdainful, supercilious Englishman.

During her stay in London the newspapers made fun of her, and even worse, claimed she was "in a very destitute condition," indicating that she was chasing Heald in order to get hold of much needed funds.

Lola's situation was in fact quite serious. Actually Heald was drinking himself to death somewhere and Suzanna Heald, by trying to have him termed irresponsible and placed under the supervision of his attorney, sought to stop Lola's access to his funds.

Unable to get anywhere with her case, Lola went back to Paris. Upon her return she found the city nearly frozen by a raging gale. Her thin mousseline de laine dress clung to her wetly as she sought to find a lodging place commensurate with her income, which was reduced to the dividends paid to her from her shares in La Presse and the theatre stock left to her by Dujarier.

From the little money left to her by Heald she made a purchase which was to prove profitable, but which, for the time being, seemed to have been a discouraging mistake. The California Gold Rush was on, and she had no sooner paid several thousand dollars for stock in a gold mine there than she learned that companies had sprung up all over Europe to sell shares in fictitious mines. It was a craze, a wild speculation. In Paris it was reported that the authorities in California were investigating these fraudulent companies.

But Lola, although she did not know it then, had bought stock in a very profitable mine, the Eureka, which a Frenchman named Lamarque had promoted. Her investment was to cause a great change in her life.

There were reports that Lola was going to America, which seem to have stemmed from her interest in California mining stocks. In New York the newspapers noted the report and called her an enchantress. There was no doubt that the whole world was interested in what she would do next.

In Nice Ludwig read of Lola's pursuit of Heald. He also noted an item from Munich stating that his son intended to put up Lola's palace at auction. Ludwig, the man of no decision in a national crisis, hurried to Munich only to discover that this story was merely a rumor. There, according to a California newspaper, he spent several days in Lola's house, surrounded by her things just as she had left them. Now that she had been long gone from Munich, people spoke to the ex-King of her many kindnesses to the poor and unfortunate. Ludwig was astonished that his former subjects who had been so averse to her when she had been in Munich now seemed to miss her flashing presence.

After finding a less expensive residence in Paris, Lola was next seen frequently in the company of Prince Jung Bahadoor, the exotic Ambassador from Nepal, who claimed that he had known Lola in India. The Ambassador, a Hindu of the highest caste, had been educated at Oxford, but the Parisians sneeringly referred to him as "the educated barbarian." To everyone's astonishment he and Lola conversed easily together in a Hindu dialect.

It was in honor of the Prince that Meyerbeer staged his last great opera *L'Africaine*.

The mood of the California Gold Rush had crept into Paris, and the opera house was refurnished in what was erroneously believed to be the style of the theatres built in San Francisco. The seats had been upholstered in crimson velvet and the walls were paneled in red silk. The paintings on the ceiling had lost their pastels, and were gilded and retouched with the brightest colors. The style was basically Victorian, and the California theatres would not catch up to it for at least two more years; then they would call it, paradoxically, the latest mode of Paris.

Lola attended the performance of *L'Africaine* with Jung Bahadoor. The Prince was proud of his race and his education and was well aware of the disdainful glances cast his way, but he met them with an impassive face. The attention of the audience was soon diverted, however, by an actress, Madame Octave, who smoked a cigar during the intermission and drew from the circle of outraged spectators a subdued murmur of disapproval. The Prince alone refrained from noticing her gaucherie.

After he had departed from Paris Lola received from him a box filled with precious gems and an India shawl embroidered in gold and diamonds. The gifts were, he wrote, "a mark of esteem."

The caustic wits of Paris could not resist comment about everything Lola did. One day she stopped on the boulevard to pet Ernir, the lion which a French officer had brought back with him from Africa and which followed him about as if it were a dog. "Ah," exclaimed a wit, "Lola is an untamed woman a lion would be afraid to pet."

Because of Lola's reduced scale of living there were soon renewed rumors that she was destitute. She became an object of pity, crushed with humiliation, pathetically friendless, given to weeping or resigned to oblivion, according to whoever was giving an account of her. One story had it that she had been the mistress of the Hindu and that she was inconsolable because he had not taken her back to Nepal with him. More astonishing was the romantic whisper that Lola Montez, worn out from her excesses, had grown penitent and was about to give up the pleasures of the flesh. She was even said to have declared her intention to retire into the house of the Carmelites at Madrid.

While Paris waited in suspense for her conversion, Lola was engaged in a complete revolution of her life and was about to emerge as a social sensation. She had only to appeal to Ludwig, and this she did. Having regained her pension from him, she was determined to surround herself once more with admirers in an impressive setting. Soon she was to be seen daily upon the boulevards visiting the leading shops to purchase furniture, paintings, looking glasses and rich carpets. She frankly admitted that she had met her friend Ludwig and that he had given her the money for her new establishment in the rue Blanche.

Once firmly settled in the house, she began to appear at public places with Michel de Coral, the most desirable beau of the fashionable world. With her wit and beauty Lola had no difficulty in snaring him, to the fury of mothers of marriageable daughters, but her real purpose was only to arouse Heald's jealousy so that he would descend upon Paris to snatch her back.

She avoided taking de Coral as her lover, partly because she hoped for Heald's return and partly because Paris no longer regarded irregular relationships with the same toleration. Men, of course, still believed in their freedom to love, but they no longer bragged or swaggered indiscreetly when they took mistresses nor did they flaunt them, even in Bohemian circles. Lola could not hope to draw to her salon the women of highest social rank because of her curious reputation as the friend of Ludwig and the bigamous wife of the departed George Heald. She was quite content, however, to enjoy the company of the men who seldom took their wives anywhere and she was careful to invite only those she could be sure would accept her invitations. In December she sent out letters of invitation for the first soirée in her new home. "*Madame La Comtesse de Landsfeld*," they read, "*à l'honneur de vous prier de passer la soirée chez elle, mardi le 6 Decembre 1850. On fera de la musique. Pour huit heures. De la part de M. de Coral.*"

So completely was the soirée a success that no invited guest declined and Lola's house was hardly adequate to hold all the Assembly members, the Élysée employees, and the more distinguished guests such as the Russian Prince, General Soltikoff; General de Grammont; the Earl of Sussex; a wealthy American, Frederick Tudor, known as the "Ice King"; and Henry Wykoff, the suitor of the great ballet dancer, Fanny Elssler, who had just bought a country villa outside Vienna.

George Trafford Heald's absence was conspicuous by implication, for the salon was over-run with fully uniformed officers of the English East India company who had turned out en masse to support Lola in her initial social venture.

The Countess of Landsfeld surprised as well as charmed them. Those who had been under the impression that she was rude, noisy, and vulgar discovered that she had the refinement, education and graciousness appropriate to her title.

Nor was Lola, presiding over her new residence, dressed as the courtesan she had been made out to be; she was unpretentious and dignified. Her hair was curled and caught back with a heavy gold chain and above this, at the side of her head, a white camellia gave contrast to the blackness of her hair. Her gown of white watered silk was modest in the extreme, and across it was the grand cordon given her by King Ludwig, with the title of nobility, which lent some authority to the prestige she boasted had been hers in Bavaria.

After the music was ended, a supper, supplied by Chevêt, the noted caterer of the day, was served to the several hundred guests. The evening was indeed a success, and when Lola announced that she would soon give another soirée, newspapermen begged to be invited so that such a socially important affair might be fully reported.

Only a few days later the *Memoirs of Lola Montez*, which had been allegedly written by a newspaperman from material supplied by Lola, appeared in *Le Pays*, but these, designed to turn Paris "upside down," did not get beyond the publication of a preface which she had dedicated to Ludwig. This was attacked as being "impudent" and without warning the paper published nothing further, saying that the memoirs would not be continued because of a "change in policy."

It was not surprising that the suspended publication of Lola's autobiography should have loosened the sharp tongues of all Paris. Rumors were launched that she had sent out letters threatening exposure to everyone with a past. No one saw the alleged letters and speculation was rife as to who had received them.

When friends told Lola of the rumor that she had been bought off, she was wild with fury. Pacing the floor of her drawing room, she proclaimed to her visitors, "I will revenge myself upon those who gossip about me"; but to identify the originator of such a tale was impossible.

XIV

WHEN LOLA began to feel certain that Heald would never return to her, she accepted de Coral as her lover. In spite of the new trend toward respectability in Paris, she decided to make no attempt to deny the connection if anyone accused her of it. Paradoxically, however, having been named as the mistress of a succession of men who had never received more than the tips of her fingers, now, when she had actually acquired a lover, no one looked upon de Coral as anything more than an escort. Yet he had even accompanied her to the shop when she had selected a graceful swan bed, which she willingly allowed him to pay for, even though she refused to be supported by him.

Michel was handsome, charming, a lover of sophistication and finesse. He was widely experienced in the art of approaching a woman, and he undoubtedly sensed Lola's outrage at any presumption of easy conquest. He won her at a moment when she longed for a physical relationship, but only after a carefully conducted courtship. The attachment was one of complete fulfillment for her, such as she had had with Heald.

The affair, which lasted about three months, terminated in the influenza epidemic of March 1851, when Lola very nearly died. Her house, like almost all houses, was closed to visitors because of the rapid spread of the virulent disease, which was to prove fatal to so many.

While she was confined to her bed, and later, lying on her chaise longue, thin and wan, she was entertained by her devoted maid, Ellen, who brought her news of the outside world. She prattled of the fair in the Faubourg St. Antoine, and even brought Lola some sausages from Strasbourg to tempt her flagging appetite. It was not until May that Lola went out in her carriage to watch a balloon ascension in what was to become a period of "balloon mania."

Her hair had fallen out in handfuls during the fever and in order to restore its growth it had been cut off. Embarrassed by this and by her thin cheeks and wasted limbs, she refused invitations to a stag hunt in the forest of Arménonville and to the races at Chantilly, where a horse named after her won the grand prize. Her friends refused to allow her to remain away from the hunt and Michel de Coral suggested that she should wear a draped hunting hat, full-skirted riding habit, and long sleeved velvet jacket to conceal her emaciated body. Thus attired, but still weak and easily tired, she finally consented to join the other ladies who accompanied the huntsmen. She was a new Lola, quiet and calm and a stranger even to de Coral. Everyone who knew her asked if something was troubling her, but she denied that she was dejected. In the long hours of her illness, when she had believed that she would die, she had thought incessantly of Dujarier and she again felt close to him; so much so that she no longer wanted de Coral and he did not again become her lover.

Her obsession with Dujarier was the subject of many of her conversations in later years with her friend, Mrs. Harriet Robinson, in California, to whom she told the story of her illness and her feeling that Dujarier was near her as she lay fighting for her life.

Three months later, having recovered her health, Lola announced that she would return to the stage. For the first time in her almost talentless career she decided to train under a leading teacher of dancing.

Immediately rumors were current that P. T. Barnum, the American showman, had engaged her to appear in New York and then to make a tour of the United States. When this news was released Lola was invited to celebrate the Declaration of Independence on July 4th with a group of Americans at a banquet at the Provençaux Restaurant. Remembering that this was the place where Dujarier had had the quarrel which led to his death, Lola declined. Persistent, the officers of an American ship, then in a French harbor, called upon her to ask her if it was true that she was coming to America, and she verified this report by saying that she expected to be there toward the last of the year.

Lola was disturbed to find that her long period of inactivity had affected her dancing, but the great teacher Mabille was quite satisfied; if she had to learn all over again, then she would learn correctly. Every day at the Jardin Mabille she practiced and exercised through the mornings. After three months of this intensive training certain drama critics were admitted to the rehearsals. All of them, without exception, considered her an adequate successor to Fanny Elssler, who had just retired.

Mabille had worked out for Lola six dances, unique in arrangement, which she executed with such delightful éclat that her audiences were charmed. She was described by one spectator as being "young," "enthusiastic," and with eyes of "startling brilliancy."

When one of the reporters told Lola that Montes, the Spanish toreador and her supposed father, had died in Spain, she smiled and shrugged her shoulders, which seemed to settle the question of the alleged relationship. Asked if Lord Byron was her father, Lola made a positive *moue* of distaste and asked how she could be the daughter of a man who had died in 1824. A rapid calculation on the part of the reporter seemed to make this very possible, but Lola, who eternally lied about her age, said she was not yet twenty-five. She seemed to have forgotten having admitted to twenty-five when she had been charged with bigamy in London two years before.

Just as Lola was about to leave for Brussels for an engagement, she received word that George Trafford Heald was dead. The pitiful and confused young man, disdaining the company or the consolation of his relatives, had been living in Lisbon. There he had continued to saturate himself with liquor as he had done in England. Lola had had no word of this, and all the time that she had been hoping for Heald's return he had been drinking his life away in despair over the ruin he had made of it.

Essentially, he was a simple man affected with a passion which he had been unable to overcome. Both by disposition and social training he was basically moderate and conventional. Lola blamed herself for being the cause of his destruction and sobbed bitterly when a newspaperman described to her how Heald, in a state of intoxication, had been rowing about the port and had been caught in the wake of a departing steamer. When the swell overturned his boat he had been too inebriated to swim and had drowned before he could be rescued.

Within a matter of weeks Lola heard that her husband, Thomas James, had died in India some time before Heald had drowned. This was the bitterest and the most ironic circumstance of her life. Heald had died because he drank and he drank in part because there could not be a legal marriage. Had she known of James' death sooner, her marriage to Heald might have been legalized and the confused young man who had drowned in Lisbon Harbor might easily have been led back to a normal life. She turned to her career again with a heavy heart, feeling that she was never to find happiness and that once more destiny had mocked her.

Lola's dancing tour was tremendously successful, but in her private life she was unhappy, as those who met her discovered. She was constantly accused of liaisons which did not exist and given little credit for her truthful statement that she had returned to the stage to clear debts she had incurred, despite her generous allowance from Ludwig. Since any number of gentlemen would have been willing to assume these obligations in order to enjoy her companionship and her bed, her avowed intent aroused only skeptical amusement.

The cities through which she traveled were all so eager to claim her as a native that a correspondent for the New York *Herald* wrote: "It is believed she was born at Seville in Spain. Many cities contend for the honor as if she were Homer, the prince of poets."

Lola not only refrained from solving the mystery, but even told the apocyrphal story that she had been forced to take up a career of dancing because her parents had been in financial difficulties. She was asked to explain her connection with India. Not a word did she say of Thomas James, although she did admit to having been in the East.

Everyone wished to look upon the famous beauty who had captivated the King of Bavaria. While still not an outstanding dancer, she was now far better trained than in her early career, and her lavish costumes, her large eyes, her flashing smile, and her grace held and charmed her enthusiastic audiences.

In America theatre patrons speculated about the rumor that she was going there to dance and followed with fascination the greatly exaggerated stories of her lovers. Had she had a lover at this time Lola would have been quite willing to admit it but, as she later explained, she felt no desire to replace Heald, with whom she had violently quarrelled but whom she had loved deeply and whose tragic death had left her shattered.

Commenting on the gossip about her love affairs, Lola once said that if she had collected all the falsehoods about herself "they would form a mountain higher than Chimborazo." The most intimate details of her life were apparently of acute interest to the public, and journalists did not hesitate to use their imaginations freely. "Lola Montez bathes in lavender water and dries herself with rose leaves," a reporter wrote in the San Francisco newspaper, the *Pacific News*, with more regard for romance than truth.

Lola returned to Paris on the 6th of November completely exhausted from her tour. Her intensive training, following upon her long illness, had overtaxed her strength even before her agent had persuaded her into a contract which turned out to be a nightmare. She had been required to dance not only seven days a week, but also several times each day, until her fatigue was such that she could scarcely complete the contract.

When she arrived in Paris her agent, M. Roux, who was collecting twenty-five per cent of all she earned, claimed he had another contract awaiting her. He was vague about the details, however, and Lola suspected that he had undoubtedly heard of her plans for going to America and was trying to hold her in France, where she had proved so enormously profitable to him.

A contest of wits now developed which amused people on both sides of the Atlantic. P. T. Barnum, who had introduced the Swedish singer Jenny Lind to the American concert stage, and who had exhibited freaks in his American Museum and hoaxed the public endlessly, also wanted Lola. In Paris, Barnum's agent, Le Grand Smith, began negotiations with Lola to bring her under Barnum's management. The thought of being associated with Barnum, however, horrified her. His headliners were Tom Thumb, the midget who was only a little over three feet tall, and those two palpable frauds: the Fiji mermaid, which was probably a desiccated human head mounted upon the body of a fish; and Joyce Heath, who was alleged to have been George Washington's nurse back in the 1730's.

"Lola," Barnum had said, "the notorious Montez, if rightly managed, will draw immensely here."

Lola resented the use of the word "notorious" and retorted, "I am a humbug enough myself without uniting my fortunes with the Prince of Humbugs."

"I will use my influence if you do not come under my management," Barnum threatened.

Lola had an answer ready: "I have met kings, politicians, and poets and have upset them all, and I will upset Barnum, too. I will annihilate this Napoleon of showmen."

Rather than admit that she had refused his offer, Barnum then declared that his agent had never entered into negotiations with Lola. "There is not a word of truth in this report," he swore on his oath, and the New York *Herald*, keeping track of the fun, said that Barnum had "thrust himself and his heart into the controversy, together with his family Bible."

But Lola was still determined to go to America, and when she learned that Roux had not yet obtained a contract for her in Paris she signed with Edward Willis, an American agent.

Her hair was growing rapidly, but it was still ragged and Lola was obliged to wear a wig which had been made for her by an

"Europe, farewell! America, I come!"—A cartoon published at the time of Lola Montez's first voyage to the United States, picturing her farewell to a group of sorrowing kings.—*The Bettman Archive*

expert wig maker in Paris. So successfully had this man copied her own hair from a painting of her that no one suspected she wore a wig. But it robbed Lola of her confidence in her appearance, and her thin body worried her even more.

When Madame Octave, the actress, visited Lola about this time and found her without her wig, she exclaimed: "Imagine you wearing another woman's hair!" Stung with fury, Lola looked at Madame Octave's shawl and replied, "Imagine you wearing another sheep's clothing!"

At this time Lola smoked incessantly, a habit she had picked up from George Sand but which she had later abandoned. Recently her ragged nerves had led her back into the habit, and she now indulged it to excess.

Anticipating the sea voyage and the long rest she would have aboard the ship, Lola sailed from Le Havre aboard the *Humboldt* on November 20th, accompanied by her maid and Edward Willis, her manager.

Behind her, in Paris, Le Grand Smith had the last word when he observed that La Montez had at last left. "She probably thought," said Smith, "that Barnum and Lola Montez, two of the greatest humbugs of the age in one pill, would be too great a quantity for the generous people of the United States to accept in a single dose."

Aboard the ship which carried her to America, Lola's flagging spirits revived. She described herself, upon her departure, as being "shattered in fortune, and broken in health." To her delight the gentlemen aboard the ship paid her constant court and Lola's confidence in herself was restored. She was even reported as being in one of her wittiest moods and kept her admirers entertained with all sorts of jokes. Caustic humor, such as the Parisians now enjoyed, would not do at all. She was sensitive to the mood of the men who surrounded her and saw in many of them, who were Americans, the influence of Victorianism, which had caused in them a revival of early Puritanism, recognizable not as austerity, which was its earlier form, but as a tendency toward reserve. Later on, her shipboard stories were told and retold and were even published in California by a news-paper owner who appropriated them for his columns.

Aboard the ship was Lajos Kossuth, the Hungarian patriot, whom Lola described as a morose man. As usual there were sub-sequent legends about her behavior toward this famous figure. It was said that she had tried to attract his attention by sitting on deck near him and casting flirtatious glances in his direction, but the truth was that he had suffered from seasickness and kept hidden. When Lola finally got a look at him she took an imme-diate dislike to him, judging him to be self-centered.

Upon their arrival in New York, Kossuth was greeted by cheering crowds and Lola's opinion of him may have been somewhat prejudiced by her observation of how he accepted the adulation for himself and failed to recognize that many of the people on the wharf had come to welcome her. The salute of thirty-one guns was, of course, in honor of Kossuth, but it was at once evident that many in the crowd had come to see Lola and that the press was as much interested in interviewing her as they were in seeking information from Kossuth. Lola could not resist turning to the Hungarian to ask him if he thought all the acclaim was for him.

Lola found out that she was obliged to defend her reputation with these New York newsmen of 1852. No, she said, she had not been the mistress of Ludwig, but his political adviser. Neither had she been the mistress of Dujarier; apparently she had quite forgotten admitting this with some pride at the investi-gation into Dujarier's death.

She told reporters how five hundred men in Paris had offered her ten thousand dollars if she would appear in one private per-formance for them, a circumstance which she had concealed from her Paris agent, who would undoubtedly have insisted on her appearance, no matter how risqué the dance.

"If," said Lola, "I was a woman of that description, would I be compelled to go on the stage to earn a livelihood?"

Lola neglected to mention that she desired an income far beyond her allowance from Ludwig. When asked questions about him, she refused to answer. Neither did she mention that she had visited him at Rome before leaving for America, stayed at his Villa Malta, and discovered him to be in excellent health and still sharply intelligent. They had spent their time together talking of the political maneuvers of Louis Napoleon and playing chess, and had walked together in the grounds of his residence.

Upon reading the newspapers the day after she had landed in New York, Lola was elated to see herself described as being "much lighter of figure and more refined of feature than the portrait painters had made her out to be."

During the interviews she had very cleverly turned aside the topic of her sexual attraction and had appealed to the patriotism of the Americans by lavish praise of their love of liberty and of the beauty of New York. How wonderful it was, she said, to live in a country which was not in the hands of tyrants who made the people their victims. Her astuteness in saying just the right things brought her favorable publicity, as she had anticipated.

XV

LOLA WAS AWARE that she was in a country which expected her behavior to be uninhibited and that if she were to counteract this conception it would be necessary for her to disprove all the stories of her supposedly shameless character, written by her former servant August Papon, and the more recent "autobiography," by her recent manager Roux, which had just been published.

She had put on a good performance for the newspapermen and they were half convinced that she had been unjustly maligned. If she could have kept to this role she would have had all America at her feet, for the New World, in spite of its Republicanism, loved the nobility of the old, even when the title was only acquired.

Lola was besieged with offers from theatre managers, but kept them all dangling while she shrewdly investigated each possibility. The mood of awful despair in which she had left France was gone and her suite in the Howard Hotel was besieged with admirers. She smoked cigarettes, served champagne—although she drank but little herself—and wore dresses which hid her thin arms but did not conceal the magnificent fullness of her bosom. Her rooms were filled with flowers sent to her by would-be suitors. Her maid, Ellen, hovered nearby, enjoying the excitement, as did Lola's spaniel Flora, which she had brought with her from France.

Every man who came to pay her court jealously vied for her attention. She sang for the company, although not too well, played her rented piano, and soon became the subject of endless gossip among New York ladies, who would have tried to copy her way of life if they had had her beauty and the courage to try for such adulation.

She was hardly established in New York when her former Paris agent, M. Roux, sued her, saying that his contract with her was not completed, since she had appeared only in Belgium and Germany. She had yet to tour France, as agreed, and he wanted damages in the amount of sixty-five thousand dollars. What he got from Lola was a cross-suit, also for damages, for the ridiculous "autobiography" about her which he had passed off on a publisher as being hers. One suit seemed to countervail the other, since nothing more was heard of either of them. Lola, however, had to overcome the slurs upon her reputation, for people in New York had obtained copies of this degrading publication from Paris.

Toward the close of December she was scheduled to make her first American appearance at the Broadway Theatre before a supposedly distinguished audience. On the night of her debut the theatre was so crowded from the orchestra to the gallery that people who had not secured tickets had to be content with standing in the foyer, peering over the heads of the audience from between drawn back curtains, or standing against the walls of the downslanting auditorium. So great had been the curiosity to see her that the tickets, instead of being sold at the box-office, had been auctioned off soon after the announcement had been made that she would appear in *Betley the Tyrolean*, a play especially written for her.

With the exception of a few brave ladies who had risked their reputations to see the "real queen of Bavaria," the audience was composed of men. The patrons proved impatient, and from the uproar they created while they awaited the alluring Lola it was evident that this was not the usual assembly of spectators who were in the habit of patronizing this velvet-cushioned theatre.

When the curtain remained down unduly long, the already restless audience of aroused males, who were obviously hoping for a wicked display of Lola's famous bosom and limbs, began to hiss the orchestra, which tried to appease them with music which was played louder and louder to drown out the din.

The pandemonium did not abate until the curtain arose. The men yelled in wild acclaim as a large ballet appeared in a tableau. The audience quieted as they stretched their necks and rose out of their seats in an effort to identify Lola Montez, but without apparent success. Then, as patrons speculated in whispers to their neighbors as to which dancer she might be, a figure appeared to the left where a path wound down in the woodland scene. A burst of applause identified this performer. With a slight curtsey of acknowledgment, Lola descended to the stage, where she came into full view. Far from the expected *deshabillé*, she wore a Hungarian jacket, cut in military style and faced with gold braid. On her midnight hair was a red hat trimmed with a feather. Behind her came a company of soldiers all dancing in unison with her in a choreographic imitation of a military march. The audience applauded wildly.

When she was fully before the footlights and performing "The Mountaineer Dance" with the corps de ballet behind her, she looked to be a very young girl of not more than sixteen. Never had she been more fascinating, with her slender form, graceful movements and superb features. Her countenance astonished the audience, for it was both aristocratic and virginal; surely she was anything but the vulgar, notorious, devil-may-care woman of endless sexual experience that rumor reported.

The spectators were dazzled at her large, dark blue eyes, at the perfect brow, wonderfully formed lips and chin, and the men clung to the hope that she would finally emerge in something that would whet their senses, even if it caused the few ladies present to blush.

Nothing of the kind occurred. Her modesty won the ladies over. Most of them were seated in the boxes and at the end of the performance they tossed bouquets to her over the footlights. She could not have dreamed of a bigger triumph; fashionable and well-to-do women were ready to defend her; she was, in spite of all that had been said about her, respectable and aristocratic in appearance.

Even the newspapers were with her, one of them saying, "It was the most modest performance of public dances we have seen for a length of time."

At the end of her first night Lola was exhausted. Fatigued and plainly out of breath, she addressed the audience, after repeated curtain calls.

With sincerity she said, in her deep voice, "I thank you from the bottom of my heart for the very kind reception you have given me, a poor stranger in your noble land." In her appreciation to people who showed a liking for her, she was close to tears. Her own heart was tender, generous and sympathetic. But perhaps only Ludwig had ever uncovered her susceptibility to genuine affection, and it was likely that only he and Dujarier had yet heard from her the story of the cruelty shown to her when she was a child. It was a story that explained why she would not talk of her early life and why she always sprang to the defense of the downtrodden so readily.

The director of Lola's play, who had never had a chance to see her anywhere but on the boards of the theatre, was dumbfounded when he joined the cast party after the opening. He was sure that Lola was merely a curiosity and not a dancer of merit and he anticipated that the play would not continue on past the time when the interest in seeing her would be satisfied.

Lola Montez off stage filled the director with despair. Nothing of her true personality, he realized, came out over the footlights. Her voice was throaty, passionate and enticing. Her eyes flashed fire. Her conversational powers were impressive, her repartee quick and clever. Without apparent effort she dominated a whole roomful of people, the greatest beauty he had ever seen with a personality to match. It was no wonder that men went mad over her and that she could kick up a revolution with the toe of her dancing slipper.

The director took immediate steps to cover up Lola's stage deficiencies. To the leader of the orchestra he said, "When you play for the Countess, follow her precisely; when she stops, do you also stop, no matter whether or not the music is finished." He was determined to make the most of Lola's fabulous personality and to minimize her obvious lack of talent as a dancer.

Just before Christmas Lola, no longer able to stand the strain of constant company, moved from her hotel suite to a private residence on Waverley Place. Here, in an elegant small house with beautiful blue and gold furniture, she thought to find privacy by having her maid say that she was out when unwanted callers came to see her. Even such important persons as Governor Anthony of Rhode Island and a French prince failed to obtain entry. Less than three weeks later, however, she gave up the house because her servants proved unable to handle so many callers. She moved back to the Howard Hotel, where visitors could be more easily screened.

As soon as she was settled down again at the hotel she dismissed her agent, Edward Willis, because of an unsatisfactory account of her earnings and her dislike of his ideas of publicity. Edward's brother Nathaniel Willis was an editor and journalist, hailed with acclaim as a poet, a friend of Washington Irving, and the best friend of Edgar Allan Poe. He called on Lola to intercede for his brother. She was adamant, saying that her real reason for dismissing Edward was that he had disgraced her with publicity about her career in Bavaria, misrepresenting what her position had been at Ludwig's court. This was something she would not stand for. He had also dared, she said, to take the position that the Jesuits had been right in demanding her exile and in depriving her of her château and the income from her estates. She had been trying to establish a constitutional government in Bavaria in order to give the common people popular rights. She wanted it understood that it was not the Jesuits who had driven her out; it was she who had driven them out. Edward had misrepresented this in the New York newspapers.

Nathaniel Willis argued that this was excellent publicity, which his brother had planned. The Americans were always ready to defend a visitor who was made the victim of foreign intrigue. If it could be made to look as if she was being persecuted, she would find that she had supporters on every side. Lola did not agree with him and the interview came to an end without her having the faintest idea that this man, currently named among the corespondents in one of the most sensational divorce suits that had ever taken place in New York, had in meeting her fallen out of love with the defendant in the case, Mrs. Katherine Forrest. Later this tall, handsome man with his wavy hair and charming manner was to disconcert her by following her across the continent in order to declare his love for her.

Lola next acquired as agent Josephus A. Scoville, noted later as the publisher of *The Pick,* and called "Reverend" by everyone because he had once replaced R. C. Cralle as the burning light of the Swedenborgian Church in Washington, D. C. Both men had then been with Secretary of State John C. Calhoun, Scoville being his private secretary, and the religiously inclined Cralle acting as Chief Clerk. Scoville could never resist making fun of other people but in this one instance the fun had been turned upon himself. Calhoun, opening his big eyes, had expressed astonishment at Scoville's untried and unrepeated talent and ever afterwards said that he had "a fair crack" at Scoville. Scoville could never thereafter get rid of the appellation and had long since given up explaining the reason for his title of "Reverend."

The "Reverend" had a racy wit, black curling hair, dark eyes, liked to write in an elegant dressing gown, and kept his cat, Hokee, comfortably situated atop his desk. He moved into the Howard Hotel with the avowed intent of protecting Lola from the kind of insults she had received when the theatre critic of the *Herald* wrote that in his estimation "her reputation is no better than she is." Scoville declared that no one was going to make any false accusations against Lola Montez.

Beyond his protective duties as her agent, Scoville found her a wonderful foil for his wit, adored her beauty and enjoyed her company. He also introduced her to many people who were later to become famous: Walt Whitman, then merely a journalist who wrote poetry; William Dean Howells, who was working in a printing office and had ambitions to become an author; and the fascinating actress, Adah Isaacs. With the latter, Lola established a friendship which was to last throughout her life.

To Lola's amazement Scoville told her that Nathaniel Willis had been right; the Americans loved to spring to the defense of anyone who was being persecuted. The new manager soon had Lola launched into an imaginary contest with the Jesuits, but this metamorphosis "from pirouettes to politics" bewildered the newspapers, who were inclined to be a trifle skeptical of so much hitherto undiscovered intrigue in New York.

In May of 1852 Lola got her name in the newspapers, not because of her quarrel with the Jesuits, but because she received by far the most amazing of all her long line of visitors. The Emperor of Haiti, Faustin I, had sent his grand chamberlain, Prince Bobo, to try to induce Lola to come to Haiti for a visit to his court. The Prince, a man with velvety black skin and large flashing eyes, stood over six feet high, as magnificent a specimen of his race as could be imagined. Lola was tempted at the thought of this unique tropical kingdom with its court of majestic beauty in a jungle setting, and it was with some regret that she was obliged in the end to decline.

XVI

By her exemplary behavior, Lola had won over many ladies of New York and every night their numbers increased in her audience, showing that they had overcome their hesitation in accepting her and had finally judged her to be maligned and innocent of many of the charges made against her. They no longer had any misgivings about her position at the court of Bavaria; the ladies had made up their minds to accept Lola's own explanation of her friendship with the King.

Later in that May of 1852 Lola got her name in the New York *Herald* in a way destined to take the edge off her respectability quite neatly. The Howard Hotel had not proven quite the refuge it was supposed to be. To it came the nobility of old Europe to pay court to Lola: barons, counts, princes; a Croatian officer, a Hungarian cavalry officer, and a brilliantly uniformed Serbian officer all thirsted for attention from this queen of romance.

One evening in her suite, contesting for her favors, was Count Zezemsky, running competition to his own son, Count Walowski. The father had come to the New World to lecture and the son was engaged in making a concert tour as a pianist.

Also present was the man Lola called Carissimo, the Prince of Como, who she had entertained at her first soirée in Paris. The Prince of Como had been in pursuit of the Countess of Paris when Lola had left France, but he had recently taken up with Katherine Forrest, replacing Nathaniel Willis as that lady's admirer.

Through her success on the stage and the recovery of her health, Lola was full of spirit and impulsively decided to give a smart evening party. Since no other ladies were present, Lola smoked with the gentlemen while she served champagne. The old Paris spirit of wit and abandon was revived as Lola's guests made their way through an underbrush of politics and came out to a clearing of scandals.

This was Lola's opportunity to get even with Carissimo, who had paid her ardent court until he had met the fascinating Mrs. Forrest. That lady had recently departed the city and Carissimo had again returned to Lola's salon, but not to her favor. When the subject of the scandalous divorce case of the great tragedian, Edwin Forrest, against Katherine was brought up, Lola sprang to the defense of the portly Mr. Forrest. Carissimo attempted to shield his absent beloved, which only served further to enrage Lola. Since Katherine Forrest had come off very badly in the divorce which made public her relationship with Nathaniel Willis, Lola seized upon this as an excuse to attack her, for she could not bear to hear praise of the woman whose charms had proved more attractive to the Prince than hers. The Prince replied, "You should be the last person in the world to make such an attack on a lady, particularly in the presence of one who has such a knowledge of your own conduct and unenviable notoriety in Paris and elsewhere." Whereupon Lola sprang from her chair and with a fury which surprised everyone, began to box the Prince's ears. When Carissimo attempted to escape by the door Lola ran behind him, slammed it shut, and locked it, tossing the key to one of the gentlemen present and asking him to ring for the hotel servants.

After being escorted from the room by the hotel employees, the Prince went to the bar-room and found an Italian friend who was willing to help him carry on his fight with the Countess Lola. They went back upstairs and were admitted to Lola's suite by Ellen, who had just come in with the spaniel, Flora, and was unaware of the quarrel. The two men rudely pushed Ellen to one side, and within a matter of moments the discordant sounds of a battle royal could be heard along the hallway of the hotel, for the door into Lola's suite had been left open by the startled maid. Voices in Polish, in Italian, in French, and in

English could be heard, accompanied by the sharp barks of the excited dog. From every room along the hall sleepy guests, pulling on their robes, found their way to the scene. Lola circled the fight, gleefully jumping up and down and clapping her hands. From the spectators gathered around the door, Josephus Scoville separated himself and with a few well-aimed blows knocked the Prince and his friend to the floor. Scoville then picked up the two fighting cocks and tumbled them down the back stairs.

The newspapers reported the fracas in its smallest detail, one of them pointedly remarking that it was to be hoped everyone in the hotel found his own bed without any mistakes.

It had taken a long time to satisfy public curiosity about Lola, but adverse publicity, immediately after a packed house following the incident in the hotel, caused her popularity to take a sudden downward plunge. Lola unfortunately made use of the incident to say that the Prince and his companion had deliberately planned the quarrel at the instigation of some Jesuit sympathizers who had followed her to America in an effort to ruin her career. This ridiculous assertion was momentarily believed by the police; Captain Rynders of the N.Y. Police Department and the heads of several civic clubs called on Lola to offer her their protection when she appeared at the theatre.

For a time it looked as if the lecturer, Count Zezemsky—the newspapers were not sure it should not be spelled Kazenski— was going to bear the brunt of the affair in Lola's salon. The Prince of Como challenged him to a duel but received a call from the police, who informed him that even to challenge anyone to such a contest in New York was illegal, leaving the fuming Prince without any means of defending his honor.

In appreciation for the protection given her by the police, Lola gave a dinner on the stage one night after the play to which she invited the police captain and the sachems of Tammany Hall, and the famous Edwin Forrest as well. Scarcely ever in New York had such speeches been heard, such homage and such tributes. Lola bubbled with wit and the Tammany officials in a glow of champagne agreed with each other that Lola should be made "Royal Squaw." Never one to drink too much, Lola allowed her enthusiasm to run so high that she was soon promising to lecture for them on "The Liberation of Bavaria from the Jesuits."

It was apparent to theatre managers and newspapermen, if not to the public, that Lola's sudden war on the Jesuits was for the sake of creating excitement over her new play, *Lola Montez in Bavaria,* in which she appeared in January 1853, as herself. Written for her by C. T. Ware, it told the story of a discontented Bavaria and the terrible Jesuits who had proven unequal to the struggle once Lola had extricated the King from their clutches and proved to him that they had gained their power over him and his people through mysterious rites. She taught him that it was more fun to pursue romance and worship Cupid than to muse upon the dreadful riddle of the grave. Hopping in and out of the drama like a delighted katydid was Lola as a danseuse, a politician, a countess, a revolutionist, and finally a fugitive, playing against the background of Lola's palace, painted on a back drop. But the newspapers began to make fun of her, and in five nights she was through. One newspaper had said that Lola was entertaining as her guest at her hotel a mysterious Mr. Davis, a "man of fashion" from Boston. There was no such person nor did Lola have any guest staying with her, but the insinuation that she had a lover was enough to ruin her hard-won reputation among the ladies in Puritan New York.

Lola should have done everything to prevent the story of the fight in her suite from being published in the newspapers. That, in combination with the mention of the non-existent "Mr. Davis," shattered her reputation, just as a misunderstanding had ruined that of Katherine Forrest. Three years previously Edwin Forrest had come upon his wife unawares as she talked to the actor, George Jamisson. He insisted that they were entirely too close together. Both his wife and Jamisson protested their innocence, but being a man who could never shake loose from an idea, he would not rest until he had finally located a letter from

Jamisson which spoke of how happy he had been in knowing Katherine. Edwin applied for a divorce and Katherine counter-suited in New York, and Lola, like everyone else in the country, was daily absorbed in reading the testimony in the case.

Currently Mrs. Forrest's good name was being further be-smirched by the testimony of an uncommonly moral neighbor who had watched her at home. This neighbor declared she had seen Katherine standing in the library of her home with N. P. Willis' arm around her waist, although there were curtains over the window and a high backed sofa was pushed against it. Katherine and her caller had moved away from the window and had disappeared from the sight of this watchful, self-appointed guardian who deemed this the very worst sort of behavior, because "Mr. Forrest was absent." Another woman who ran a boarding house and who thought one of her roomers "might have been Mrs. Forrest under another name" testified that the roomer had been "so immodest as to have two gentlemen locked in the room with her at one time." This vague story was only one of many brought out at the trial. A few newspapers announced that they were compelled to forego pub-lishing anything more about the case because it was "too im-moral."

People capable of creating so much scandal out of so little would scarcely be less ready to suppose that the "Mr. Davis," called into being out of nothing, but real enough to the public, was in Lola's hotel for no good reason. What he was there for was all too easy to guess. The damage was done and it was irre-mediable. Lola sought out an attorney and had him prepare a suit for libel against the New York *Times*. The *Herald* was next on her list but she did not go forward with these suits immedi-ately because she was due to leave New York on a tour.

On May 4th she departed to take her show on the road. Just as she had been about to leave her hotel a man tried to hand her a document. The usual number of her admirers were on hand and they seized the suspicious-looking character, sure that he

146

was a Jesuit in disguise intending some harm to the dancer. Lola herself was so tangled up in the fiction of being surrounded by Jesuit sympathizers that she found it difficult to isolate the real from the feigned in her own mind. When the bewildered man proved harmless, she accepted the paper, which turned out to be only a summons for a bill which she had neglected to pay.

In Albany, where she appeared with twelve dancers of her ballet, the audiences were enthusiastic over her, even serenading her after one performance. Her next stop was Philadelphia, where the audiences were distinctly cold to *Lola Montez in Bavaria*. When she danced between the acts they hissed her, but not without reason, for the orchestra, with which she had rehearsed only briefly, ended by either being conspicuously ahead of her or belatedly behind her so that Lola frequently found herself abruptly without music, one of her dainty feet suspended in midair, or ready for applause while the orchestra still played. She lost her temper and was so furiously angry that she stamped at the conductor after her performance and accused him of having Jesuits hidden in the orchestra.

Provoked and indignant, she left Philadelphia behind determined to rouse Washington by some audacious act which would attract the attention of the senators and congressmen who, she had learned, were so busily quarrelling among themselves over the coming election that they could think of nothing else. She resolved to put on a fight so startling that the politicians would be diverted from their own rampage.

Abandoning the black dress and red flower in her hair, which she had adopted in Paris as symbolic of her grief after Dujarier's death, she appeared in dresses designed to excite the men. She exposed enough of her bosom to reveal its enticing portions, cinched her small waistline to make it even smaller, and pinned diamonds, like so many snowflakes, in the shining waves of her hair. Soon the gentlemen were in ecstasies over her as they saw her being driven about in an open barouche. The time had now come to advertise who she was.

She needed something to make the gentlemen of the town spring to her defense, having learned that in America men loved coming to the rescue of a beautiful woman. A quarrel with her manager was just the thing. He acted his part to perfection as she stamped her foot, declared her outrage at his failure to protect her, and threatened to horsewhip him for not guarding her honor. A woman so concerned with her good name was indeed admirable, and this was exactly what was needed to turn the tide of public opinion in her favor. When she appeared the house was crowded and the men showed themselves so much in favor of her that the next day she was invited to the House of Representatives and to a reception afterwards in her honor.

On the closing night of her play her uncertain temper detracted from the charming picture of herself which she had created in the public mind. She was increasingly ruled by wild caprice, in spite of her real desire not to make herself vulnerable to those who provoked her. Below her, as she took her final bows, she saw a man put his thumb under his nose and waggle his fingers back and forth in a coarse and offensive way, suggestive of a common school-boy's misguided attempts at profanity. Instead of ignoring him, she stepped out toward the footlights, and looking directly at him cried out, "Sir, I did not come here to be insulted."

The theatre patrons shouted their approval of her spirited self-defense and a number of men descended upon the offender to escort him from the theatre. General Roger Jones, seated nearby, stood up in his seat and called for order, distracting attention from what might well have developed into a fracas. After a round of cheers was given for the General he reseated himself and Lola reappeared from the wings, holding up her hand for silence. "Ladies and gentlemen," she said, "I return you my most grateful thanks for your kindness to me during my sojourn in your magnificent and extraordinary city."

Unfortunately for Lola it was not her performance that was to be remembered, but her burst of rage, and this was to gain more and more notice, until an accumulation of such incidents

148

gave her an unenviable reputation throughout the theatrical world.

By the next month Lola had reached Boston to appear at the Howard Athenaeum.

XVII

LOLA WAS in a city quick to take offense at someone like herself who was an alleged demi-mondaine, a name Alexandre Dumas had attached to all women of questionable reputation.

The people of Boston had a strong sense of their own superiority which was in part based on a belief in their racial purity. Thomas Jefferson had once said that the people of New England believed themselves to be absolutely apart from the rest of the country. This attitude made them unpopular away from home. Boston was, however, remarkably free of moral wickedness. Once they formed their opinions, Bostonians were rigid in maintaining them, but they did not accept reports of calumny without subjecting them to study. There had always been prejudice in New England against the theatre and its performers, but a respectable play, especially if accompanied by music, usually found an audience.

They had an abiding hatred of injustice and felt a responsibility in correcting uncalled-for persecution. Lola Montez had scarcely arrived in Boston when the Boston *Transcript* launched a violent onslaught of unfavorable criticism against her, inspired by a visit she made to the city schools. An invitation had been extended to her by a prominent member of the school committee, who, with the other members, believed it would be interesting to have her lecture to the various language classes. In addition to addressing the French class in French and the Spanish in Spanish, she surprised and delighted everyone by conversing easily in Latin with the Latin class. When she at last addressed the English class, she betrayed an odd accent which seemed to be neither French nor British. The members of the committee learned that she had altogether an easy com-

THE YOUNG LOLA MONTEZ

An early photograph by South-
worth and Hayes.

THE BETTMANN ARCHIVE

Lola in riding habit, 1840.

THE BETTMANN ARCHIVE

"British actress and adventuress." Photograph ca. 1855.

THE BETTMANN ARCHIVE

The duel in the Bois de Boulogne in which her fiancé Alexandre Dujarier was killed.

George Sand. Engraving by Alexandre Manceau from a portrait by Thomas Couture, 1844.

Franz Liszt as a young man. From a rare photograph.

King Ludwig I of Bavaria. Portrait by Wilhelm von Kaulbach.

Lola Montez. The Command Portrait painted at the order of King Ludwig, Munich, 1847.

The Orleans Hotel, Sacramento (third building from left), where Lola stayed in 1853.

CALIFORNIA STATE LIBRARY, SACRAMENTO

Lola Montez. From an original painting in the Carthay Circle Theatre, Los Angeles.

COURTESY MISS CAROLYN WENZEL

Lola performing her famous "Spider Dance."

SACRAMENTO BEE

Lola Montez, San Francisco, 1853.

The Metropolitan Theatre, San Francisco, showing the stage on which Lola danced.

Grass Valley in the 1850's.

Lola Montez and her husband Patrick Hull entering Grass Valley, 1854.

The home of Lola Montez at Grass Valley, showing Lola and her bear at extreme right. From a contemporary wood engraving.

Lola's house today.

Nevada City (top) and Marysville in the 1850's when Lola Montez visited them.

mand of eight languages and spoke a ninth "with a little difficulty."

The *Transcript* decried her visit to the schools as being almost a debauchery of their youth. Turning on the *Transcript*, Lola remembered Victor Hugo's saying, "Silence under attack," which was in effect an admonition that no person in public life could afford to reply unless he had the gift of caustic wit. Mr. Sargent of the *Transcript*, who had attacked Lola's past as if he had a divine right to censure her because he was himself impervious to criticism, now found himself accused of being ill-bred and ungentlemanly to the visitor. A rival newspaper invited him to throw the first stone.

In defending herself with witty sarcasm Lola had acquired a staggering number of defenders, most of them gentlemen. Priding itself on being a city of intellectually superior people, Boston was ready to declare for a woman who could reveal a mentality as rare as Lola's, and their previous concept of her as an artiste of a less than perfect talent was overshadowed by their recognition of her quick mind.

They were willing to believe in her expolits as a political adviser to Ludwig and even spoke of her as being the widow of a British lord. She was undeniably a fit subject for history.

Her costumes for *Carnival at Seville* were described, her modesty and aristocratic bearing were remarked upon and praised. Her determination not to be browbeaten, her independence in insisting that she earn her own living were formidable arguments in her favor.

While the theatre was filled with gentlemen for her first performance, the increasing presence of respectable ladies on successive nights reflected the exasperation most Bostonians felt for the criticism to which she had been subjected.

She had never had a more successful run and people went to see her, not because of the scandalous rumors about her, but for that remarkable beauty, those magnificent black fringed eyes, her gracefulness, and the extraordinary variety of her dances. Her modesty and her earnestness in trying to project her flashing personality marked her as thoroughly capable of defending her reputation with either a pistol or a horsewhip.

It was in Boston that people told Lola that she would have a great appeal in New Orleans, where there was always merry-making, and in California, where there was much enthusiasm for stage actresses. When she again headed for New York on May 25th she was considering this excellent advice. There was always, in the back of her mind, curiosity about the mine near Grass Valley in which she had invested while still in Paris, for it had turned out to be an investment of major proportions.

In July Lola appeared again at the Bowery theatre in *Lola Montez in Bavaria* before the kind of audience which despised people of nobility, but loved anyone who was supposed to have a scandalous reputation. These transformations of her character for public consumption bewildered Lola, but the theatre owner, Tom Hamblin, knew his audience.

He took this opportunity to redecorate his theatre, to enlarge its seating capacity, and provide seats with velvet cushions. An increase in prices eliminated an element of rowdy patrons who had long made it their headquarters. Hamblin did not attract quite the fashionable audience he had hoped for, but the house was packed to capacity for every performance throughout Lola's engagement.

Upon her return to New York Lola sued the *Times* for $65,000, and the other newspapers who had calumniated her speculated upon her intentions toward them. Most of the papers resolved either to ignore her or praise her as an artist while leaving her private life strictly alone.

In August peace between Lola and the newspapers was ingeniously brought about by Scoville. Because of his obligations to his newspaper, *The Pick*, he had been unable to continue as her manager since she had left New York. Having established his reputation as a wit when he had been on the New Orleans *Picayune*, he had acquired a large circulation within a short period. The beloved Scoville, called "Pick" by his New York friends, was the inspiration for a celebration held by his admirers who had formed themselves into what was called the Pick Club. The event, held on the 26th of August, consisted, as Scoville put it, of "27,221 subscribers, 83 advertisers, and 209,-000 readers." Everyone agreed, from the number of prominent people who had promised to attend, that the affair was likely to become "immortal." Suitably enough, it was to be a picnic.

Waiting at his newspaper office for his friends to gather, Scoville was at first disheartened, for "it rained in torrents" and was "perfectly awful," he said, "for any two-legged arrangements, except ducks." At five A.M. the "clouds were down as low as the gas lamps," and the committee he had appointed were "doubtful whether to go or stay," but by six A.M. the rain had ceased, the clouds had rolled away and the day promised to be magnificent.

An hour later a gun was fired to announce the departure of the steamboat *Hero* from Brooklyn. The *Hero,* trailing a series of barges, picked up guests at a number of points until it reached the foot of Christopher Street. A band came on board and the *Hero* idled alongside the dock until finally Lola Montez arrived, accompanied by the President of the newly formed Pick Club. Seated near the capstan and smoking cigars were P. T. Barnum and Horace Greeley of the *Tribune,* whom Lola barely greeted. She hurried past them to the stateroom that had been provided for her use and did not emerge from her quarters until after the Grand March around the deck was over. She then danced in the quadrille while artists sketched her and prominent newspapermen sat around watching her.

At Yonkers the passengers disembarked. Lola was taken in a carriage to Kellinger's Hotel, where some of the guests preferred to eat before departing for the Grove, where the picnic was to be held. Everyone but Lola and her maid, Ellen, walked from the dock to the hotel. As the great crowd of people climbed the hill Scoville found himself behind Barnum and Greeley and close enough to hear what they were saying. He promptly brought out a notebook and took down their conversation for his newspaper.

After a little good-natured bantering, Greeley turned on Barnum with an air of suspicion and said, "What did you come up here for today?"

Barnum promptly replied, "Partly to have some fun, and to have a quiet talk with Lola Montez. I promised Mr. Pick, who is a very nice and very respectable person. He said he would try and reconcile me and Lola. But what are you driving at?"

"Well," replied Greeley, "the fact is, Barnum, I have made an infernal ass and Judy of myself about Lola Montez and I intend to make it up and do that gifted lady the most ample justice. I took a solemn oath that I never would allow her name to be printed in the columns of the *Tribune*, but I broke the oath because circumstances changed. Upon my soul, Barnum, I believed Lola Montez to be a slandered and injured woman. I had a cursed narrow escape. Jemmina and crikey, hain't Raymond put his foot into it nicely! I do believe any honest jury will give Lola $50,000 sure," he added, referring to Lola's suit against the *Times*. Greeley then warned Barnum to be careful what he said against Lola, and charged the showman with "unmanly persecution of an unprotected female. Put that in your pipe and smoke it!"

"Come, come, Greeley," replied Barnum, "this is putting it to me a little too strong! Draw it a little milder, if you please." It was a good thing, he said, that the editor of the *Times* couldn't hear them. "I'd a blamed sight rather be *Herald*-ed than *Pick*-ed up!"

"Why, old calf," exclaimed Greeley, "you are getting witty in your old age."

At this point Scoville was tired of writing and joined the people converging on the Grove where "dancing, eating and drinking" were "all going on at the same moment." Lola had provided champagne and everyone toasted her, although she had not yet put in an appearance. Sometime later she was observed on the platform where the band was assembled and she was followed there by Scoville. The crowd, which greeted each speaker with cheers, was addressed in turn by Scoville, Lola

Montez, who carried a beautiful silk banner in her hands, Bennet of the *Herald*, Fuller of the *Evening Mirror*, Dr. Ingraham and Maitland of the *National Democrat* and Raymond of the *New York Times*.

The thousand or so people who had attended finally departed on the steamboat, with its trail of barges, and everyone danced by moonlight most of the way back. Horace Greeley was said to have got so excited that he threw his white hat down on the deck and jumping on it, gave forth a loud Cossack huzzah. Barnum meanwhile held forth with a lecture on zoölogy and humbug which lasted a full hour.

Later in the evening Scoville escorted Lola back to New York by railway. The day had been a triumph for her and she was in high spirits, telling some of her funniest stories and keeping the car in an uproar.

At Pfaff's Café the next day Lola was seen surrounded by newspapermen and there was no more talk of libel suits. They were joined by Adah Isaacs and Cornelius Vanderbilt, the flaxen-haired, blue-eyed promoter of a steamship line to Nicaragua. Absorbed in his talk of the gold fields of California, Lola scarcely noticed the newspapermen's efforts to attract her attention.

A few nights before her departure for St. Louis, Lola took part in a dramatic festival held at Castle Garden to commemorate the introduction of drama into America in 1752. Castle Garden was thronged with eight thousand people and the dressing rooms back-stage were impossibly crowded. In the dressing room she shared with several others, Lola took off her bonnet and laid it down on a little table. On stage a scene from the *Merchant of Venice* was being played and when Mrs. Vickery, who was playing Portia, entered the dressing room, she pointed to the bonnet and said, "Whose bonnet is that? Does it belong to that creature in the chair?" Ellen, who was standing behind Lola, said later that she had fully expected Mrs. Vickery to be "eaten alive." Instead Lola made room for the actress by offering her a chair and said in a mild voice, "You wished to know who I am. As we are rather cramped here, we had better make ourselves agreeable—I am Lola Montez."

Scoville entered the room just in time to capture the scene for his newspaper. He stayed in her dressing room to chat with her after she had done a sailor dance, received an ovation, and been showered with bouquets. They talked of the day's news, Scoville reported that Horace Greeley had at last ordered a new suit. It would have one sleeve made of Irish linen, and the other of American cotton with "one pocket large enough to hold a German pipe and bottle of lager beer, and the other breeches pocket will be capable of containing a temperance pledge, a volume of Sermons upon Peace, a revolver and the Life of General Scott. The buttons will be miniature spittoons." From this rather bewildering description Lola gathered that Greeley was thinking of going into politics.

Lola's stay at St. Louis was marked with the usual "horse-whipping" of her theatrical manager but Lola ended by wielding a candlestick in a fury and breaking the manager's nose. Pictures of Lola brandishing a horsewhip had been used in advertisements to suggest the zeal with which she protected her moral reputation. Somewhere on her tours, she had received a real insult and her tempestuous nature led her to administer an actual horsewhipping. Forever afterwards during her theatrical tours she was quick to take offense against actual or fancied slur. Once more she forgot the importance of using her wit rather than her temper in defending her honor. Her unbridled temper irrevocably lost her friends and did nothing to establish her as a chaste and misrepresented woman in the eyes of the public.

In New Orleans she apparently felt the need more than ever to convince the public that she had been maligned. As the easiest and quickest way to destroy the impression that she was a scandalous adventuress she announced it was her intention to enter a convent. The effect was electric. It was believed to be, in part, the culmination of wounded feelings, for it was reported that a New York newspaper had said that she smoked cigars, swore like a trooper, and spent her time enjoying men.

New Orleans was at the height of its prosperity. It was the quintessence of gaiety, festivity, and optimism, with no more thought for the future than Lola had ever had. Many plantation owners who lived far from the city owned magnificent town houses overlooking Canal Street. On the plantations they entertained lavishly, carrying on an intense social life of house parties, dinners and dances.

Along the oak-shaded bayous, eerie with Spanish moss, stood the Greek revival houses, facing the water. On a long drive, and again on a boat trip down the river, Lola saw the lofty columned houses: Oak Alley with its Doric columns, houses styled in Steamboat Gothic, houses with galleries, others which resembled the Greek temples she had once seen with Ludwig.

She visited the old St. Louis Cemetery on Basin Street in order to see in practice the strange custom of New Orleans families who on Sunday afternoons sat on elaborate cast iron benches before their family sepulchres greeting other visitors who passed by. This odd custom seemed to bridge the chasm of death between the departed and the living in a city famous for its plagues and epidemics which had wiped out whole families in twenty-four hours and filled her cemeteries.

Due to the depredations made by the plague of 1837, Lola was to acquire a new maid whose background was not at all unusual for New Orleans. She had scolded Ellen and the maid refused to remain with her longer. When she quit, Lola refused to pay her and Ellen went to court to demand her salary. When the warrant was served upon Lola she locked herself in and refused to accept it. Finally a policeman was sent to the theatre. Lola not only refused to accompany him, but engaged in ridiculous dramatics. She drew out a dagger, and when she was seized by her companions in the theatre and the dagger taken away from her, she used her teeth on the officers. Her fellow actors endeavored to quiet and reason with her, but she escaped from them in a rage and grabbing a bottle marked "Poison," drained the liquid. "I shall be free," she cried as she lost consciousness. The police officer was stunned, the actresses screamed and an actor ran for medical help. Whether Lola had known it or not the bottle had been a stage property and contained nothing more harmless than water. She was revived and was considerably chastened and even ashamed of her hysterical behavior; she promised to appear at the hearing instituted by her maid.

Within a matter of a day or two she had acquired a young colored girl who came to have a remarkable understanding of Lola Montez. The girl's name was Hyacinth. Her surname, probably mispelled, was Fhlerey. Her mother had been one of the quadroons set up in a residence by the son of a planter. Because of the young man's love for his mistress he had never married. In the epidemic of 1837 both the planter's son and his mistress had died, leaving behind them their small daughter, Hyacinth. The girl had been taken in by kindly Negroes and been trained as a maid. She was in her early twenties, ashen in color, with oddly colored blue-gray eyes. Lola, because of their shade, dubbed her Periwinkle, and Periwinkle she remained ever after.

To Periwinkle many of Lola's whims were deliberate bids for attention. Lola had carried the theatrical into her real life and become enslaved by the process. Often she found herself really angry when she had only meant to pretend to be vexed, or smoked a cigar because it shocked people and then she would acquire a taste for it, or planned a battle simply for its publicity value and then would become emotionally involved in its outcome.

A few weeks later Lola, with her new maid, departed for California. Even her fellow performers in New Orleans were grateful to see the last of a woman who went to such extremes in her passionate rages.

XVIII

AN ENGLISHWOMAN, Mrs. Seacole, in writing of her adventures, claimed that she had seen Lola Montez at Cruces on the Isthmus of Panama when the latter was bound for California. "Came one day," wrote Mrs. Seacole, "Lola Montez, in the full zenith of her evil fame, bound for California. A good-looking, bold woman, with fine, bad eyes, and a determined bearing, dressed ostentatiously in perfect male attire, with shirt-collar turned down over a velvet lapelled coat, rich worked shirt-front, black hat, French unmentionables, and natty polished boots with spurs. She carried in her hand a handsome riding-crop, which she could use as well in the streets of Cruces as in the towns of Europe; for an impertinent American, presuming, perhaps not unnaturally, upon her reputation, laid hold jestingly of the tails of her long coat, and, as a lesson, received a cut across his face that must have marked him for some days. I did not wait to see the row that followed, and was glad when the wretched woman rode off the following morning."

This account Lola emphatically denied. She claimed that she was "never in Cruces" at any time and that she had gone by way of Nicaragua.

Regardless of whether or not Lola made use of her whip upon a man who was too familiar with her, she did travel by this route and she did dress as a man, as a number of witnesses all too excitedly described. She even admitted it to a few intimates, giving as her reason that she wanted to protect herself from being bitten by the many annoying insects. By keeping herself covered she perhaps unwittingly saved herself from the danger of yellow fever, for no one at that time knew that the mosquitoes were the agents that transmitted this fatal disease.

The two lines of steamships which were in operation advertised that their passengers would be delivered to Chagres on
the Atlantic side of Panama. Stormy weather from the
"northers" and outgoing currents from the Rio Chagres, however, often caused the drowning of people in small boats trying
to make a landing. The passengers were therefore taken to
Aspinwall in Navy Bay, only a few miles away from the town
of Chagres, peculiarly situated upon both sides of the river and
overshadowed by the Spanish fortress of San Lorenzo atop
the promontory. Aspinwall, located upon Manzanillo Island,
was an ugly town built on stilts over what had once been mostly
swamp. Lola stayed at the City Hotel, set down among
the warehouses and shops and miserable houses which covered
the island. The hotel was inadequate for its business in spite of
accommodations for two hundred people who could be served
at once time in its dining room. If Lola had a room to herself it
was secured by bribery, for many of the guests had to sleep on
canvas cots jammed edge to edge on the balconies that girdled
the building.

When Lola came to Aspinwall the Panama Railroad had been
completed only as far as Gorgona. The road ran through tropical jungles above which the coco palms towered. The tops of
many of the low-growing trees were laced together with vines
which had not climbed up their trunks. Like every traveller,
Lola was bothered by this mystery. How could the soft, limber
vines have shot up in the air when they had nothing to cling to
on their way upward? The answer was simple, Lola learned.
Birds carried seeds into the trees and from there the vines sent
flexible roots straight down to the ground.

Upon reaching Gorgona there was a twenty-mile trip to be
made by mule. It was up to the traveller to find a trustworthy
guide for the journey and to make arrangements for the transportation of his luggage and equipment. Warned of the natives'
habit of stealing luggage from the unwitting traveller, Lola,
keeping her whip in hand, made the journey with her ex-

tensive wardrobe lashed to the backs of donkeys, so that she could keep it in sight at all times.

The trip was an exhausting one, although the trail as it continued became easier to travel. At Panama, where there was a wait of several days for a steamer, Lola wandered about the city, which was inhabited by a filthy, disease-ridden, apathetic populace, without courage to attempt to better its condition. The natives, a combination of Indian, Spanish and Negro strains, would never be any different. Their ambition, if indeed they had any, was to outwit by theft or cheating. Yet they were a sad lot, ill-fed and miserably housed, and the only people who ever concerned themselves with their betterment were missionaries, who seemed to fail in all their efforts.

On the 5th of May Lola left Panama on the *Northerner,* which sailed at nine P.M. with four hundred passengers, among them some of the most prominent men in California. The ship also carried the greatest number of bags of mail yet transmitted to the gold country.

For many years the true story of the arrival of Lola Montez in San Francisco was almost lost in legend. There were stories that the schools were let out so that the children could strew flowers on the street before her; that the firemen turned out in their full regalia; that every band in town was on hand to greet her with music; and that all the prominent citizens formed a welcoming committee in her honor.

Nothing of the sort really happened, nor was the other extreme true—that Lola appeared unexpectedly and took everyone by surprise. A month before her arrival there were reports in California newspapers that Lola intended to come to California and every ship that conceivably she might be aboard was thenceforth eagerly watched. Countess or danseuse, politician or drawing room hostess, wielder of whip or pistol, she was the object of widespread curiosity.

By 1853 in San Francisco there was an influx of wives arriving to join their husbands, and many coming there for the first time were bringing their families with them, even though the wicked city of San Francisco was regarded with apprehension, and everyone who came planned to stay only long enough to make a quick fortune. In spite of this, San Francisco was beginning to have an air of permanency, for many had settled down there as merchants. Soon the wives of prosperous men were thinking of improving their wardrobes. Practically every fashionable matron in the city had read of how Lola had looked when she had been in New Orleans. Lola, read the ladies of the Bay City, had been dressed in China grass linen, the color of dried straw. Upon her head she wore a bonnet of matching Tuscany straw decorated with black lace. Over her shoulders was an elegant black shawl of soft Canton crêpe, deeply fringed. When they read of Lola being hauled into court on a charge of assault and battery brought against her by an actor, they admired her spirited defense: "I have been kicked by a horse," she was quoted as saying, "but never before by an ass."

The latest story to reach San Francisco was that Lola had kicked the prompter of the New Orleans theatre, that he had kicked her back, bruising her considerably, and that her agent, hired in New Orleans, had taken a dim view of her behavior and refused to represent her any longer.

San Francisco had little reason to condemn anyone, for the town was still lawless, even though flourishing with prosperity and politicians. Unmarried men found an endless round of pleasure in the saloons and gambling halls, with their music, their games of chance, and the women of easy persuasion.

Burglary was a nightly event in San Francisco and fires repeatedly levelled the town, yet those who had begun to think that they might remain in San Francisco were putting up buildings of substantial material. The main streets—Commercial, Clay, Washington, Montgomery and Merchant—had begun to look permanent. Almost no women, however, walked alone along the streets. The few who had carriages never rode in them alone but waited to be accompanied by husbands or fathers, for the streets, filled with drunken men, were the scene of continual fights and violent scenes with squatters and itinerant miners.

Only a year before, the streets had been unplanked, filled with mud in wet weather and deeply rutted when the thoroughfares had dried. Sometimes the mud became such a quagmire that merchants threw all their trash out in the streets to fill up the holes. Even garbage which befouled the air was often added to the refuse, and among the rain-stained buildings of that period rats in great numbers foraged for food.

Notwithstanding outhouses, the difficulties in disposing of garbage, and the lack of water, which had to be conserved in case of fire, the city was cleaner now. There was talk of laying a sewer pipe under Montgomery Street and lighting the city by coal gas. This had already been introduced in two large mercantile establishments as well as in one of the leading hotels, but the theatres had not yet installed gas-light. Lanterns were still hung outside business establishments at night and people carried lanterns with them after dark.

Down by the waterfront there were still many buildings of warped clapboards affixed with rusty nails. Most of these had been built on stilts, for those that had not were sometimes swamped with water.

A number of wharves jutted out into the water and all of them were crowded with people leaving for the gold mines, coming back from them or simply hanging about the wharves for the arrival of vessels. Few ever left San Francisco to return to their former homes, but the incoming ships were constantly bringing new arrivals. On the docks the men who awaited the ships were usually dressed either in buckskin coats or black broadcloth suits. Men departing for the mines could be easily identified by their calico shirts, which had replaced in fashion the red shirts worn at the beginning of the Gold Rush.

This was the scene that greeted the new arrival as the ship was warped up to the dock. Rising in back of the city were the brown hills of San Francisco, covered with heather and green gorse. Off to the right of Long Wharf, where Lola would arrive, were the ships which had been deserted by their gold-hungry crews during the year 1849. They had since been surrounded by footbridges and were being used as warehouses or boarding houses.

During the fourteen days Lola was aboard the *Northerner* she had found more to entertain her than the excitement attendant upon the passing of the ships *Isthmus* and *Pacific*, both of them southward bound. She had met a man who was the living image of Alexandre Dujarier and who was also, surprisingly enough, half-owner of a newspaper for which he worked. Patrick Purdy Hull, reputed to be related to Patrick Purdy Brontë, the father of the Brontë sisters, was Irish, had a deep, smooth voice, a fund of witty stories, and was endlessly entertaining. It was his wit which originally drew Lola's attention to him. She then noticed that his hair was the same shade of seal brown as Dujarier's had been and his eyes gray-green. As she grew to know Hull better she found him to be increasingly like her former lover. He was proud and brilliant, and a little restrained with women. One night soon after they met she invited him into her cabin when he stopped by to return her shawl, which she had left on deck behind her. That night she found that the two men made love to her in the same way, with reserve, tenderness, and increasing passion.

The passengers, who naturally suspected the new relationship, described Lola as being beautiful and bewildering but relaxed. There was now no show of temper. There was merely a sudden indifference to the men aboard. If they looked at her boldly she paid no more attention to them than if she had been a Greek statue mounted upon a high pedestal. Her attention was riveted on Hull, but she was playing an old game with new rules. She had learned a harsh lesson when she had pursued Heald. Any man she now accepted could never stop wooing her if he expected to keep her. Let Pat Hull burn to be in her arms again;

he wished to marry her, but she was not sure that she wished to lose her freedom. All men of any worth were dominating, managing, ready to establish their rights over the women they married. They interfered with independence, self-thinking, pursuits, likes and dislikes, and even dictated the hours of arising and retiring.

Yet, as she was later to relate, her opinions parallelled his in many ways, for she and Hull had the same interests in politics. Hull had taken a very prominent part in the campaign when Zachary Taylor was elected President of the United States. As a reward, Taylor gave Pat Hull the job of taking the census in California.

After completing the census of the state, Hull remained in San Francisco to become editor and part owner of *The Whig*. Together with his business partner, Colonel James J. Ayres, he joined in civic affairs. In the organizing of the Vigilance Committee, that group of forthright citizens in San Francisco who were determined to correct legal abuses and curb crime, Hull took active part.

Hull's political philosophy was based on the principle that the natural leaders of men should never be dragged down to strengthen the hordes of the weak. Lola had heard George Sand expound a like philosophy, for the latter had said, "Keep the peasantry occupied and they will not have time to think of ways to bring themselves up to the level of their superiors." For hours aboard the ship Lola and Hull discussed the difference between the Old World, where people of royal blood, by right of birth, had held the wealth and the lands, and the opportunities of America, where affluence and position were to be gained solely by a man's endeavors. Hull was never intense as he expounded his beliefs; his way was pleasant, dispassionate, reasoning.

What Lola did not then detect in him was his enormous pride, which matched her own. He could not stand humiliation any better than she. In other ways they were also alike—in wit, in humor, in sudden moods of depression. Perhaps they were too much alike.

Before the *Northerner* had docked in San Francisco, Hull had found out from Lola the truth regarding her puzzling past and, like Dujarier, kept the confidence.

XIX

When Lola's ship docked at Long Wharf she and Hull stood on deck looking over the rail at the crowd. It was only six in the morning, but already the sun was up. Lola had come on deck after an early breakfast so as not to miss the sight as they reached the narrow passage that was the Golden Gate and entered the harbor. She was soon joined by Hull, who had also hurried through his breakfast, not to look at the view which he had often seen, but to be with her.

At the side of the ship, as it was being warped up to the dock, there was a gathering of people from every country in the world, men and women of all races who had been drawn to California by the Gold Rush. They awaited relatives, families, friends, business associates or the mail that the ship had aboard her. Among the prominent men returning on the *Northerner,* was the ex-governor and noted attorney, John McDougal; the United States Marshal, W. Richardson; and Samuel Brannan, a civic leader in San Francisco, who had been paying court to Lola aboard the ship and ignoring her evident interest in Pat Hull.

Brannan had come to California as an elder of the Mormon church, bringing with him a group of settlers. He was the publisher of the first newspaper in California, a prosperous owner of real estate, and he was also known as the man who had actually started the Gold Rush. When gold had been discovered by James Marshall at Coloma, the gold nuggets had been taken to Brannan's store at Sacramento. Brannan displayed the find in San Francisco and started the international scramble for the precious metal.

The news that Lola might arrive any day had made San Franciscans alert, and Hull's partner, Colonel James J. Ayres, later wrote that while he had been at the dock waiting for Pat, he had first spied him standing beside the rail of the wooden side-wheel steamer, and had then noticed his companion. Ayres asserted that he had seen Lola Montez once previously and had at once recognized her. It was he who then uttered the exclamation which became a stock phrase that was carried out of San Francisco and repeated from one gold camp to another: "Lola has come!"

Immediately after Ayres had exclaimed at the sight of her, the public began to cry out her name, and the crush against the gangplank was so great that Sam Brannan and Hull had to use their arms as a guardrail about her before she could descend. As Lola stood holding her full skirts up out of the dirt, men ran to the end of the wharf where a public carriage was waiting. This was impulsively disengaged from its horses by Lola's admirers and dragged toward her through the milling, shouting mass of men. Through close-packed crowds, increasing in size every minute as the news of her arrival was carried from one person to another, they moved slowly, first along Sansome Street, and then along Montgomery, where finally Lola's cortege was unable to move.

She then had her first taste of the attitude of the rough element among the miners toward a sophisticated woman. A few years before, the sight of a woman had moved the lonely gold seekers almost to tears. Upon seeing a woman appear in the streets, men expressed their reverence by stepping off the long planks that served as a sidewalk and doffing their hats. They did this silently honoring the mothers, the wives, or the sweethearts they had left behind them at home. But by 1853, when Lola arrived, the attitude had changed. Although there were more than twenty men to every woman in the population of San Francisco, men had altered their moral outlook. A man now had no hesitancy in forcing his attentions upon any female available. If the lady was married she was at extreme pains to ignore all the covetous looks cast her way. Sometimes the opportunities for a weak woman were tremendous. Respectable women for the most part refrained from walking the streets alone, for they laid themselves open to the bold stares of those men who did not care to associate with prostitutes and who were nonetheless driven through natural desire to look for feminine relationships in some other quarter. Women shopped in the company of their husbands and contented themselves with a social life which consisted mainly of either giving dinners or going to them. When they occasionally went to a play it had to be entirely proper. But there were, of course, many women of less moral persuasion who had come to San Francisco with the hope of gaining quick wealth.

Between the chaste woman and the prostitute there was another class who indulged in the evils offered to them because they had no restraints, such as family ties, dread of scandal, or natural moral purity. Usually they were widows without children or women whose husbands were away in the mining country.

Lola was in an anomalous position; she was neither prostitute nor wife; she was a widow without family, and a woman whose reputation was somewhat of a riddle. Men were bound to regard her as vulnerable and many hoped they might be attractive to her.

A great change had come over Lola's moral standards since her earlier Paris period when she had associated with George Sand. Those were the days when women were bold, outrageous, and devil-may-care. Romance was an intrigue, and to snatch an admirer from some other woman was sport, not merely a flirtation but a triumph born of the desire to share in a novel experiment. It was perfectly permissible to shop around for a lover, to take one on approval, and to keep trying until perfect satisfaction was found. Lola had not played this game to its full extent by any means, but after trying out Alexandre Dumas and Franz Liszt, she had found the perfect lover in Dujarier. Yet the latter relationship had a curious effect upon her outlook, since she had first become engaged to Dujarier and would have married him.

For her this proved a transition stage against further moral laxity. Her later marriage to Heald, in spite of its unhappy outcome, had endowed her with a desire for respectability. She had learned all too late, however, that she could not establish an aura of propriety. A reputation like hers could never be so perfectly mended that the repairs were invisible. Men were disappointed when a notorious woman showed signs of wishing to improve —and women never believed that the improvement was anything but a sham.

As she was lifted into her carriage on the shoulder of Hull that day in San Francisco, the hands of many men had reached out to receive her and set her down upon the cushions of the conveyance in safety. What happened she never did explain clearly, but apparently more than one lewd and offensive liberty was taken. Once in the carriage she recovered her poise and endeared herself to the men surrounding her by throwing kisses, her fingertips daintily pressed to her lips. On the way to the Russ House, where she was taken by the human horses pulling her carriage, she was surrounded by a crowd of men said to number five thousand.

Once she arrived at the hotel she retired to her suite with Periwinkle and did not emerge for five days. Sam Brannan with his elegant carriage, coachman, and fast horses failed to persuade Lola to go driving with him. She knew he was a married man and would not be seen with him.

Outside in the street before the hotel the passage of traffic was impossible. Men by the hundreds stood there at all hours, a day and night vigil was directed at Lola's windows on the second story in the hope that she would make an appearance there. Eventually the patient admirers grew a little suspicious that she might be trying to snub them.

As Lola had left the wharf, two important citizens had received a rebuff from these same watchers. Senator Gwin and Congressman Weller had known that many in the crowd on the wharf were there to greet them, but the surprising appearance of Lola had automatically turned attention away from them. Even surpassing this circumstance in its departure from the ordinary was the unheard-of lack of interest in the mail. At the mere sight of a ship people used to line up for blocks before the post-office, but the alluring Lola had made them all forget that the *Northerner* had anything else aboard but her. And now she was cheating them of the sight of her.

Probably Lola was offended by the experience she had had in being handled by the men who put her into her carriage. In any case her attitude toward the total male population was without doubt partly good showmanship. The leading citizens of San Francisco were welcomed to her suite as visitors; the others should be made to pay to see her. Meanwhile Tom Maguire and John Lewis Baker, San Francisco theatre managers, were contesting for her. Downstairs in the lobby of the Russ House newspapermen envied Hull and waited without reward for a glimpse of Lola.

"This distinguished wonder," said the San Francisco *Herald*, "this world-bewildering puzzle, Countess of Landsfeld, has come to San Francisco and her coming has acted like the application of fire to combustible matter. She sways hearts and potentates and editors and public opinion."

Just how precarious her position was with the San Franciscans Lola did not realize. The great rank and file of men were sensitive to the slightest disdain, and they would base their attitude toward Lola Montez upon how she regarded them. They could be generous with their praise and adulation and money and they were excessively tolerant of any weakness. If a man fell down in the mud because he was drunk others hurried to help him. Whenever a family was burned out in a fire, all homes were hospitably opened to the victims as a refuge. If a tradesman's goods were being stolen, everyone turned on the thieves. Even in the gold country a persistently unsuccessful miner was often given a tip about where he might find gold.

The citizens of San Francisco could also be aroused to deal out punishment for injustice, to apprehend criminals, and to stop abuses in their fledgling government. They would leave their card games in the gambling halls or saloons to fight a fire, help reconstruct a building that had been razed, or bring a criminal to justice. Because of this common ground upon which all men met in brotherhood, no one could afford to feel that he was better than his fellows, and the punishment for such presumption was deadly. If a gentleman parading the streets, dressed in the height of fashion, wearing gloves and carrying a cane, exhibited undue haughtiness toward anyone who spoke to him, some huge miner, dressed in the usual rough clothes, would follow after him, giving a perfect imitation in pantomime of the contemptuous fashionplate until spectators lined the street in his wake, howling with laughter. Thus did they successfully bring anyone down to their level.

So now if Lola showed that she worshipped California and the Californians, they would adore her. Meanwhile they refrained from criticism of her seclusion, reserving their judgment until she made her attitude toward them clear.

Some said that Lola had gone into retirement out of respect to the family of a former agent who had died, but since Edward Willis, the man with whom she had quarreled over her publicity in New York, was the deceased agent in question, the circumstance could scarcely have had any bearing on her remaining in her suite.

In the hotel she kept her shades drawn, and her suite, lit by bracket lamps, was a wonder to her callers. The contents of the fifty or so trunks she had hauled over the Isthmus were lavishly displayed. Her bed was hung with silken draperies and her sitting room was decorated with a mahogany and gilt mirror and numerous tiny French pillows. Her wardrobe, to the few ladies who saw it, was sensational. Her jewels were greatly admired, even by the gentlemen, who were especially taken with a set of pigeon-blood rubies which she wore with a robe of matching color.

If the man in the street and newspapermen had any complaint against her as yet, it was that only the most prominent Californians had been admitted to her presence. Supposedly among her visitors were Governor Wainwright; the Honorable Alexander Wells, Associate Justice of the Supreme Court of California; Alexander Abell, who had been recently Consul for the Sandwich Islands; A. Bartoll and H. M. Gray, both ex-presidents of the Board of Aldermen; the Honorable George W. Baker, Custodian of Public Records; The Honorable Judge Parsons.

Yet if this list tended to stamp Lola as a snob, it soon became evident that she was seriously interested in Pat Hull and was willing to accept his friends, for when he visited her he was accompanied by the associate editor of *The Whig*, Louis R. Lull. Another of Hull's friends, H. J. Clayton, brought his wife to call, and soon other ladies made their appearance in Lola's makeshift salon. The wife of the Governor called and other less important personages, including various actors. All were equally welcome and the word spread abroad that Lola was wonderfully intelligent and fascinating, even if she was a little unrestrained in her gaiety.

Pat's wit and conversational abilities, which were equal to Lola's, gave an added touch of distinction to the salon. Lola sent for a piano and the impeccable Fred Woodworth came to see her, for he owned the only piano company in town. An ardent pianist, he was soon playing for her when she practiced her dancing. Woodworth was one of the most honored citizens and an astute business man, having been the first in San Francisco to see the possibilities of erecting his building out over the water line. There in his warehouse, concerts were often given and Lola promised to dance at a large benefit then being arranged. Just to be accepted by Woodworth was a great mark in Lola's favor.

But it was after Woodworth had departed that Lola sat one day with Hull and smoked a cigar. Periwinkle had never seen her do this before, and was shocked.

"Mam'selle," she protested, "that is the tip of the devil's tail!"

Lola winked and went right on smoking.

XX

IN SPITE of Lola's aloofness and her failure to capture the popularity of the proletariat, the city paid her homage. Merchants hurriedly redecorated their windows, always previously overstuffed with a hodge-podge of rakes, hoes, ironstone china, solar stands, gold pans, wheelbarrows, and perhaps an embarrassed sunbonnet or two, since ladies who did not make their own were considered poor excuses for women. Lola's arrival created a lasting change. Merchants contemplated the results of their hasty attempts to display feminine fashions and were elated with the sudden press of business. All the shawls, silks and boots were suddenly "Lola Montez Fashions," in spite of the fact that Lola wouldn't have been caught dead in any of them. A man named his yacht after her and won a yachting cup, and a horse named Lola Montez won a race at the Pioneer Race Course, much to everyone's amazement. The name became identified with good luck to everyone but its bearer.

Lola was incapable of thinking of herself as blessed with future happiness. The thought of marrying Hull filled her with misgivings. Her past was merely the exemplification of what was to come. It was a bitter truth that nothing she ever laid hold of could last. There was the ever-recurring thought that if she loved a man she could not have him. She had never been consoled for the loss of Dujarier, and although Heald had often irritated her because he was so juvenile in his ways and so conventional in his ideas, she had loved him. Until she had learned that he was dead, she had never given up hope that he would return to her. Long ago she had struggled, too, to hold Franz Liszt, the first man she had ever loved, but his slack morals and determination to keep his freedom foretold from the outset the early conclusion of their relationship. Discontented as she was, marriage with Hull might very well lead to unhappiness if she once committed herself to this decision.

Of more immediate importance was her acceptance of the contract offered by John Lewis Baker, manager of the American Theatre. She was to make her debut in Sheridan's play, *The School for Scandal*, as Lady Teazle. So great was the demand for tickets that they were sold at auction, the best seats commanding sixty-five dollars and even the poorest bringing five.

The moment Lola appeared on the stage in her initial performance, there was clamorous applause. It was much too noisy and prolonged. Lola had had experience with impolite audiences, but not with patrons who were crude, loud-mouthed, and ill-bred, while at the same time gay, enthusiastic, and uncritical. Looking her very best, Lola accepted the ovation with a deep curtsey, displaying nothing of her repugnance toward men who too easily betrayed that they lived under the strain of being starved for women. Lola sensed the slight mass hysteria aroused by the sight of a woman who disturbed them and she was naturally repelled. It was fortunate that Lola's curtsey, with her head bent and her curls falling forward, was taken to mean that she was grateful and touched by their ardent response.

Although she had talented actors to support her and the play was a classic, her own deficiencies as an actress could not be concealed. Yet her audience was at such a pitch of excitement, and so gratified to have their anticipation at last satisfied, that merely to see her was sufficient reward for most of the patrons. They noticed only her intense earnestness and desire to please, and waived all critical judgment of a woman who had been the talk of two continents for a long time before her actual arrival. Even the newspapers refrained from anything severe in the way of judgment. One paper spoke of her as being "deficient in training," as if the fault was scarcely hers, and at the end of the performance she was called out again and again to receive the plaudits of an audience that showed itself to be in love with her.

The play was not repeated and the next night Lola appeared in *Yelva*, in which she played her part in pantomime. Between the acts she was to do her "Spider Dance."

Once again the house was overflowing with the largest audience that had ever been packed into any theatre in the history of San Francisco. *Yelva*, which Lola had had to translate from the original French in order to produce it in California, was not inherently a play of much worth, but Lola made it effective as she played the part of a dumb girl, dependent entirely upon the expression of her face and the pose of her body to convey her thoughts and feelings.

The great Fanny Ellsler had originated the dance, "La Tarantule," but the San Franciscans in their enthusiasm for Lola swore that she was unequalled. Her dance costume was Spanish in design, with full, short skirts under which she wore flesh-colored tights. The ladies in the audience, of which there were quite a number on this second night, caught their breath at the daring exposure of limbs. None of them, even getting in and out of a carriage, dared reveal more than an ankle, but the men expressed approval by loud applause the moment she appeared. Lola had some time since abandoned the use of a wig and her hair, grown to shoulder length, was caught back and fixed with a wreath. The full perfection of her face was revealed as she swung gracefully to the center of the stage and paused for a moment. Then as she moved she made it evident that she was entangled in the filaments of a spider's web. In a dancing step she portrayed that she was more and more confused as the fibers wrapped themselves about her ankles. The music slowed as she discovered a spider on her petticoat, which she attempted to shake loose with graceful leaps into the air. Then she discovered other spiders and, examining her skirts, she shook them to reveal petticoat after petticoat, each one a different color. The fight against the spiders grew more hectic as she danced with abandon and fire, and at the conclusion she had succeeded in shaking all of them out upon the floor, where she stamped them to death.

The audience was held spellbound, and somewhat horror-struck, but when the dance ended the applause was thunderous, and as Lola addressed the audience after numerous curtain calls, bouquets were showered at her feet.

The theatre-going public had long heard of the success of *Lola Montez in Bavaria,* and they now began to clamor for it. It seemed to promise huge success, for when it was announced, there was such a demand for tickets that a great overflow of people were turned away, even though the play was to run for a week, an extraordinary length of time for San Francisco with its population of thirty thousand.

Every effort was made to reproduce the Bavarian scene authentically with the best scenery and the finest furniture available, yet the time for rehearsals was inadequate and the prompter was kept busy correcting a constant succession of mistakes by the supporting actors.

Backstage and in the dressing rooms, Lola acted like a pyromaniac trying to set a blaze. She quarrelled with everyone, including her agent, J. S. Henning, and the theatre manager, and caused much unpleasantness by her persistence in bringing to rehearsals whatever gallant was in attendance upon her.

One day when she was accompanied by a count the manager reminded her forcibly that visitors were not permitted. Suddenly haughty, as if she had just remembered that she herself was a countess, Lola exclaimed, "The play will not continue until you apologize to my friend!" Far from apologizing, Baker told the count to go, and Lola retaliated by constantly interrupting the rehearsal until she had alienated nearly everyone in the supporting cast.

Throughout the run of the play, no opportunity was lost by fellow artists to belittle Lola and to make sport of her conferred nobility. One of them deliberately baited her by asking her if it was *true* that she had been made a countess. "Indeed I was," retorted Lola, "with the titles Countess of Landsfeld, Baroness

Rosenthal, and Canoness of the Order of St. Theresa, as well as estates and two thousand people under me." To this her tormenter replied, "I calculate you don't recall whether he gave you any royal ancestors or not, do you?"

The climax to her scenes at rehearsal came during a quarrel with her agent. She stamped her foot, let loose with epithets unbecoming to a lady, and made such a rush at Henning that he fell over backwards. She was down on her knees instantly, pounding him so furiously with her fists that he was unable to arise. He finally managed to get to his feet only because the actors nearby caught Lola by the arms and restrained her. Henning tried to placate her by handing her a check, but she promptly tore this up and scattered it like confetti into the air. "Filthy lucre," she screamed, "is no object to me!" She then told him he was dismissed.

That day in a saloon a man who had heard of the row put a champagne glass upside down on the bar and made it leap in an identifiable imitation of Lola's spider dance. In another saloon, known for its rowdy atmosphere, the bar-keeper affixed a wire spider to the ceiling and let it down by a string onto drunken customers' heads. In a sly way Lola was being subjected to lower-class San Francisco's usual treatment of anyone who put on airs; she was being made fun of.

Shortly after this episode, Lola made her first appearance on Montgomery Street, San Francisco's shopping center. She had sent Periwinkle to buy her some stockings, but as the girl had been unable to find the right kind, her mistress decided to look for them herself. At this time, merchants often used the planked sidewalk as a warehouse and people were forced to step out into the rutted street in order to get around the piled-up boxes. Not the least disconcerted, Lola picked her way to a leading merchandise store. The owner waited on her. Lola said she needed very long hose for a stage costume and the merchant showed her his stock. "This hose isn't long enough," she protested. The merchant had evidently heard of her tantrums in the theatre, and replied, "Then I suggest if you need longer hose you call in at the nearest fire hall." Fortunately Lola laughed and the man was so endeared at her taking his sarcasm so well that he afterwards described her as "sweet and lovable."

Her appearance in public did much to mitigate her reputation as a snob and from then on she was constantly seen in the streets, although this alone did not suffice to overcome the damage she had done by losing her temper. Repeatedly newspapers had tried to interview her about Ludwig, but Lola reacted with ill-concealed indignation. She had always been lacking in tact and it did not seem to occur to her that she need only suggest that they come and see her in *Lola Montez in Bavaria* to get the whole story. Appreciation of the interest shown in her, demureness, anything would have been more acceptable than hauteur.

Even more offensive was her failure to offer her hand to the men who were introduced to her. In San Francisco this was tantamount to an insult. Yet the more serious breach of convention in visiting a gambling house in the company of Sam Brannan did not reflect to her discredit, for no one was a greater champion of public morals than Brannan and the respect in which he was held made it impossible for people to criticize Lola for being seen with him.

Another mark in Lola's favor was that she was invited to stay over a week end at the house of Dr. and Mrs. William Robinson. Everyone knew that Mrs. Robinson, in spite of her husband being an actor, had little respect for actresses, yet Lola accepted the invitation, and much to everyone's amazement the two women spent most of the time repairing Lola's stage costumes. During the week end they were entertained at the homes of other actors whose cottages were strung out near Dr. Robinson's on the eminence of Telegraph Hill, and the visit wound up with a picnic on a ridge overlooking the bay. Lola showed all the lovable qualities in her nature at being received so cordially by her various hostesses. It seemed that she wanted nothing more than to be accepted and liked for herself. Nothing was visible of the tempestuous, fire-breathing demon she was alleged to be backstage at the theatre. Nor was she the thrilling, passionate, dominating woman, famous for her intellect and her Republicanism. Lola followed the conversation rather than led it, and appeared to enjoy herself thoroughly among these people, to many of whom she was a virago during the week.

The outcome of this week end was soon apparent; a newspaper the following day referred to her as "high-souled," and with her morning coffee she received baskets of flowers, most of them accompanied by notes expressing admiration and affection.

She was now rehearsing for *The Maid of Saragossa* and seemed to be considerably quieter. In a new type of bonnet which rested upon the back of the head and demonstrated to the surprised ladies of the town that their poke bonnets were now out of style, Lola allowed herself to be seen more and more about the town. She wore the most chaste clothes in public, dresses tight-closed about the throat and a shawl which concealed her perfect form, although she never went so far as to look as if she belonged to a family circle, which most of all would have charmed the San Franciscans. But she was democratic enough to be seen with an admirer having a drink of sarsaparilla at Samuel Adams'—the only druggist who served such a drink—in an atmosphere of powdered sage, cod liver oil, port wine, and Osgood's Chologague.

Lola beat the drum for the emancipation of women by appearing in the late afternoon at Peter Job's on Portsmouth Square, demanding that she be served an ice. Other ladies soon followed suit, stepping down from their carriages into the fearful dirt of the street which politicians and office holders said could not be cleaned because the city treasury was empty. Nor was Lola afraid to appear, surrounded by men, in the dining room of the International Hotel. She even began to eat at a restaurant not yet penetrated by ladies, known as the Poodle Dog, a French rotisserie run by a huge and unkempt French woman who had named her place of business after her equally huge and unkempt dog.

XXI

Durıng the run of *Lola Montez in Bavaria*, Lola, having "shaken all the spiders from her dress," decided to conquer audiences with another of her dances. This, the "Sailor's Hornpipe," brought as much applause as had its predecessor. Ever since the early days, when the lonely gold miners had sought the cheer of any entertainment available, they had been enthusiastic over the crudest scenery, were content with the light from spermaceti candles, and expected little in the way of costumes, which the actors had to carry with them on horseback. This deficiency in properties had led them to concentrate upon the quality of the acting, which had made them shrewd natural judges of talent.

By the use of every device to cover her inadequacies, Lola hoodwinked her audiences to dazzling effect. Others had done the dance much more brilliantly, but Lola scored a triumph. Dressed in a blue jacket with a broad collar and a boy's tarpaulin trousers—to the delight of the gentlemen—she danced against a backdrop of a ghostly wrecked ship. Flashing lights, the sound of the surf beating at the shore, and a howling wind were all novel effects to the San Franciscans, and they were delighted.

One result of the increased enthusiasm for Lola was a veritable deluge of verses written in her honor. Most of them were sent directly to her, but others found their way into the newspapers, revealing the pathetic loneliness of the men who penned them. The poetry critic for the San Francisco *Herald* placed a cigar box with a hole in the top in Barry & Patton's refined saloon on Montgomery Street, in which habitués were invited to deposit their poetic efforts. Some inebriated gentlemen, a little confused, deposited money instead of verse, and it was said that the saloon was always so crowded that the poets had difficulty in composing.

Gentlemen who drank only bimbos fared better. This drink was the height of fashion, described to a visiting legislator as consisting of three parts root beer thickened with soft squash and water gruel strained through a cane-bottomed chair. The majority of contributions were regretfully rejected by the proprietor and the newspaper poetry critic yielded to his superior judgment, but one day they were delighted to find a poem signed "M. W.," and knew the initials concealed the identity of a worthy local statesman, an impulsive fellow who had seen Lola dance and was known to be hopelessly infatuated. With the assistance of bimbo and passion he had dashed off an effusion on the back of the playbill from the American Theatre, and it was published next day without comment.

> Fair Lola!
> I cannot believe as I gaze on thy face
> And into thy soul-speaking eye,
> There rests in thy bosom one lingering trace
> Of a spirit the world should decry
> No, Lola, no!
>
> I read in those eyes, and on that clear brow,
> A Spirit—a Will—it is true;
> I trace there a Soul—kind, loving e'en now;
> But it is not a wanton I view,
> No, Lola, no!
>
> I will not believe thee cold, heartless and vain!
> Man's victim thou ever hast been!
> With *thee* rests the sorrow, on *thee* hangs the chain!
> Then on thee should the world cast the sin?
> No, Lola, no!

By June 7th Lola was appearing in the *Maid of Saragossa*, and the critics declared that she was particularly well cast as a maiden in the Peninsular war. In those scenes where she urged a cowardly lover to be brave and noble she was agreed to be inspiring, and this critical acclaim brought her huge audiences. She added to her performance the Andalusian dance "El Ollé," which created such a furore that she was obliged to repeat it.

Three nights later she shared in the benefit given for the first Hebrew Benevolent Society, when the most noted actors of the day gathered to appear in selections from their repertoires. Never before had anything like this been seen in California. Enthusiasm knew no bounds and the theatre became so over-crowded that its doors were thrown open and spectators looked in from the street. Lola danced three times and the bouquets that fell at her feet roused the jealousy of the other performers, who included Caroline and William Chapman, two well-known performers who were brother and sister, Dr. Robinson and the violinist Miska Hauser. Hauser in particular had been poorly received in the gold-mining country, where his too obvious attempts to appeal to American patriotism with such selections as "Yankee Doodle" had not found a gullible response. He had been reduced to giving concerts in Woodworth's piano show-room and Lola's reception that night filled him with such bitter envy that he and Dr. Robinson began to seek a chance to turn Lola's popularity to their own advantage.

There was another benefit on the 18th, this time for the San Francisco Firemen's Fund, instituted and arranged by Lola. The firemen came in full dress, and the Chapman troupe put on a burlesque. Other actors gave such performances that the affair was acclaimed a veritable feast of drama. Yet when Lola appeared to do her spider dance the firemen, having applauded the preceding numbers warmly, got to their feet and broke into an uproar of enthusiasm.

When Lola finally began to dance she changed the divertisse-ment to an exhibition which Hull's partner was to describe as "grotesque and amazing." Her makeup, he said, "caused one to shiver." It was apparent, as she darted from side to side of the stage, that she was imitating the movements of the tarantula weaving a web. Then abandoning the spider role after the web was finished, she pulled off the mask that had been over her face and became the beautiful captive caught in the woven lure. One by one she broke the filaments, and as she emerged triumphant and killed the spider, the firemen began to throw their helmets upon the stage. Amid wild tumult she snatched one of them up and retreated to the wings. When they brought her back with a curtain call she had the hat clutched to her heart. With her feet buried in bouquets she told her audience she was happy because "I have the firemen's hearts as well as their hats."

It was the last performance Lola gave in San Francisco, but *tour de force* though it was she was to pay for her success. While she was taking twelve days' rest before going on tour, she learned that Dr. Robinson and the Chapmans had been rehearsing a burlesque, written by Robinson, which was designed to make fun of her. When it was produced, feeling ran high, for through Lola's endeavors thirty thousand dollars had been put into the Firemen's Fund, and not only the firemen but several of the newpapers objected to the ridicule she was subjected to. The play, a burletta founded on *Lola Montez in Baravia*, was called *Who's Got the Countess?* And Lola's spider dance was turned into the "Spy Dear Dance." Even Baker, the manager of the American Theatre, came in for a sarcastic portrayal, and the quarrel that Lola had had with her agent, J. S. Henning, got full treatment.

Who's Got the Countess? filled the theatre most of the time that Lola remained in San Francisco, but on the whole the audiences did not like it. Lola could not understand why she had been made the butt of Dr. Robinson's wit and turned to Mrs. Robinson for an explanation, but when that lady had no adequate answer Lola appears to have shrugged off the slight. The ovation she had received from the firemen had convinced her that she was cherished by the San Franciscans, and she felt that people loved her not only for her beauty but for herself. She had been accepted for her intelligence, for her wit, and for her personality. The burletta was unkind, but it was merely professional jealousy and didn't matter. All the most prominent people had called on her when they might have taken her past reputation as her measure. They had judged her for themselves, and never had she felt so much a part of the people among whom she was living.

Meanwhile the ruddy-faced Hull, with his wealth of funny stories and his many friends, had begun to seem to her the end of all her searching for satisfaction. But although she dreamed of a home and a circle of friends, she was still afraid to commit herself. Her first husband had deserted her for another woman; Heald had been lost to her; Alexandre Dumas had predicted that she would bring an evil fate upon anyone she chose to love. She had grown superstitious about wanting happiness. If she married Pat Hull she felt sure something would happen to ruin the marriage.

It was during this period of uncertainty that she visited Madame de Cassins, the popular diviner, who could speak several languages and who read her fortune in French. At that time it was quite the fashion in San Francisco for men to consult fortune tellers before making business decisions, and the predictions of these prophets was taken so seriously that they even affected mining and banking transactions. Whatever Lola was told, it was shortly after this visit that she reached a decision.

On the evening of July 1st, Fred Woodworth, accompanied by some companions, went to a restaurant in Commercial Street. "Clayton," said Woodworth to the owner of the place, "we have a secret for you, a Masonic secret." "I am not a Mason," Clayton replied. "But if it's a secret worth keeping, I can keep it." "Be at the Mission church tomorrow at matin bells, but don't tell anyone why. We don't know if this will come off, and we may all be sold." He then whispered in Clayton's ear.

When Clayton went home, he told his wife that he wished to be wakened early next morning. Mrs. Clayton expressed surprise but he evaded a direct explanation and merely said that he wanted to walk to the Mission for exercise and was therefore trying to avoid one of his friends, who might stop by and ask him to ride.

With this flimsy explanation Mrs. Clayton seemed strangely content, and at dawn next day when Clayton walked past the Mission Road toll house he was surprised to see a great number of carriages ahead of him, as well as men on horseback. Reaching the old adobe church he found about twenty people, including Governor and Mrs. Wainwright, walking about the grounds.

Just then a carriage arrived which was recognized as belonging to the Adams House. Abraham Bartol emerged, followed by Pat Hull, and a moment later, Lola Montez. She immediately entered the church, and the Wainwrights hurried with Clayton through a side door. As they were about to seat themselves, Lola turned and indicated that she wished the main doors of the church closed. There were already about forty people seated and among them Clayton recognized Judge Wills, Captain McMichael, the Honorable Beverley Saunders, the Honorable Alexander Wiles, and several other equally prominent politicians.

Lola held two white vases filled with flowers, which she presented to Father Fontaine at the altar, and as Bartol moved up beside Hull it became apparent that this was indeed a wedding ceremony in spite of the fact Lola wore only a plain gray dress and matching bonnet. At the close of the brief ceremony, Hull kissed Lola with a tenderness quite foreign to his usually rather rough ways, and Lola then signified to the guests in the pews that they were to follow her into the ante-chamber.

Here, to Clayton's utter surprise, was his wife, who had been asked by Lola to arrange the refreshments and was much amused at having deceived her husband.

The light shining on her black curls and lighting up her huge blue eyes, Lola was besieged with congratulations. More daring than the others the Governor kissed her. Clayton followed suit "to make the occasion memorable," and Lola responded with a smile, "It is the custom of my country." The people who had been walking in the grounds now joined the party and were eagerly greeted by the bride, if not by Hull, who kept his arm firmly around Lola to prevent any other man from kissing the woman who was now his wife.

Among the guests were many of the men who had called on Lola when she had first arrived in San Francisco, but noticeably absent was Samuel Brannan, who, having failed to win Lola away from Hull, did not attend to give the marriage his blessing.

Finally Lola whispered to Hull that she would like to invite their friends to take breakfast with them, and his close friend Louis Lull observed a frown cross Hull's face. Lull knew, as he was to write in later years, that Hull could not possibly afford such an expense but Lola, who had, it was said, been receiving over four thousand dollars nightly in the theatre, could easily do so. Hull's masculine pride was obviously hurt, but he overcame it, even when Lola suggested an expensive restaurant.

Neither Lola, Hull, nor Hull's friends have left any account of the breakfast which followed, but the long parade of carriages into the city drew so much attention that by noon the news of the marriage was widespread, and returning to the house of Mrs. Gates, where she had recently been living, Lola was besieged by callers. As soon as she had changed into travelling costume, she was again joined by Hull and they held an impromptu reception, Hull's friends having hurriedly provided champagne.

Lola's eyes sparkled with happiness at the kindness showered on her by so many people. Such prominent men as the Honorable John B. Wells, of the United States Senate, San Francisco's mayor, George W. Baker, and the Honorable Judge Parsons came to congratulate the bride and groom.

In the afternoon they sailed for Sacramento on the steamer *Arrow*, a memorable occasion in itself, for the *Arrow* was on her maiden voyage. Hundreds of people who had come to see her depart had the added thrill of seeing Lola and her new husband standing on deck.

XXII

LOLA LEFT San Francisco with such feeling of kinship for the Californians that she was moved to tears at her departure, and when a San Francisco newspaper which reached her a few days later contained a eulogy of admiration and affection, she felt that she had found herself at last. It was even more satisfactory when other newspapers reprinted the article. "Lola Montez," said the item, "during her short stay in our city has by her many good acts so won the esteem of our citizens as to have made herself a general favorite with every class in the community and it is with a feeling of regret that we noticed her last appearance on the boards, previous to her departure for Sacramento. You will find her a noble-hearted and generous lady well worth the warm reception which the citizens have at all times bestowed upon members of the dramatic profession."

When the captain of the *Arrow*, A. D. Averill, invited Lola and Pat to his quarters to share a bottle of champagne in double celebration of their marriage and the ship's maiden voyage, Lola expressed her desire to make California her permanent home. Since both she and Pat were fond of hunting and the outdoors, they would probably settle in some place in the mountains, she said, for she had a husband to take care of her now.

But that evening at dinner, when her husband questioned her about a topaz necklace she was wearing, and she replied that it had belonged to Heald's family, Hull's face darkened, and he demanded why she had not returned it. "What for?" she retorted. "So that old maid aunt, Suzanna Heald, could wear it around her scrawny neck?"

With this small contest of wills the tenor of the marriage was set and it did not forecast equanimity. The atmosphere throughout the rest of the dinner remained as cold between them as the imported Alaskan ice in their water glasses.

Lola was to find she had misjudged the huge Irishman she had married, for while he was gay and witty on the surface, he could be belligerent when crossed, was self-centered, and as rough as a mountain lion. He liked nothing better than to ride horseback and to hunt, but Lola was an excellent horsewoman and almost unmatched as a marksman, so it seemed that their community of tastes would make their life together congenial. But Hull's friend, Henry Tinsley, wrote that Pat had fallen in love with Lola "on sight," while Lola had been charmed by Hull only because he was "witty, had a musical voice, and smooth conversational powers." This was Lola's overt evaluation of the attraction he had for her, but there was another reason underlying her sudden decision to marry him. Although she had been Hull's mistress aboard the *Northerner,* she had not dared to spend time alone with him in San Francisco. Marriage was the only way they could indulge their mutual passion. It was only when Hull had her in his arms once more that the wide gap between them was forgotten.

Sacramento had rapidly progressed from the tent town it had been during the Gold Rush. It was not even half as large as San Francisco, but its buildings were now constructed of brick, all built within the past year. The streets were vastly better than those of the great port of the Pacific, for they were graded and were in the process of being planked, with great piles of lumber stacked at every corner ready to be laid down. In Chinatown there were so many stacks of lumber waiting for the industrious Chinese to put up their buildings that some wit had dubbed them the "great wall of China."

The heavy rains of the previous winter had put the city under water, but levees had been built and the business houses as well as the two thousand or so frame houses were fairly secure from the threats of the river on which the city was built.

Theatres in Sacramento were now comparatively luxurious, especially the Sacramento Theatre, where Lola was to appear.

The audiences, however, were still the rough, floating population of miners down from the mountains, who came into town with their gold pokes to be entertained in saloons, gambling halls and theatres. Performers were apprehensive of their ribald humor and dreaded the cat-calls or the vegetables pelted at them on the stage, although if they were pleased the audience could produce bouquets with equal alacrity. They liked variety, scorned far-fetched melodrama, were fond of Shakespeare if adequately played, and had a doughty contempt for any amateurish performer, man or woman.

The kind of humor that most appealed to them was exemplified by one of their favorite stories of a miner who advertised in the Sacramento *Union* for a wife: *Any girl what's got some pots and pans, a good feather bed and all the fixings can get me for her husband.* As Sacramento then had only six hundred residents and the sight of even one woman caused a furore, the advertisement was judged to have been placed by some wag with a highly developed sense of the absurd.

The first rumor that Lola was to arrive in Sacramento was launched by Mr. Chawill, who owned a boarding house on I Street at which Hull had made reservations. No one knew until her actual arrival that she had married, and Chawill's was commensurate with Hull's income. But much to his mortification, Lola scorned it. Instead, she insisted upon staying at the Orleans, the most elegant establishment yet constructed. No place in town had a more splendid saloon, which was brilliantly lit by four chandeliers, the gas being supplied by means of oil burners, an innovation from New York.

Whether Lola already knew that this hotel was the center of social life in Sacramento or whether she heard of it upon her arrival is not clear, but she managed to persuade her somewhat sulky husband that it was good showmanship to stay at the most popular place.

The choice was probably shrewd, for the *Democratic State Journal*, always alert to comings and goings at the Orleans, heralded Lola's arrival with the announcement: *The curious will have the opportunity of beholding the famed Lola. Blessed privilege!*

For her first performance in Sacramento Lola chose her famous "Spider Dance." The house was packed, many men paying the full price of good seats for the privilege of standing. But at the moment when she discovered the spiders in her skirts, there were loud guffaws, and when she pretended to shake them off there were cries of "Higher up, Lola! Look higher up!"

An eight-year-old girl was to follow her several months later, doing the identical dance, and no one saw anything untoward in the performance, but in Lola, with her wild reputation, every movement was taken to be suggestive. The house was filled with men smelling of liquor and strong tobacco who appreciated to the full the sight of beautiful limbs, the incredible breasts that shook as she leaped wildly upon the spiders, the small waist that almost any man there could have spanned between his hands. The cat-calls finally died down and she finished in a silence which showed the absorption of her audience. Then there was deafening applause, and bouquets and even a fireman's belt were tossed at her feet. Lola lifted the belt to her lovely lips and kissed it as she retired from the stage.

She was followed by Miska Hauser, the violinist, who still had not profited by what he should have discovered at the concerts he had given in Woodworth's wareroom at San Francisco. There, in the belief that he was playing to a superior audience, he had performed Mendelssohn and bewitched his hearers. He underestimated the standards of Sacramento patrons by bringing forth all the stale compositions every hack violinist sawed at, and got scant notice in the newspapers next day, one of them remarking with disdain that his was "adequate entertainment."

Out of jealousy Hauser was to give an account of Lola's second performance in which he lauded himself and made it appear that she was left grovelling for favors. It was true that she lost her temper next night, but Hauser had been engaged by her merely to fill out her program, and in the light of her repeated generosity to him, his behavior was inexcusable. Out of sympathy for his disappointments at Sonora, Columbia, Jamestown and other mining towns, Lola had sent him a large basket of flowers at Woodworth's, and on another occasion had presented him with a silver pen in a holder filled with gold dust. Yet in spite of these well-meant gifts the bald, pudgy little violinist hated her.

On the evening of this fiasco in Sacramento Lola wore a fairy-like costume instead of the revealing one she had worn the previous night. She looked so beautiful that a gasp of delight ran through the audience when she appeared, and a number of people threw bouquets at her feet. But as Lola began to dance a man started to laugh, and others soon joined him. She stopped, bade the orchestra cease playing and, stepping toward the footlights, addressed the audience, her eyes blazing with indignation.

"Ladies and gentlemen!" she exclaimed. "Lola Montez has too much respect for the people of California not to perceive that this stupid laughter comes from a few silly puppies."

There is no doubt that the group was making it their business to ridicule her simply because they had been expecting something vulgar, and were disappointed to see a woman poised upon the stage with the lovely fragility of a dragon-fly, and wearing a costume which though sheer was not diaphanous. She had also, it later transpired, offended others in the audience by stamping on some of the bouquets.

As they continued to laugh, Lola looked toward the group, who should have been put out of the theatre, and said, "Give me your men's trousers and take in their place my woman's skirts; you are not worthy to be called men."

The scoffers laughed even louder, joined by others who were amused at her challenge, and Lola's eyes flashed as she defied them. "Lola Montez is proud to be what she is, but you haven't the courage to fight with her—yes, this woman, who has no fear of you all, despises you!"

Lola was now facing what had been successfully avoided in San Francisco, and she could not understand it. She did not recognize it for what it was, a combination of disappointment over the evident modesty of her performance and a desire to put her, a countess, in her place. As she stood there in the center of the stage, silent because she could no longer be heard above the din, the vulgar element in the theatre took over. She was pelted with decayed apples and eggs, and unable to defend herself, had to retreat to the wings, beside herself with fury. It now seemed that Sacramento audiences came prepared either to cheer or to jeer. When she had stepped out on the stage a scattering of bouquets had greeted her, but if they ostensibly entered the theatre carrying bouquets, their pockets were filled with material for a riotous time at the expense of performers they did not like. One actor had continued to play, with the remains of rotten vegetables affixed to his costume, and another had left the stage only when hit directly in the eye with a cabbage. For the most part the theatrical people ignored the challenge of abuse and went blithely on, pretending that nothing had happened, which had the usual effect of calming the audience after they had run out of their supply of weapons.

In an effort to restore order, the manager of the theatre sent Hauser out to play his violin. Hauser later claimed that the audience was so charmed by his music that quiet descended immediately. More likely the pause was due to the fact that everyone was waiting to see if any Chinese firecrackers were to be thrown upon the stage, since this was the ultimate in insult. The audience did not pause any length of time to listen to Hauser, but started for the boxoffice to get their money back. Hauser was grinding away at "Yankee Doodle" when Lola, with admirable courage, reappeared and went through her dance to the end, ignoring the tune that Hauser was playing, as well as the orchestra which was accompanying him. The theatre manager, looking at this erratic double performance in which the participants acted as if they were totally unaware of each other, groaned and fled out into the street. The audience, meanwhile, having found the boxoffice closed, came back into the auditorium to knock over the benches, break up the chairs in the boxes and throw them through the windows. Hauser's broken English, as he appealed to the theatre patrons, did not help matters. The vandalism went on until they were satisfied they could do no more.

In the meantime, Lola had gone to her hotel, and the mob, enjoying itself enormously, was soon outside the Orleans. Very quickly a band was assembled with instruments of pots and kettles beaten with ladles and sticks, the mob screaming out a kind of rhythm. Unafraid, Lola calmly opened her window and crawled through it to stand on her balcony. In her hand was a lamp which she held aloft to show that she was there and equal to outscreaming the charivari.

"You cowards, low blackguards, cringing dogs and lazy fellows! I would not despise a dirty dog as much as I do you." She was amazed when the crowd dropped their kettles and pots and ceased beating the drum which had been adding to the confusion. There was nothing the miners loved better than this sort of courage, and to a man they applauded and cheered her, although one of them climbed up on the balcony and put out Lola's light.

News of the riot had reached Sacramento's fledgling Vigilantes, but by the time they came to her rescue, she was laughing and throwing kisses to the crowd.

The next day she said to Hauser, "I have added another to the list of my adventures."

XXIII

THE DAY FOLLOWING what had been virtually a riot, Hull's friend, Lemuel Snow, was confounded to see Lola and Pat out walking on the Sacramento streets as if nothing had happened the evening before. Lola wore an elaborate black dress and a magnificent black bonnet, lined with pink. "She is a wonderful and enchanting creature," wrote Snow; his friendliness evaporated when he later learned that she had persuaded Pat to give up his newspaper. Nevertheless, he confessed that she dazzled him, as she did everyone else.

A Sacramento newspaper gave an inaccurate account of the demonstration at the theatre, in which it was stated that Lola had had a fight with the orchestra. She was quoted as saying that certain persons, amused at her withering glances at the musicians, had started the laughter, and that she had left the stage after saying she would not dance to its accompaniment. Since the account related how easily Hauser had quieted the audience by playing a favorite air, it cannot be doubted that the point of view was his.

The night following the fracas, Lola had an audience which overflowed into the street. While some people were willing to concede that she had won the people over by her courage, others felt that the multitude had poured into the place solely for the purpose of hoping there would be another row which they would get to see. The Marshal, however, made his appearance, backed by the city's full police force posted inside and out, ready to quell any repetition of the previous riot.

There were certainly some who came because they admired Lola's bravery, and among them was Major General John A.

Sutter, upon whose property the gold had been discovered which had started the Gold Rush, although he himself had lost his land to squatters. At the sight of this popular man, everyone cheered, and as other prominent men came into the theatre, it was observed that they were accompanied by their wives, proving that the ladies were there to support Lola in her contest with the churlish element. After the overture was played, the manager came out on the stage, made a bow, and said that Lola Montez wished to explain what had happened the night before. When the audience applauded, Mr. King left the stage and returned leading Lola by the hand.

"Ladies and gentlemen," she addressed them, "I am overwhelmed at your reception of me this evening and feel it my duty to explain to you the misunderstanding which occurred last night. I have ever been accustomed to be well received and loved by the public of the United States, wherever I have appeared before them, and these recollections will ever remain in my mind and endear America to me. I came before you last night with the same confidence in your kindness and the utmost desire on my part to make my performance pleasing to you. Two or three individuals insulted me grossly by sneering and laughing at me. I was more sensitive, perhaps, than most artists upon such an occasion, for the reason that I am persecuted and followed by certain persons and their agents, because I made political enemies in Europe who follow and annoy me upon every occasion. I know that no American would gratuitously insult a woman. You have too chivalrous and gallant natures, and women are far more respected in America than any other country in the world. And now about the bouquet, which I am so severely blamed for trampling upon in the 'Spider Dance.' You must know that a spider is supposed to be upon the ground, and it is very difficult to procure a living spider, and therefore I leave it to the imagination of the public to substitute one. It sometimes happens that some of my facetious friends deposit bouquets at my feet which I stamp on thus."

At this point Lola stamped as if killing a spider, lifted herself upon her toes and then looked toward the audience. The patrons applauded her uproariously.

"As for the circumstances which occurred after the performance closed," she finally continued, "I wish to draw the veil of oblivion over them. It does not become me to speak of, or you to listen to, them. To conclude, let me again return my sincere thanks for your kind reception, and I hope that we shall be all good friends together, and that I may feel that same regret at leaving my friends at Sacramento as I have experienced elsewhere in America."

The next performance Lola gave was for the benefit of the manager of the theatre, Charles A. King. The Sacramento Theatre had just been finished at a cost which had far exceeded expectations. It was among the permanent and well built structures in the city and the bricks for its construction had had to be imported at great cost, together with workmen who had received the unheard of sum of ten dollars a day for their labor. The carpenters who had finished it had been paid almost as much, and King, after the theatre was erected, had had no funds to put in upholstered seats such as the patrons were accustomed to in San Francisco. This was why ordinary chairs had been used in the boxes and wooden benches in the auditorium. The theatre also lacked an adequate drop curtain, an enthusiastic amateur artist having painted one that depicted a lurid view of the Sierra Nevada mountains in brilliant purples and yellows when the sight was actually one of great splendor, the elevations etched in misty blues against a brilliant blue sky with fleecy white clouds.

The smashing of King's windows and the wrecking of the seats had been still another blow to the harassed man. When Lola was asked to contribute to a fund to be given to King, she sent a letter to the committee of merchants behind the movement and offered to give a benefit, saying she would be happy to contribute one evening's performance because of her "high esteem for that gentleman."

The only remarkable circumstance of that evening was Lola's

introduction to George B. Gammons, a prominent merchant. He was a huge but excessively handsome man with thick, dark curly hair, mischievous black eyes, and a full face with ruddy cheeks. Because he was fashionably dressed in a black broadcloth suit, Lola did not immediately identify him with the gallant Sacramento volunteer fire department when he was introduced to her as Captain Gammons. At the end of the performance, when the company appeared upon the stage with Mr. King, Gammons, accompanied by another prominent citizen, presented King with a snuff box of California gold as an additional token of esteem.

During King's speech of appreciation, Gammons kept his eyes fixed upon Lola and she met his bold look with a mischievous smile. She was to see him again during two subsequent visits to Sacramento, but the moment of challenge between them which took place that night was never repeated. Had she been free he might well have become her lover, for the look that passed between them was unmistakable. Instead he became the lover of that sinister woman of color, Mammy Pleasant, who controlled many of California's leading citizens by blackmail for a period of thirty-seven years. Gammons was often to speak of the effect that Lola Montez had had upon him; sometimes he even teased Mammy by claiming he could have had Lola if she had not had a husband to keep his eye on her.

A few nights later, on an excessively hot evening, Lola gave a benefit performance for the fire companies of Sacramento. She collected a large sum of money for them, received an ovation from her audience, and was called upon to make a speech by the cheering members of three fire companies, present in their full dress uniforms.

As soon as the curtain had fallen for the last time, the firemen emerged from the theatre to form into rank and march to the Orleans Hotel. There they stood while a band played until Lola arrived from the theatre. When she made her appearance on the balcony outside her room, the band serenaded her, and at the finish she unfolded an American flag which she had carried with her throughout her tour, and dropped it into the waiting hands of Gammons.

Hull, who was standing below with the firemen, invited them into the saloon of the hotel, saying, "Boys, the drinks are on me." There in the oppressive heat they quenched their thirst with sherry cobblers.

Upstairs, in a thin mousseline de laine dress, Lola stood with Periwinkle on the balcony in the bright moonlight. Out in the surrounding country the farmers, who had been unable to work because of the intense heat of the day, were cutting a bumper crop of grain by moonlight. But the day did not end happily for Lola; Hull accused her of having flirted outrageously with Gammons.

San Francisco was keeping track of her career in Sacramento and one of the newspapers was contemptuous of the rival city. "Lola is great but the Sacramento people are unstable. One night she is hissed, booed, and insulted, and the next she is applauded and glorified by the same people."

Indeed, it seemed that Sacramento newspapers were like Sacramento audiences, for an article appeared charging that the enthusiasm for Lola Montez in Sacramento was all sham; she had hired people to applaud her.

Lola was quick with her reply. "Sir," she wrote, "the extraordinary article concerning myself which appeared in your paper this morning requires an extraordinary answer. I use the word 'extraordinary' for I am astonished that a respectable (?) editor should *lie* in such a barefaced manner and be so devoid of gallantry and courtesy as yourself. I am a woman. I do not advocate women's rights, but at the same time I can right myself by inflicting summary justice upon all jack-a-napes!!! After such a gross insult you must don the petticoats. I have brought some with me, which I can lend you for the occasion— you must fight with me. I leave the choice of two kinds of weapons to yourself, for I am very magnanimous. You may choose between my duelling pistols, or take your choice of a pill out of a pill-box. One shall be poisoned and the other not, and the chances are even. I request that the affair may be arranged by your seconds as soon as possible, as my time is quite as valuable as your own. Maria de Landsfeld Hull (Lola Montez)."

The challenge was not accepted but it delighted the men in the mining towns. Soon thereafter, whenever a fight occurred, they would declare that it could only be settled with "pistols or pizen."

In a city already famous for unheard-of behavior and originality, Lola's hit a new high. The raciness which marked her every appearance assumed almost epic proportions in the annals of the city.

On July 15th, accompanied by Pat, Periwinkle and her troupe, Lola departed to fill an engagement fifty miles north of Sacramento at Marysville, a mining town of nine thousand. The stage was so crowded that two of them were obliged to ride with the driver, and although the road was smooth and easy to travel they suffered greatly from the heat, with the temperature at 106 degrees.

Whether Lola was tired from the trip or whether she was antagonistic to her audience was not clear, but at Marysville everything seemed to go wrong. For a mining town, Marysville had a great number of families of some culture. The theatre, still very new, was large and covered with a dome, which impressed visiting performers. But in spite of the eagerness to promote the arts in Marysville, few wives attended the theatre and the cruder element was in ascendance.

Hauser led off in Lola's engagement by displeasing the audience with his violin selections. He was at a disadvantage because the night before, in this same theatre, a particularly naïve-looking young lady had aroused sentimentality and homesickness in the miners' hearts by singing ballads of great tenderness in a sweet and perfectly toned voice. By comparison Hauser's attempts to play such music became merely mawkish and affected.

Nor was Lola pleased over the reception given her spider dance. The men saw it only as something erotic and they grew disorderly, resenting it when in response to their lewd remarks she blazed out at them in a furious tirade.

Hull, who thoroughly understood the defensiveness of the Californians, attempted to explain to Lola that the men came from all walks of life and all nations. Some were educated and some were not. In the gold country a famous general had sluiced for gold beside a man who could neither read nor write. Here all men were equal: the French count, the German baron, the New York doctor, the unsuccessful husband of a boarding house keeper, the ex-saloon keeper from the East, the man who had had to change his name because of a crime back home, the transient who gambled his gold away on Saturday nights. They were united in trouble and in luck, fighting the fires, the droughts, the floods, the heat of summer and the snows of winter, meting out justice with a hanging, and sitting together the next night to forget their troubles in a theatre which, however elegant it seemed to be by comparison with their surroundings, was crude, built of splintery lumber, and smelling of pitch and of kerosene that burned in the bracket lamps affixed to the walls.

But never did they make fun of each other, unless someone came among them whose manner was haughty or who refused to help others in emergency.

Hull explained in vain that Lola could not treat the men with disdain and that if they told her where to look for the spiders they were, however vulgar, only taking part in the performance and thoroughly enjoying themselves.

At her hotel after the performance she had a violent quarrel with Hauser because he would not listen to her suggestions regarding what he should play. Although he had been without engagements of any kind when she had invited him to join her company, he was not going to take orders from her. The argument waxed so heated that everyone in the hotel could hear them as the stubborn Norwegian tried to yell louder than Lola and she attempted to box his ears. Someone suggested that the sheriff should be summoned, but Hull said that he would see what he could do to quiet them. When Lola turned on him, he marched downstairs and out to another hotel. Hauser packed and took the next stage out.

Lola went on with her performances, but her audiences did not yield to her determined efforts to make them behave. Every night she was subjected to what was now ridicule and she never succeeded in winning them over as she had done in Sacramento. Her only champion seemed to be a young lawyer named Stephen J. Field, who defended her vigorously. He was to continue to be a friend as long as she remained in the gold country.

Not too far away was the Eureka Mine in which Lola had purchased an interest when she had lived in Paris. This, together with another circumstance, brought about her decision to go to Grass Valley. After an interview with the San Francisco newspapers in which she was quoted as saying that she wanted to have a home in the mountains of California, she had received a letter from a Mrs. Dora Knapp, whose husband was acquainted with Hull.

Mrs. Knapp urged Lola to come to see this important mining town if she was considering a place to live. The town, urged Mrs. Knapp, was unique, the social life quite lively and relaxed, and many notable Frenchmen and Southerners lived there. She suggested to Lola that she would, perhaps, be acquainted with some of the mine owners who had come from Paris. Mrs. Knapp later said she had invited Pat and Lola to visit her "never thinking they would take me at my word."

When Lola took the stage for Grass Valley she found Hull awaiting her at the stage station and asked him to forgive her for her loss of temper. They were both in a gay mood and Hull kept his wife entertained with funny stories he had gathered in Marysville. They stopped at the Empire Ranch stage station for dinner, then passed through the town of Rough and Ready, in which only fifteen houses remained after a recent fire which had wiped out the business section and the toll house. People were clearing away the blackened remains and already had started to rebuild.

Four miles from Rough and Ready they entered the town of

Grass Valley. It was a real '49er town, having been settled by five immigrants who had pitched their tents in a thicket near Wolf Creek. Soon others had come to look for gold and to help each other in the weary round of getting food, fighting the cold, and the constant danger of being killed by Indians as they had gathered firewood or fished the stream. Finally a store had been established, although it dealt only in heavy clothing, cotton duck, and boots. Little was to be had in the way of groceries except pork and beans, but cheap whiskey had been plentiful. The men had been dependent upon their axes for their fuel, and upon their fishing poles to fill their frying pans.

But by the time Lola arrived there was a population of around sixteen hundred, two hundred of them women who had come there to join their husbands. The richest mining district in California, it was unique. There was a town marshal and two constables who had little to cope with in the way of crime, most of the men being so occupied with getting gold that they had little time for crime or amusements. It was more usual for them to take a holiday in Sacramento or in San Francisco and spend their time in the saloons and gambling halls there than to seek the relaxations to be had in the large Alta Saloon at Grass Valley, and even there the behavior of the miners was peaceable enough.

This prosperous and busy town was situated in a beautiful valley, surrounded on all sides by gently rolling, pine-covered hills. Through the center of the town, which was three miles in length, flowed Wolf Creek. Unlike most of the barren mining country, Grass Valley, lying snugly in the shadow of the imposing Sierras, was in a section of dense trees, and adjoining meadows were laid to the plow.

Breathing in the scent of the pines which stood tall and close together under the intense blue heavens, Lola was irresistibly drawn to the mountains. In the hills, rushing streams, cutting down through the red earth, were bordered with alders and willows. Trails wound between the pines and the manzanita bushes, and mistletoe decorated live oaks. There was the scale-running cry of the misty blue quail as they were flushed from their ground nests, and stout grouse running to cover. She saw herself fishing with Hull for trout in the transparent cold waters. They would cut dead pines for firewood and eat their catch under the stars and afterwards, pressed down against the mosses, they would sink into heavenly sleep.

Lola decided in an instant that this was the place where she wished to live. She saw herself as a part of the village, taking her place among the other wives, joining the country dances, the quilting bees. She would no longer discuss political problems, the latest novel, the book that Victor Hugo was writing in which he would give Napoleon his due. She would not need to be brilliant and clever, but only relaxed, listening to the women tell of children, grand-children, marriages, engagements, illnesses.

But Hull had married a woman whose life had been a succession of perfumed boudoirs, silk-draped beds, tables set with Dresden china lit by candlelight, and this was how he had envisioned his life with Lola. He did not believe, as he watched her embroider samplers during her leisure hours, that this new occupation betrayed a longing for a home, for a normal life, lived peacefully amid happy surroundings. Perhaps she even saw herself in a family circle, for she was more than once to speak regretfully of having no children, in spite of her three marriages. Her thoughts were undoubtedly concerned with withdrawal from a life of elegance and the smart but empty wit of the drawing room. She dreamed of making jam from the wild blackberry, of having a cow to milk, of chickens sitting on their eggs to hatch broods of fluffy yellow young, of putting bread to rise, of raising hollyhocks against a fence, perhaps even of making a cake to serve at a country dance.

But when she did actually lean over a cast iron pot hanging from a crane in a sooty fireplace, Periwinkle, that elegant and handsome lady's maid, would shoo her out of the kitchen, telling her that such pursuits would dry her skin and ruin her beauty. Soon an Indian woman named Maria was found to take over the kitchen.

In spite of the invitation to stay with the Knapps, Lola and Hull decided to stay at the Robinson boarding house. This proved to be something of a mistake, for Mrs. Knapp belonged to that very strata of homely society for which Lola most longed. Although the two women were eventually to become fast friends and Lola was to be defended by Mrs. Knapp, in failing to stay with her Lola rejected the social life of normal pursuits. Instead, by going to the Robinson's boarding house, she aligned herself with the "rebel" element.

Mrs. Harriet Robinson, the wife of a miner, and Lola's own age, owned the largest house in town and the only one with any pretensions to elegance. Two stories high, it had originally been built by her brother-in-law, Zenas Wheeler, on what became known as the Mill Road, for close to the house he had built a large planing mill. Galleries on both floors, supported by pillars two stories high, ran around the front and sides. When the Wheelers left Grass Valley, the house had been sold to Mrs. Wheeler's sister, Mrs. Robinson, who had added a large kitchen at the back of the house in the shape of an L.

The Robinsons had come from Maine and Mrs. Robinson, for a short time, had been on the stage in San Francisco. Whenever theatrical people came to Grass Valley to perform they stayed at this spacious house on the Mill Road, where there was a social life not understood by the other women of the town, in which talk of plays and the theatre engaged Mrs. Robinson and her guests while they put a necessary stitch to stage costumes. So interested was she in the life she had left behind her that she kept a trunk, filled with all sorts of materials, which was invariably hauled out when there were costumes to be repaired.

Also sharing this fringe of theatre life was the keeper of another boarding house just down the road. This place, a large, square, plain house of two stories, was run by a tiny, determined and ambitious woman with auburn hair and a grim expression whose name was Mrs. Mary Ann Crabtree. She was a recent arrival and she had come by her boarding house through what had been a bitter disappointment. John, her husband, was running a profitless bookstore in New York City at the time he first heard of the Gold Rush in California. "Nothing would do but that he must go," Mrs. Crabtree was fond of saying. The matter of getting started proved to be a prolonged affair and John did not set forth for California until 1852, after most of the gold fields were overcrowded.

A year later Mrs. Crabtree followed, having received news from her husband that if he remained in California he would make a fortune. Mary Ann set forth, taking with her her petite daughter, Lotta, a sturdy child of six, with bright red hair and merry black eyes. John Crabtree failed to meet his wife and daughter upon their arrival in San Francisco and they were forced to take refuge with their only friends, the Kents, who were delighted to have them stay as long as they pleased at their home near the Presidio.

Mary Ann was not entirely dismayed at her husband's disregard for her welfare, for she had a way of making the best of any situation. Her mother before her had made a poor marriage and her father had disappeared, leaving behind him a large family. With the help of her daughters, Mary Ann's mother had run an upholstering shop and often when Mary was sent out to deliver furniture covers, she would return to the shop to delight her family with imitations of the customers.

Little Lotta had inherited this gift of mimicry and her mother even then may have thought that the child had a talent which might be developed. It was said that Mrs. Crabtree, after her arrival in San Francisco, worked her way into the favor of a theatre owner by offering to work on the scenery in exchange for passes. In the months she waited to hear from her husband it was certain she became familiar with many phases of the theatre and this knowledge was to stand her in good stead when she later launched Lotta upon her almost unparalleled career as an actress.

When two months had passed, John Crabtree had belatedly bethought himself of his family, and assuming that they would have found their way to the Kents, sent a letter telling Mary Ann to come to Grass Valley. He gave as his excuse for not meeting her that he had been in the Sierra Nevadas and had a plan for making a fortune.

Mary Ann set forth with her little girl, travelling up the Sacramento River and across the level plain that led to the mountains. Upon her arrival, her first words to her husband were: "Are we rich?" His reply was to take her down the Mill Road to see his "gold mine." She learned that Crabtree, as she always referred to him, had acquired the large house just down from the Robinson's place and that he expected her to run it as a boarding house. Mrs. Crabtree had a fiery temper, but she quickly recovered from the disappointment, for she was devoted to her tiny daughter and perhaps forgave Crabtree his aimlessness because he was Lotta's father. Without complaint she took over the running of the boarding house. The merchants of the town who were unmarried or whose wives had not followed them to California stayed at the Crabtree house, but mostly the boarders were men who had come down from the mines.

Whenever she had a free moment, Mary Ann slipped over to the Robinson house to share in the excitement of meeting visiting actors and actresses. In this way she met Lola and became her staunchest friend. Never at any time would she permit anyone to criticize Lola in her presence.

When Lola decided to settle in Grass Valley both Mrs. Robinson and Mrs. Crabtree urged her to rent the furnished Stoltenberg cottage just up the road from them. It would be only a temporary residence, but it would give Lola the opportunity to look about for a place to buy.

In a short time Lola and Pat moved into the nearby cottage. Lola was almost deliriously happy as she unpacked her many trunks and distributed about the house the mementoes of her life in Europe and the valuable bric-a-brac so carefully wrapped in newspapers. Even Periwinkle liked the change from being a theatrical dresser and unpacked Lola's extensive wardrobe as if they were going to stay there forever. Only Hull showed restlessness, but even this disappeared when a number of Europeans, who had heard of Lola elsewhere, came to call, and several Southern gentlemen appeared, declaring that they were tired of primitive homes decorated with calico. Hull, who had always been surrounded by friends when he was a bachelor, and who had lived a particularly gay life as a San Francisco resident, enjoyed the role of host. With the stimulation of a crowd about him he grew expansive as he served wines in a house lit with glittering candelabra, presided over by a great beauty who was in her unquestioned element as hostess.

Each morning Lola went riding or hunting with Hull in the mountains. When the weather grew excessively hot they left the house in the late evening and slept in the hills on the red earth beside a stream. They had neither worry nor tribulation. Lola had made a great deal of money during her American tour, clearing for herself an average of about seven thousand dollars a week, it is said. This had been wisely invested and she still had on deposit in New York over twenty thousand dollars and in San Francisco another fourteen thousand. After forming her own company in the Bay City she had been her own manager. With her current funds she had paid off her company on leaving Marysville, and she now invested the remainder in the Empire Mine near Grass Valley, where a consolidation of claims and sufficient capital had made possible the driving of tunnels and shafts to obtain gold which was far underground.

Hull, too, had quite a bit of money to invest. He had sold out his half interest in his paper to Colonel Ayres, and had also sold a quarter interest in still another paper, as well as stock in a third publication. He had then invested the money in gold mining companies and had enough money on which to live comfortably without having to be supported by Lola.

XXIV

A WEEK after her arrival in Grass Valley the local residents urged Lola to give them an entertainment. The Alta Hall, which was used as an assembly room, and which occupied the second floor of a building housing a large saloon, was turned into a theatre for the occasion. It was a building of shakes with its interior walls covered only by canvas. When the tickets were placed on sale for five dollars each, with the seats in the front rows going for ten, all in town lined up to buy them, for any theatrical, ballet, or concert performance was always welcome as a change from the violin or guitar playing which provided their only amusement in the camps. Within two evenings everyone in the region, with the exception of those who were bedridden, and one disdainful minister and his wife, had seen Lola perform.

In spite of the crude surroundings, Lola did everything possible to supply a satisfying performance such as she had given in the great cities, and she had never had a more intent audience. The inhabitants knew that she had decided to settle among them, and greeted her as one of themselves. There were no crude sallies, no disconcerting laughter. The applause was prolonged, and if Lola had ever loved any place in the world it was this town of Grass Valley, which had opened its heart to her and whose people had accepted her so speedily.

Perhaps if Lola had not been tempted to take other engagements in the gold country, she and Hull might have remained happy and the outside world would never have heard much about her again. As it was, they had been in Grass Valley but two weeks when she consented to perform in the large mining town of Nevada, only four miles northeast of Grass Valley and the merchandising center for the surrounding gold country. The town was nightly filled with gold-miners, whose purchases of equipment kept teams of oxen hauling in machinery for the quartz mills and wagons bringing merchandise from Sacramento. Two stage coach lines from Sacramento, one by way of Grass Valley, and the other by way of Marysville, brought the miners and business men to town, while other stages went in every direction to the gold country camps snuggled in the recesses of surrounding mountains.

Nevada was anything but beautiful. Its wooden buildings had false fronts facing the streets and were packed solidly together. The town had never been properly laid out because the mineral deposits were so plentiful that the roads about the city had to circle the workings in order not to interfere with their profitable operation. To enter Nevada, vehicles had to cross a bridge over Deer Creek, which flowed through the town, and had been the source of much trouble, since whenever the snows melted in the mountains broken branches and heavy logs were washed down the swollen stream to pile up against the foundations of the bridge. An assembly hall, called the Jenny Lind, which had been used for theatrical performances, had been erected just beside the bridge, and twenty-three months before Lola's arrival it had collapsed into the current during a storm.

The first building to be erected solely for use as a playhouse in Nevada was the Dramatic Hall. Dr. Robinson, the San Francisco actor who had contrived burlesques of Lola's plays in San Francisco, had been one of the first performers to play there, bringing his equipment in two wagons. Since that time the theatre had been much improved and there had been consistently full houses, for the town was always crowded with men in from the mines shopping for supplies, many of them preferring the theatre to the saloons and gambling houses.

Lola could not resist the temptation to play before people who were so fond of the theatre, and she and Hull stayed in Nevada for a number of days while she played to packed houses.

Then she decided to accept still another engagement at Downieville, a long, hard day's ride by stage coach. The road climbed up gradually out of Nevada and wound through the mountains past tent camps. It was scarcely more than a mountain trail as it ascended and descended in its windings through the mountains, steep, narrow, dusty and rocky. The country was timbered in oak as well as pine, and despite the altitude, the day Lola and Pat made the trip the weather was hot. The stage, carrying passengers and empty gold boxes, lumbered upward, crossing the forks of the Yuba, until there were occasional views of distant forested ridges and even the snow-capped High Sierras. They passed through one mining camp after another—North San Juan, Camptonville, Goodyear's Bar —passing mules laden with merchandise following in the wake of men on horses. The lone traveler was in danger, for many had been killed on the ridges by bandits and few travelled by themselves.

Downieville consisted of a group of rough buildings strung along the bank in the steep canyon of the North Yuba River. The National Theatre had been completed only a few weeks before and Lola was eagerly awaited, and the news of her impending arrival had been carried ahead of her with the old excited cry: "Lola is coming!"

Seldom had any performer created such an impression as Lola did here, for the men were highly susceptible to Lola's voluptuous beauty as she performed her famous "Spider Dance."

In Downieville she met men who were to become noted in after years; Colonel E. D. Baker, a close friend of Abraham Lincoln; John W. Mackay, future Bonanza King; and the large, tall, handsome German baron who had dropped his title in the gold country and preferred to be known as simply "Doctor" Adler. He was not seeking gold in the mountain but amusing himself hunting and fishing, and he began to court Lola, ignoring the fact that she was married. Hull discovered that in taking Lola as his wife he had not bridled her; often she had said, "I am a free, independent being," and this was exactly how she felt and intended to behave.

Had Hull handled the situation with finesse and taken stock of Lola's constant desire to draw attention to herself, he could have made her avoid Adler's advances. Had he ignored the Baron's attentions and shown marked favor to one of the other women staying at the hotel or in town, Lola would have dropped everything in an effort to recapture what was hers. Instead Hull foolishly quarrelled with her. She lost her temper and went off hunting in the mountains with Adler.

As a companion she found Adler more interesting than Pat, and after two or three trips together on the forested heights, she decided she preferred to be with the Baron. Adler could tell her the names of the birds of the region, and when he picked a wild flower from a crag inaccessible to her, he would place it in her hands and identify it by name.

One day, lying stretched out on the ground on a ridge overlooking the road which led to Downieville, waiting with their guns in their hands for a flock of grouse to flush, they were startled to see a masked man hiding behind a tree across the road. When the stagecoach came around the turn, inexplicably the man made no move to stop it. Instead, he waited behind the tree for some time, and when no other coach or traveller came by, finally removed the handkerchief from his face, mounted his horse and rode off in the direction of Downieville. Lola and Adler had a good look at his face.

According to the story she told Mrs. Robinson, Lola next day encountered the man on the street in Downieville. On an impulse she stopped him and said she would like to gamble with him for the possession of his gun. He obviously knew who she was and that she was given to bizarre behavior, and when Lola told him she had witnessed the scene on the ridge, he had no choice but to consent.

In the subsequent card game she played with him Lola became convinced that George Walker, who posed as a miner, was head of a gang, for two other men came to watch with tense faces. She won the gun, and as long as she lived in the mountains she carried it with her whenever she went into the hills. It is not known whether she ever learned the eventual fate of Walker, who was finally captured and hanged for highway robbery, but there were times after she had left California when she told the story with much amusement.

Lola and Hull seem to have become reconciled soon after this, for on August 21st, having returned to Grass Valley, Lola bought a house on the Mill Road a short distance from that of the Robinsons. Originally the cottage, set in a grove of tall sycamore trees, had been the office of a lumber company. Subsequently it had been sold to a beautiful and somewhat mysterious Irish-born woman named Jennie Moore, whom the natives called Jennie-on-the-Green because she ran a faro table and the table upon which she dealt the cards had a green felt cover.

Jennie, a slight woman with dark brown hair, enormous deep blue eyes, and soft melodious voice, had drifted in with the gold miners. She had first appeared at one of the gambling halls in Grass Valley and soon afterward acquired the reputation of playing a straight game. Her behavior was quiet, ladylike, and her manner, characteristic of the confirmed gambler, was remote.

In 1852, about a year after the lumber company moved out of its office, she had bought the building and divided its spacious interior into three rooms. Along the outside she had built a wide veranda extending around three sides of the structure, its roof supported by perfectly plain pillars. The rough plank walls of the interior were covered with wallpaper, and the large room to the left of the front door was turned into a gambling room. In New Orleans it would have been called a "shot-gun cottage," with its hallway cut straight through the middle of the dwelling and ending at the back door. To the right was another room, about the use of which stories were soon circulating.

In that heavily curtained room there was always a girl available for any man whose conduct was gentlemanly and decorous and whose desires had so far overridden conscience and judgment that he was willing to dig into his pocket in order to satisfy them. The customers were said to have been carefully screened by Jennie, who was always on hand to greet them. When a man was accepted he would only be admitted after gambling had stopped for the night and the customers had departed. But whatever girl occupied the room on the right, it was never Jennie herself. She was considered to be unobtainable.

One evening a man came to gamble whom Jennie had never seen. He had handsome, classical features but his eyes were cold and chilling, and he introduced himself as Curly Smith.

"Give me a stack," said the stranger, "I feel like sitting in on a friendly game."

The men in the room waited in sudden silence, for they had already recognized the visitor, and there were suspicions that he was the bandit who had been holding up stage coaches near Robber's Roost on the road to Auburn. He was credited with being ruthless, but he was also exceedingly elusive and no crime had ever actually been proven against him. Jennie looked at him for a moment and the two seemed to take each other's measure. At last she said, "Why, sit in, Curly. You're welcome."

Sometime thereafter the patrons of Jennie-on-the-Green knew that Curly had become her lover, and it was generally believed that she had made up her mind to reform him.

Now suddenly Jennie sold her house to Lola and moved to the town of Rough and Ready, just west of Grass Valley, where she bought a cottage in the hollow just back of the Toll House. Why she had moved no one knew, but Lola was delighted to acquire a decent structure in a town where so few were available.

Lola spent almost two months overseeing the rebuilding of her house. Not wishing the place to look as crudely finished as the interior of the Robinson house, which had been built by the inferior workmen in Grass Valley, she sent to San Francisco for carpenters. The plain uprights were removed from the veranda in favor of more elegant pillars; the small windows of the cottage were cut down and turned into French windows with cut-up panes, the trim above them suggestive of the pediment of a Greek temple; a new front door was ordered from San Francisco and this was set back into a panelled recess; above and at either side of the door panels of glass were installed to give light to the hall; and above the doorway at the other end of the hall a simple niche was set into the wall to hold a small bust of Ludwig.

The large room at the left was divided by sliding doors, forming a drawing room, and behind that a dining parlor which boasted a fireplace to be faced with marble. The ceilings of both rooms curved to meet a picture molding which was covered with gold leaf. Below the molding the walls had been papered in a delicate Empire design of classic pattern.

A long, narrow wing was added behind the dining parlor to provide a kitchen and a bedroom for Periwinkle. On the other side of the hall Lola wanted a bathroom attached to the bedroom. No one had such a thing in Grass Valley, but Lola had it added in the form of a small extension, and a bath tub, which had to be filled and emptied by hand, was ordered from the East.

While Lola and Pat were standing one evening in the unfinished kitchen discussing where the stove should go, a drunken miner came to the door and said he had come to stay overnight with "the girl." Hull got rid of him with difficulty, but several nights later another man appeared and the incident was repeated. Seeing they were going to have trouble living in a house with a past, Lola hit upon a peculiar solution to the problem of dealing with men down from the mines who did not know Jennie had moved.

When a miner came into Grass Valley with a brown bear he had tamed, Lola offered him a large sum for the animal, called Major, and chained it to the stump of a tree near the entrance to the cottage. Major quickly scared off the unwanted callers, and Lola soon became passionately fond of the animal. Much to Pat's annoyance she insisted on taking him along on walks over the hillside, and almost daily she could be seen with a whip tucked under her arm, the bear shuffling along behind her on his chain. Captured as a tiny cub, Major gave them little trouble, but Hull disliked the creature intensely and never became reconciled to him.

Almost daily Lola and Pat went riding out into the hills, Lola dressed in a trim riding habit and often smoking a cigarette. The whole district near the cottage had been mined, and unless they went high into the hills they could see little but great heaps of earth and rocks, stamp mills and mine dumps, for there were more than a hundred mines strung out east and west along Wolf Creek and north and south along the northern mining district within a few miles of Grass Valley.

At home Lola spent a great deal of time at her desk, keeping up voluminous correspondence with Ludwig and old friends in France. As winter approached, people began to notice that Hull was constantly coughing and that Lola increasingly showed irritation when he had a coughing attack in public. More and more, during an attack, Hull went outdoors in order to avoid offending her. He grew thin and as the winter advanced his illness was diagnosed as chronic bronchitis. Lola had not observed this during the heat of summer when she had married him, but the damp weather in the mountains and the increasing cold of the air seemed to irritate the condition. Friends talked of Lola's evident nervousness when she was with her husband and the gossip was carried out of Grass Valley. To Pat's humiliation a San Francisco newspaper contained an item that a rupture between them was expected. There was an even more personal comment in a column given over to news from the mines. The *Golden Era* leaped to the conclusion: "Lola has taken a dislike to Hull." Another paper reported that she was spending more and more time at her desk and less time with Pat.

The break did not occur, for no matter how annoying Pat's ailment might be, Lola was neither cruel nor selfish. She was deeply concerned for Hull's health and kept the Indian cook, Maria, forever busy making him hot drinks, warming the blankets at night, and bedding down the fires so that they would not go out during the early morning hours.

During the early part of October Lola packed for a trip to

San Francisco, and Hull went with her. A worse time for their trip could not have been chosen, for they were beset with calamitous incidents. But the beginning of the journey was pleasant and interesting, since neither Lola nor Hull had travelled this route before. All the way from Grass Valley to Sacramento on the Concord-type stage, with its curving body and enormous wheels, they travelled a winding road over gently rolling hills. Along Wolf Creek miners were panning for gold, the stream running sometimes beside the road, then between pine-covered hills, and finally curving away to the west where it joined the Bear River. After crossing this stream the road twisted through the oak and pine-clad hills to Auburn, where they changed coaches.

As they coursed down the ridge with the horses at a brisk trot, the coach swung around a turn and, thrown out of its course by careless driving, a wheel mounted the stump of a tree beside the road. The top-heavy stagecoach on its high wheels turned over on its side, but the driver, keeping a tight hold on the reins, jumped into the road so that the horses, in spite of their freight and twisted gear, were under control. The ground was soft and damp from recent rains and as a result nothing was broken. The passengers emerged somewhat bruised, but their injuries were, on the whole, only minor. The stagecoach was righted, the luggage and the boxes of gold, which had tumbled off the top, were reloaded, the somewhat muddy passengers climbed aboard, and the journey continued.

Two children in the overcrowded stage had to sit on the laps of passengers, and one of them sat on Lola's lap through the remainder of the trip. She always remembered with pleasure the lovely, perfumed lady who had kept her warm and cozy and showered her with attention.

Although badly shaken up, Lola insisted on continuing on into San Francisco. She and Pat managed to board the steamer *Antelope* at Sacramento, just before her departure at two o'clock in the afternoon. The side-wheeler, newly refitted and refurnished, was comfortable and elegant, but her first class cabins were forward, the most dangerous place in a ship in case of an accident.

Every river boat in those days vied with others for swiftness of transportation, and heated races between steamers of rival lines were not at all unusual. The captain of the *Antelope*, however, was not given to reckless racing and pursued the course with caution rather than speed. As the steamer reached the point in Suisun Bay opposite the mouth of Suisun Slough, a dense fog rolled in and the *Antelope* moved even more cautiously.

But looming up in the haze, another steamer going in the opposite direction came at them without warning, travelling at great speed. This steamer, the *Confidence*, struck the *Antelope* amidships, just forward of the gangway. The impact cut through the guards of the *Antelope* and penetrated the ship to the bilge caissons. The *Confidence* did not stop to inquire if there was any damage but pulled away as the *Antelope* began to fill with water. The captain called all hands and they spiked oakum into the openings so the ship was saved from foundering until the captain could run her aground on the mud flats.

The *Antelope* blew her whistle constantly and soon another steamer, the *Senator*, came to the rescue. There had been no time to get the boats lowered from the davits and the listing of the ship made it almost impossible to get them down without their overturning.

The shock of the collision had left most of the two hundred passengers dazed and they filled the companionways, not knowing which way to flee from the incoming waters.

Since it was eight o'clock in the evening the majority of the men aboard were in the saloon or out on deck. The forward cabins, one of them occupied by Lola, were accessible only through the forward companionway, and when the crash occurred they were cut off from the companionway, which had been broken clean through.

Lola was always credited with tremendous courage when calmness and heroism were most needed. The ladies and their screaming children in the cabins adjoining hers were quieted by her admonitions to hang onto the sides of the berths. She then lowered the window in a cabin overlooking the bow and asked one of the men to help them out, but since part of the bow was already submerged, the descent was dangerous.

Eventually the passengers were taken off the wrecked ship and driven to Benicia to be transferred to the Stockton boat, which was on its way to San Francisco. Lola had suffered little from the two disasters of the day, but Pat, bruised from the stagecoach accident and again injured when he was hit by wreckage aboard the steamer, was put to bed in the California Hotel as soon as they arrived in San Francisco.

Word of Lola's arrival soon spread. When she finally emerged from the hotel to do some shopping, the street outside was filled with people hoping to catch sight of her. Lola had learned her lesson since the day so long ago when a miner had lifted her off the ground and held her up in the air. Then she had offended the crowd by kicking at the man. Now when they stared at her she smiled, and was greeted with cries of, "Welcome, Lola!"

XXV

Lola had come to San Francisco for two reasons. One was that Nathaniel Willis, the man who had been named as corespondent in the notorious divorce case of the Shakespearean actor, Edwin Forrest, had written that he was to be in the Bay City, although why she should have cared to meet a man whom she had rejected was not clear. She may have merely consented to see him from a desire to talk of old times and the people they mutually knew in New York. So while Pat was still confined to his hotel room, Lola met Willis for dinner. But she gave no indication in her many letters of the period that she saw him more than once.

Her other reason for coming to San Francisco was one which caused a new rift between her and her husband. When she had decided to remain in Grass Valley she had written to Ludwig at Nice to ask if she might not have some of her most cherished possessions from her little palace in Munich. During the intervening years newspapers in California had published stories of Ludwig's odd sentimentality about her, one manifestation of which was his insistence on keeping her house just as she had left it. Only at her instigation was it disturbed, Ludwig returning to Munich to do her this favor, and by October the shipment of her property had arrived. Among the things sent was her swan bed with its silken draperies, the drawing room furniture of ebony inlaid with pearl, and the matching chairs and sofa, upholstered in a brilliant shade of crimson shot through with gold. He had also sent her a pair of console tables with their companion nine-foot mirrors. Ludwig had included the two pieces of French furniture he had given her for her boudoir in Munich: a magnificent gold leaf cabinet decorated with pastoral paintings and delicately painted garlands of roses surrounding the curved glass door; and its companion piece, a square table of pearwood with ormolu mounts on the legs and a pastoral scene painted on its top.

A love seat of delicate design and a gilt mirror brought tears to Lola's eyes as she remembered the man she so much admired, for they were new and she knew they must have been specially purchased.

The various pieces were done in red, cherry, antique gold and almond green, and the hand-woven carpets, subtly combining all the colors, which Ludwig also sent, later proved a perfect background for the furniture. Curtains also had been included in the first shipment and were of the sheerest deep cream lace, overlaid with a baroque pattern of white.

After opening all the crates, Lola had the shipment repacked to await her departure by boat for Sacramento, whence she intended to send all her things by wagon to Grass Valley. She spent the intervening time shopping for everything needed for her household and purchased the best china, linens, and ornaments available.

Her shopping completed, she presented a letter of introduction she had received from Colonel "Ed" Baker of Marysville to his two friends, the elegant, auburn-haired Southerner, Archibald Peachy, and Frederick Billings, a vigorous New Englander. Together with their partner, Henry Wager Halleck, who was to become Abraham Lincoln's Chief-of-Staff during the Civil War, they were the most famous attorneys in San Francisco, being authorities on land titles, then the most important legal problem in California because of the legal difficulties attendant upon the acquisition of California from the Spanish and the poorly defined deeds held by the original Mexican and Spanish settlers.

At that time the members of the firm were putting up the first of many magnificent buildings to be erected in San Francisco, soon to become known as the Montgomery Block. Lola watched the workmen erecting the Doric columns at its entrance, and

Peachy and Billings urged her to stay over for the formal opening two months hence.

Through the rest of October and well into November Hull did not emerge from the hotel, and when he was finally well again he was emaciated and irritable. News of almost torrential rains in Grass Valley, followed by a heavy snowfall high in the mountains, kept them in San Francisco. Pat was better off there, and although she was restless to get back home, Lola remained with him. She occupied much of her time with reading and buying books from John Hamilton Still, who had founded the first book store in San Francisco and who was now established with a partner on Montgomery Street. Her purchases that winter included some of the Waverley Novels and Thackeray's *Vanity Fair*.

As Pat grew better he went out and about with old friends. Peachy also invited him to dinner and one evening at the Ivy Green, a fashionable restaurant where prominent men of the town gathered, Lola, included in the invitation, insisted on taking with her a small cinnamon bear cub which she had purchased that day from a miner. The restaurant owner looked on this odd pet with apprehension, but Lola settled the animal under the table and as it seemed content to remain there, she confidently took off its chain. When they were halfway through their dinner, she heard a startled cry and to her dismay saw her bear running across the floor. He encountered the legs of a waiter who was carrying a loaded tray of filled dinner dishes and the man was brought down with a crash of broken china and spilled food.

Most of the patrons, under the mistaken impression that the bear had attacked the waiter, jumped up from their seats ready to flee. Lola recovered her pet, but Hull was furiously angry. He paid the restaurant owner for the damages, but afterwards told her in no uncertain terms that he would have much preferred to attend the dinner without her.

He was scarcely happier when Lola was also included at an open house which the lawyers held in December to celebrate the completion of their Montgomery Block. The reception was held in the second floor lobby, which had been elegantly decorated as a public gathering place, with lounges and potted palms and a red carpet on the floor. Once again Pat felt that Lola was out of place in the company of men who were mostly drinking too much and telling off-color stories. A few days earlier the leading ladies of the city had been taken through the building at an open house held especially for them; they had been permitted to inspect the frescoes on the ceilings, to walk through the billiard room, and even to take a discreet peek through the door leading into the magnificent Bank Exchange Saloon before it was yet opened. This had sufficed for the ladies, and it was all too clear to her husband that Lola was there not as Mrs. Hull but as Lola Montez, the woman of sensational legend. It was significant that the only other women present were leading actresses from the American and Metropolitan theatres.

During their stay in San Francisco, Lola had found a dry-sink of hardwood and a wash-stand for her bedroom, and had persuaded the busy colored man, David W. Ruggles, to put together a kitchen stove for her. Few of these were shipped in from the East, and Ruggles had been the first man in the city to assemble them from materials that could be obtained locally. Finally satisfied, she set forth again for Grass Valley.

Somehow it had so far escaped the San Francisco papers that she had acquired an assortment of pets, but now the Sacramento *Union* reported that Lola Montez had purchased two dogs, a cinnamon bear cub, and a parrot. Nothing would do but to have the animals and bird crated and shipped with the furniture, and she engaged two wagons to haul her tremendous shipment from Sacramento to Grass Valley while she and Hull followed by stagecoach.

The day after their return, Lola and Pat attended a performance in which Caroline Chapman, the homely, gypsy-looking queen of burlesque, made fun of Lola in another satire on *Lola Montez in Bavaria*. The skit was called *Actress of All Work* and would have been a fiasco if Lola had not been amused.

Dressed in a new tilted hat from San Francisco, the like of which had never been seen in the gold country, she sat beside Pat and applauded loudly, setting the tone for the reception of the play. The second evening, when Lola was not present, there was a decided coolness on the part of the audience toward the ridicule of a local resident.

Lola was determined to be in her home for Christmas, and as the holiday drew near everyone helped—the Robinsons; the Chapmans, who were staying over with them; Mrs. Crabtree, who ran her boarding house with such determination that leisure was found with difficulty; and Mrs. Knapp, who continued to be a friend of the "Rebels" even if the other women of her set were not.

Working with Lola to arrange the silken draperies of the drawing room over the lace curtains, Mrs. Knapp asked her if she missed the gay life she had lived in Europe.

"Never," replied Lola. "Ah, you little know, Mrs. Knapp, what sorrow and distress everyone has in such gaiety. I am only sorry that I never had a little home like this, and friends who really loved me before I became so notorious—for notorious I have been, and never famous."

All Lola's activities were reported in some manner. If the newspapers failed to note them, Grass Valley residents wrote letters to their friends and relatives about her elegant house and her current attitude toward her husband. Frenchmen like Lamarque, who had sold her an interest in the Eureka, Jules Fricot, André Chauvanne, and others connected with nearby mines made it a point to call on her and wrote letters back home about her. A number of Southern gentlemen, who would not have been suspected of being gossips, passed on information about her.

Some of this crept into the San Francisco newspapers in late December and one rumor had it that Lola was going to divorce Hull. To Lola it seemed that no one wished her to be happy. She believed that she had found herself and she was determined to remain sequestered in this tranquil life. At Christmas she had never looked more handsome. In a white dress of silk moiré trimmed in red, and wearing her rubies, she played her melodeon while the company she had invited sang Christmas carols and drank champagne in a revelry which was to be long remembered.

But in Bavaria, almost two months before, a strange incident had occurred which was to bring an end to Hull's part in Lola's life.

At the castle of Acheffenburg, where Theresa, Ludwig's queen, was in residence, a lady dressed entirely in black with her face heavily veiled suddenly appeared before the Queen's two nephews. When they spoke to her she did not answer but passed into a nearby room where some servants were seated. The princes followed, only to discover that the servants had not seen her. They then went to the Queen and asked if she had seen a black-clad woman. When they saw the frightful effect their question had upon Queen Theresa they realized that she believed the specter to be the Black Lady whose appearance foretold the death of a member of the Royal Family.

The next day Theresa returned to Munich. Ludwig was also in the capital, having returned there for the purpose of shipping Lola's furniture, and the news of his queen's preoccupation with the weird apparition was carried to him. The story spread quickly throughout Bavaria and recalled the legend of the Black Lady. A princess of the royal house, she had been dead for a century. Once she had been seen dancing among the guests at a ball, and immediately thereafter a member of the royal house of Wittelsbach had died.

People speculated upon who would die now. Would it be Maximilian, the reigning King of Bavaria? or his son Louis? or perhaps old ex-King Ludwig, or Otho, the ruler of Greece?

Instead, it was Theresa. Within twenty days from the time the apparition had been seen, she was dead of cholera. Ludwig was free to marry again.

XXVI

The new year, 1854, did not begin auspiciously for Lola. The weather in the mountains was intensely cold, Pat was miserable with his bronchitis, and Lola could no longer stand his constant irritability. Nothing pleased him, neither the efforts of the obliging and affable Maria, nor the ministrations of the endlessly patient Periwinkle. He could no longer attend to the fire, so Lola found a young Kanaka, unsuccessfully working in the mines, who was willing to come and work for her as a houseboy. Because of the bitter weather, Lola had a square building erected at the rear of the property for the bears, its peaked roof decorated with a large dove cote. Here at night the bears were comfortably housed, and they did not follow their natural course of hibernating. Daily Lola took them out and chained them to the porch.

One afternoon Pat Hull ventured out on the porch and did not notice the cinnamon bear, which nipped him in the ankle. Furious, he strode into the house and got the gun that Lola had won from the bandit. Without thinking how his action might affect Lola, he shot the bear dead.

The violent end of her pet, Pat's waspish disposition, and his lack of regret at having killed the bear all combined to make the final break between Lola and him a mere matter of time. Maria got tired of conjuring up delicate dishes for a man who never showed the slightest appreciation. Periwinkle merely scrambled out of the room whenever Lola and Pat showed signs of being intolerant of each other's company.

By January 12th the weather was so cold that there was sufficient ice for skating on the swales, which were ordinarily covered with water. The days were clear, the sun shone on the snow, but its warmth was not felt.

During the previous summer Lola and Hull had both invested money in a gold dredging operation at a site near Marysville. The company which was operating it had called upon the investors for more money for further work, but Lola was not willing to risk her capital without inquiring into the prospect of future profit. Hull blamed Lola for having invested in the venture in the first place and wished he had bought a newspaper with his money instead. But when Lola wished to go to Marysville and also to see the steamer *Linda* in operation on the Feather River, Pat, in spite of the below freezing weather and the coldness between them, insisted on going along with her.

At Marysville, where they stayed for a week at the Exchange Hotel, an agent sent by Ludwig found her. He informed Lola that Queen Theresa was dead and that Ludwig wished Lola to join him at Nice, where they could be married. The agent, as well as Ludwig himself, seemed to be under the impression that Lola had divorced her husband—a not remarkable conclusion, since stories to that effect had been copied from the San Francisco newspapers and republished in Europe.

Hull's fury knew no bounds and Lola sprang to Ludwig's defense.

"I love him," declared Lola, "as I would love my father, if I had one. I am not ashamed of my love for him."

Hull took the position that the whole thing was dishonorable and that Lola was to blame. The furniture sent by Ludwig had already roused his animosity, and a magnificent gold comb made in the form of a crown, which had just been given Lola by the monarch's agent, proved the last straw.

The whole story of the final quarrel between the dazzling beauty and her husband has never been told. It is only known that Hull did not succeed in exorcising Ludwig, and that Lola, in a burst of rage, raised the window of their hotel room and tossed Hull's clothes out onto the snow.

Hull's friend Lemuel Snow heard this story from Lola. Snow knew the day they were to arrive back at Grass Valley and was at the Phelps Hotel to meet the incoming stage. "Lola got out," as Snow related the incident, "and told me that a week before at Marysville she had thrown Pat's clothes out of the window of the second story.

"She was never with him again, nor mentioned him."

A few weeks later Lola went to San Francisco again to stay at the Russ House, and there she obtained a divorce from Hull. He, meanwhile, remained at Marysville, where he went to work on a newspaper and was considerably more satisfied with his life than he had been for some time.

News of the divorce reached Dr. Adler at Downieville and the handsome Baron, who was given to amorous attachments, lost no time in seeking Lola out. She, characteristically full of violence one moment and tender the next, returned to her beloved home at Grass Valley and soon made Adler the companion of her pleasure. Although the neighbors remained unsuspicious of the attentions of the Baron, since he seemed to be an employee and busied himself in erecting a stable on the corner of her property and directing the building of a wine cellar, Lola later admitted that Adler had been her lover. While a fence was being placed around her property and the servants were out on errands or outside watching the workmen, Adler and Lola were together secretly and hastily.

The weather was still very cold, so cold that Lola did not accompany Adler when he went hunting. One day the news was brought to her that the Baron had had an accident. With what agitation Lola received the news the outside world never knew.

That she suffered over his death, alone with her grief, must have been true, but she perhaps suffered more over the painful realization that anyone she loved must be taken from her. She felt that a curse had been placed upon her.

For a time Lola dropped all social activities. Then one day she was seen in a sleigh drawn by a span of horses, the harness becomingly decorated with bells. Lola wore a hooded fur coat which looked as if it might have come from Russia. "She flashed like a meteor through the snowflakes and wanton snowballs," said the Nevada newspaper. She made a tour of the stores of

Nevada, purchasing supplies, and then turned back toward Grass Valley. It was then that snowballs were playfully thrown at her, and, better adjusted now to the Californians, she laughed as she dodged the hard-pressed spheres of snow.

Mostly she spent her days inside her house, leading a quiet life, writing letters to Ludwig, to the actress Adah Isaacs, to other New York friends, and to Victor Hugo. Often she was immersed in thought, perhaps playing with the idea of returning to Paris. Sometimes she sat contemplating the fire in the little dining parlor and smoking incessantly.

Although the letters which came from Europe seemed to lift her spirits, she evidently came to the conclusion that she loved her home in Grass Valley too well to leave it, and by the end of February of 1854 she determined to create a salon—or the nearest possible equivalent. The little cellar which Adler had built below ground, to take advantage of a natural spring which flowed out at that point, was filled with wine bottles chilling in the running water. Here was the necessary liquid refreshment, and since she considered Maria's cooking to be inadequate to the entertaining she wished to do, she sent for a French chef who had been working as a miner nearby.

Her first party was momentous. Sam Brannan came up from San Francisco. Stephen Field, the young attorney who had been her staunch defender at Marysville, arrived by stage coach. And William M. Stewart, another attorney, followed. Those local people who were known as the "Rebels" were also invited and the comfortable little house was overflowing. People played cards, Lola entertained with music, and the dinner was served after everyone had drunk much champagne. Someone asked Lola if it was true that the bandit Joaquin Murrieta had told her that she was too wild for him and that he was afraid of her. With a furtive smile, later noted in a letter by one of the guests, Lola said that it was true she had seen Murrieta, but that it had been in a side show and all she had seen of him was his head—in a bottle.

Soon Lola's soirées became an institution. Lemuel Snow was

sometimes there and he wrote of how gay everyone was as the latest jokes were told, the newest songs tried out, and card games were played. Lola was sometimes persuaded to give some of her dances, with Periwinkle acting as her dresser and enjoying the novelty of getting out Lola's costumes. In the midst of these retreats into her bedroom to don a costume, Lola would grow serious and say to Periwinkle that such happiness could not last. She would remark that she brought death and disaster to those who loved her.

In the time between these social gatherings Lola seemed quite spiritless and for hours on end sat musing. The latest novel, ordered up from San Francisco, lay unread in her hands. Then sometimes an Indian would appear at the back door to beg for sugar or salt, and Maria would come to ask Lola if she might give them to the petitioner. Lola would rise from her chair, and going to the kitchen door, would urge upon him all that he could carry, telling him not to let his people suffer but to come to her when they were in need.

Maria seldom gave any sign of how she regarded Lola's kindness of heart, but what she felt was reflected in touching ways: a brick heated to place at Lola's feet on cold nights, or some odd mountain shrub decorating the dinner table, or smoked fish suddenly appearing for supper, supplied from some secret source Maria did not reveal.

Lola always defended her servants. One day she sent her Kanaka boy to Othet's store to do some shopping. The editor of the Grass Valley *Telegraph*, Henry Shipley, a large, arrogant man from Missouri, was also in the store. He shoved the boy rudely away from the counter, and calling him a "damned nigger," told him to get out of the place. When the boy returned and told Lola what had happened, she threw her cape over her shoulders, picked up her riding crop, and strode down the Mill Road to the store. Shipley saw her enter and caught sight of her angry face and the tightly held whip. He turned white, let out an exclamation of surprise, and before Lola could get near him fled out the back door of the hardware store. Her eyes still flashing, Lola brought in her houseboy, who had been waiting outdoors, and stood with the whip tucked under her arm while he was waited upon.

It was the first time she had ever appeared with her whip in Grass Valley and all the town discussed her fiery temper, but they also admired her courage in defending her help. The story spread through the mines and even down to Sacramento, though Shipley avoided any mention of it in his own paper. The real fight between the editor and the ex-dancer had, however, just begun. Stories of it were to engage the attention of the whole country as far east as New York.

The perspective of Lola's life, which she had voluntarily restricted, quite unexpectedly found dimensions previously unnoticed right at her front door. Just beyond her house was Miss Lang's "School for Young Children." Watching the children going to school became a daily event which always lifted Lola's spirits, however depressed she felt.

One of the small students there was Lotta Crabtree, whose home was only a few hundred feet away on the other side of Lola's cottage. One afternoon, after school was dismissed, little Lotta turned into Lola's yard and called upon the Countess. Soon the week-day visits of the sturdy, bronze-haired seven-year-old became important to Lola and did more for her than the continuing friendship of the Robinsons and the other "Rebels." Afternoon tea was postponed until Lotta's arrival, and the personality of the child began to impress itself upon Lola. Lotta gave imitations of her teacher, the strict, pedantic Miss Lang, until Lola was convulsed with laughter. The Chinese washerman of the Crabtree boarding house was the subject of another sharp, accurate caricature, complete with oriental jargon, slinky walk, and an imaginary bobbing cue. Lola soon realized whence little Lotta had inherited her talent, for Mrs. Crabtree, in spite of her grim face, still engaged in this sort of thing when encouraged to do so at the Robinson house. Lola had seen her give an imitation of the self-righteous minister whose church was nearby. Although Mary Ann Crabtree was not the least beautiful, in spite of her diminutive Dresden-china figure, her bronze hair and snapping black eyes, in Lotta this same coloring was a little lighter and her eyes were full of mischief, her cheeks dimpled. She was tiny, pretty, and irrepressibly gay, with a laugh which was musical and captivating.

It occurred to Lola that she might teach this wonderful child to dance, and a music box was set going. Lola danced and soon the tiny seven-year-old came beside her and not only copied her steps but very shortly surpassed her, for it was as natural for Lotta to dance as to walk.

Within weeks Lola was also teaching Lotta to sing, and Mrs. Crabtree was called over to see what had been accomplished. Thereafter the harassed Mary Ann, who hated her days of boarding-house slavery, came whenever she could to watch the progress of her daughter's lessons. The Robinsons were invited to witness the child's perfect execution of the "Sailor's Hornpipe," and there was scarcely a step in Lola's repertoire that she could not immediately grasp: ballet, fandangos, Scottish reels.

More and more Lotta became Lola's charge, and as the weather grew warmer the Countess would take her small friend horseback riding. Finally she provided her with a pony. When neighbors told Mrs. Crabtree that the Countess of Landsfeld had been a notorious woman, Mary Ann set her strong jaw and stoutly sprang to Lola's defense, saying she was perfectly capable of judging her friend for herself.

Nor did Lotta's training end there. Once Lola shook off her depression, many of the theatrical people who came to perform at Grass Valley frequented the house. Notable among them was Laura Keene, the actress who was to be remembered less for her great talent than because she happened to be playing in Ford's Theatre at Washington on the night when President Lincoln was shot. Also a guest of Lola's was Edwin Booth, brother of John Wilkes Booth, who fired the fatal shot.

Sometimes the comic performers put on acts in Lola's living room solely for their hostess's entertainment. Leaving the Chinese help to do her work for a while, Mrs. Crabtree often came to watch with the Robinsons. But Lotta's irresistible laughter entertained Lola more than the tricks of famous comedians. There were times, as the theatrical people would often relate, when she would say that Lotta was a small edition of herself and that she wished she were her mother.

Other children soon came, too, and Lola made them welcome, even giving birthday parties for some of the pupils at Miss Lang's school. Their mothers, loath at last to criticize a woman whose behavior seemed unassailable, gradually ceased to censure her.

Stories of Lola's many kindnesses began to circulate clear to Nevada as she often replaced an exhausted mother through several nights at the bedside of a sick child. She was also known to have ridden far into the mountains to take food and medicine to a miner lying ill in an isolated shack.

Yet more remarkable was Lola's emergence as a woman of exclusively domestic interests. When peddlers on muleback came to her door carrying yardage and dress trimmings and trinkets, she went out to them and purchased calico dresses to wear in the garden, wool with which to knit her own winter undergarments, or the latest book by some California author. Callers who saw her in the afternoon often found her knitting or doing samplers.

As the weather improved she planted her yard with rose trees, had poplars put in beside her house and then, on horseback, searched the mountains for plants for her garden, bringing back wild lilacs and other native shrubs. Wearing a calico dress, which she might have made herself, and a bonnet with long ribbons tied under her chin, she planted cactus in the corner of her garden. This astonished everyone, for at that time no one but Lola had seen any beauty in these plants.

"How can she fold her wings in such an eyrie?" wrote a newspaperman, for even while she was settled quietly in this rustic retreat the smallest detail of her personal life was still news to the outside world. Only once did she go to one of the village dances and then she knew she had made a mistake. Her plainest dress from her former life was, in spite of simplicity of design, of material too elegant, and her contribution to the supper, a French dish made by the miner-chef, too European to be appreciated. What was worse, she became the center of masculine attention at once, and all the men surrounded her, eager to dance with her. She made all the other women seem drab and uninteresting.

"The Countess was a marvelously beautiful woman," Mrs. Knapp later wrote, and explained Lola's popularity by describing her vivacity as infectious.

One day about this time Lola was feeding her bear when Major, now full grown, rose to stand like a man. He put his paws about Lola and hugged her so hard she screamed. Hearing her terrified cries, some men who were on the Mill Road came to her rescue and beat at the bear until he released her.

News of the incident was carried to the mines nearby, and one evening a large group of miners appeared at Lola's house to say they had come to set up a court to try the bear. Keeping a straight face, Lola led her bear to the Alta Hall, where a "Kangaroo Court" was set up, one miner acting as judge, another as prosecutor, and still another appointed as defense attorney for the bear. The case was opened with proper legal procedure before a hall jammed with spectators, and the trial, known as *State versus Bruin* was carried out much as any other. The final outcome was that the jury acquitted Bruin of the charge of attempted murder on the grounds that he had ample provocation, for the "temptation to hug Lola was excessive." In the words of the *Golden Era*, Bruin was "a beast of sentiment as well as taste."

XXVII

Soon after the bear incident, Lola took Lotta with her when she made a trip to the mining camp with the intriguing name of Rough and Ready, to enjoy the beauty of the scenery. The country along the road at this season was splashed with color as fields of buttercups painted the scene in yellow and wild lupin bordered the road in masses of bluish purple. Live oaks, burdened with the parasitical mistletoe, and tall pines traced an outline against the brilliant blue sky.

Rough and Ready was well named. Miners poured in from the diggings with full gold pokes, eager to have a rousing time, and the town abounded in saloons and gambling halls and fierce fights. Often the dances were interrupted with gunfire.

Lola had been told that in 1850 a dispute over a nearby mining claim had led to one of the most unusual incidents in American history. A local character, Uncle Joe Sweigert, was one day working his claim when a man from Cape Cod came by, saying that he had heard Sweigert wished to sell out. Uncle Joe told him the price was three thousand. The Cape Cod man said, "I'll offer you a sporting proposition. I'll dig the hole for one day and if I take over two hundred dollars out it will be yours. If I take less than two hundred dollars' worth it will belong to me." Joe made the newcomer sign an agreement and only later that day realized no provision had been made for the number of hours the man was to work. Not unnaturally, the man loafed on the job.

In Rough and Ready the miners hated slickers. A meeting was held and the Cape Cod man was given a chance to return the mine and the gold he had removed, but he refused and when ordered to leave town said he was an American citizen and knew his rights.

Another mass meeting was held and the old grudge of the population against the United States Government for not allowing representation for their town was well aired. It was finally decided to secede from the Union and the "Great Republic of Rough and Ready" was founded, comprising one hundred and twenty-five square miles and five thousand citizens. A constitution was drawn up, an army formed, and the Cape Cod slicker was run out of town.

The Rough and Readiers then decided they would make a raid on the town of Nevada and take it into their republic. Word of this reached Nevada and the Sheriff posted notices calling on everyone to defend the town. Women and children were sent to Banner Mountain and a sentry with a musket was posted on the road leading into Nevada.

When a gang of men arrived from Rough and Ready they were ordered to halt. "Who goes there?" cried the sentry.

The reply was unexpected: "Friends with a jug of joyful for the sentry and the Sheriff."

To this the sentry replied, "Advance, friends with the jug of joyful, and to hell with the countersign!" When everyone got drunk the war was over.

The first sign of dissatisfaction with the new republic came two months later, when the nearby mining towns of Red Dog, You Bet, and Timbuktu asked Rough and Ready to join them in celebrating the 4th of July. Rough and Ready then decided to go back into the Union, but neglected to inform the government at Washington, and eventually the whole incident was forgotten. It is said that Rough and Ready was still not officially part of the United States until a hundred years later, when a fascinating character named Andy Rogers decided to apply for a post-office with his wife, Geneva, to become postmistress. A letter from the Assistant Attorney General informed them that the uprising of 1850 was forgiven and that Rough and Ready was once more a member of the Union.

This was the town that Lola and Lotta now entered to seek a blacksmith's shop where Lola wanted one of her horse's shoes fixed. She selected the shop of W. H. Fippen, to become famous for what was now to happen. To amuse her, the blacksmith showed Lotta how she could produce notes by striking the anvil in various places, thus playing a tune, a performance which always drew a crowd of idlers on Main Street.

As the music was being played, Lola lifted the petite Lotta onto the anvil, the blacksmith continued the tune, and Lotta danced for the first time in public to the delight of the spectators. She had at first resisted, for she was naturally shy in front of strangers, but once set going she bubbled over with the fun of dancing as her tiny feet kept time to the music.

This was the beginning of the career of one of the most remarkable of all American stage performers. The story of her remarkable talent was carried through the mining camps and nearby towns, but Rough and Ready was the birthplace of her fame, and the anvil was to be shown to every future visitor.

It would be another year before Lotta Crabtree went on the stage, and meantime the newspapers constantly reported that Lola was thinking of reviving her career. When any performer she knew appeared at the Alta Hall, she attended. Dr. Robinson of San Francisco came, and forgiving him his imitations of her when he had donned a short skirt over his pants and struggled with a rubber spider, she went to the performance. He refrained from mimicking her.

One evening she braved the muddy road to Nevada on horseback to see the Montplaisir Ballet Company. To Lola's embarrassment there was more attention given to her than to the performance. She had slipped in quietly, but the audience soon learned she was present and she was cheered so enthusiastically and her name called so repeatedly that finally Madame Montplaisir was obliged to invite her up onto the stage. To quiet the audience Lola addressed them so that the interrupted performance could continue, and graciously confined her remarks to saying that she wished the ballet company great success on their tour.

When D. V. Gates, noted for his tragic and comic impersonations, arrived in the mountains he heard of this ovation given to Lola and stopped at Grass Valley to try to persuade her to go on tour with him. Lola denied she was still interested in a stage career and emphatically refused to listen to Gates, saying she was supremely happy with her quiet life, but in spite of this Gates announced that she was considering his proposal, and the news appeared in all the papers. Most of them were skeptical, the *Golden Era* saying, "We can hardly credit this, for the Countess seems delighted with her mountain home," and Lola assured the correspondents that she had no intention of leaving Grass Valley.

In June of 1854 Lola went on a brief trip to San Francisco to buy camping equipment, and a month later, in the company of three others, she went by horseback for a three-week trip in the Sierra Nevada. A few ladies were undoubtedly among the company but the newspapers did not mention them. Alonzo Delano, the noted newspaperman, William Stewart then acting Attorney-General of California, a Dr. Delevin, and other prominent citizens were of the group.

As Lola appeared with her party, miners named places after her: Lola Mountain, Lola Montez Diggings and so forth. When she herself was asked to name a beautiful, clear lake up among the pines, where the company stopped to camp, she picked up a pebble, threw it into the water and, as it disappeared below surface, she said, "This is the Fourth of July. I call thee Lake Independence"—the name it was ever afterwards to bear.

During the trip Lola betrayed that her temper had not been entirely cured by her life in the mountains. Claiming he had in some way insulted her, she quarrelled with Dr. Delevin, and the altercation between them lasted the whole of one evening until the campfire had died out.

The next morning Lola was alarmed to discover that the doctor, in pique, had deserted the party and had set forth for Grass Valley alone. She could not bear the thought of Dr. Delevin being set upon by bandits and being without supplies of any kind, and in remorse she persuaded two of the gentlemen of the party to go with her. Leaving the others to continue the trip, they started out without breakfast to search for the lone traveller, but shortly afterwards all the other members of the party joined them. The disgruntled doctor had loaded and led off the mules bearing all the provisions and cooking equipment. The party consequently gave up trying its chances of hunting and fishing and returned to an outpost of civilization twenty-four hours later in a state of exhaustion. But the doctor, when found, denied that he had tried to "tame the spunky Countess by starvation."

Before going to the mountains Lola had promised the miners she would give a performance of her "Spider Dance," but her return more than two weeks earlier than she was expected, and her offer to appear with a visiting company took everyone unawares. The weather was exceedingly hot and few men were in from the mines. Seeing that there would be a poor response, Lola withdrew, but a dozen or so of her favorite admirers who lived in Grass Valley insisted that she dance for them and Lola decided to give a performance in her own drawing room, with the small, select audience seated in the dining parlor.

Those not invited were jealous. One even wrote a letter to San Francisco to a friend to say that she had performed the dance with additions and had "taken the rag off the bush." Another disgruntled and imaginative letter writer recorded his opinion that "All that was *seen* has not been divulged." Still another Grass Valley resident wrote, "My, what they saw!"

One local man who had been invited, however, described Lola as being dressed in a full-skirted Spanish dress, giving a lively and graceful performance which was pleasing and modest.

The group of singers who were appearing at the Alta Hall had been invited by Lola to be her guests, since they were short of funds. Alonzo Delano, who was at that time writing his famous *Pen-knife Sketches*, gave accurate accounts of Lola's activities including the story of why she had not appeared at the Alta Hall, of her reviving her "Spider Dance" for a few friends, and of her kindness in taking in the singers as her guests.

But Mr. Wilson, the minister, preferred to believe that Lola had danced half nude and said she deserved to be run out of town. Then Henry Shipley, the editor she had quarrelled with over the Kanaka houseboy, published a blast criticizing her three singer guests.

Lola took him to task in a letter which the Nevada paper was willing to publish: *A short time since a lady and two gentlemen artists came to Grass Valley to give a concert. Having had a few days of professional engagements they were anxious to see our far-famed mines. Artists are proverbial for slender purses and to pay the expenses they gave two concerts here. I was not present on the second, being confined to my room by an indisposition. But if they pleased or not, oh readers—have consideration and kindness to the artist.*

Less than ten days later Shipley picked up an item from a New York newspaper which actually had little to do with Lola but which he could use as an indirect criticism of her.

"The New York *Times,*" said the item, repeated in the Grass Valley *Telegraph,* "speaks in harsh terms of the present condition of Spanish affairs." The article went on to deal with Queen Christine and her habit of contributing articles to newspapers which she kept gagged. "I doubt," continued the writer of the article, "if she could earn her bread by her pen if deprived of her notorious character. There is such a Lola Montez-like insolence and bare-faced hypocrisy in her lines that the ex-King of Bavaria might be delightfully mystified by them."

When Lola saw the article she dressed, put her cape over her shoulders, and concealed under it the horsewhip which she had in her hand.

She came abreast of Shipley on the main street and, walking up to him, cried, "You vile man! You coward!"

A crowd of men soon collected, having seen her coming and noticed her excitement and angry, flashing eyes. Lola lifted her whip and rained blows upon the editor while he raised his hands to protect himself and tried to snatch the whip from her. She leaped about like a gazelle and kept striking Shipley, who finally took refuge in a saloon, hiding behind the bar. Lola, who had broken the whip, pushed open the doors of the saloon and threw it at him.

Newspapers in Nevada and San Francisco as well as Sacramento gave accounts of the affair, one of them quoting Lola as having said that Shipley was "a very commonplace kind of being in intellect."

Shipley published his own version, giving himself the edge on respectability and calling Lola "ludicrous."

Once more Lola retaliated by turning to the Nevada paper. *This morning*, read the letter she wrote, *the newspaper was handed to me as usual. I scanned it over with little interest, saw a couple of abusive articles . . . prepared by the clever pen of a great statesman of the future and present able writer as a climax and extinguisher of all the past and future stories of Lola Montez. I wonder if he thought I should come down with a cool thousand or two and cry "Grace! Grace!"*

This is the only attempt at blackmail I have been subjected to in California and I hope it will be the last one. I read the newspaper till I saw my name in good round English, and allusion to my barefaced "hypocrisy and insolence."

Newspapers sprang to her defense, one saying that Lola had retired to a quiet life and no one, therefore, had any right to publicly attack her.

"Let Lola alone, so long as she is not at present on the stage," agreed another publication. The San Francisco *Herald* concurred in this opinion by saying Lola was living a "cozy life, surrounded by her pets. Strange metamorphosis for this world-renowned woman!"

Lola won her fight when Shipley resigned.

But another attack was soon launched upon her by the Reverend Wilson, who cried out from his pulpit that Lola Montez was "a shameless devil in the guise of a beautiful and fascinating dancer."

This renewed and unprovoked campaign against her roused Lola once more, for fate seemed to be determined to keep her in a state of agitation and she had never been able to appear resigned when she thought she was the victim of an injustice. What the minister did was supposed to be right and proper. Whatever she did would be taken to be perverse.

Once more Lola strode out in anger to defend her honor. She selected an odd manner of bringing her present enemy to heel, for beneath her cape she wore the costume she had used when giving the "Spider Dance" in her home.

She rang the bell at the minister's house and when his startled wife opened the door Lola walked past her into the parlor to confront the Reverend Wilson, who stood up to face her.

She let fall her cape. "Well, Mr. Wilson, how much of a devil am I?" she asked.

The embarrassed clergyman could only murmur a feeble apology to the woman who refused to allow him to be her censor. Instantly Lola forgave him what he had said about her, and impulsively pressed a large contribution into his hands for his church. Mr. Wilson backed up his apology by inviting Lola to stay to tea.

Unfortunately for both of them the story was told by the Wilsons' maid-servant, then was repeated and elaborated upon until little of the truth was left. It ran to such extremes as to claim that Lola wore her most daring costume and did her "Spider Dance" in the minister's parlor.

These untoward incidents left an indelible mark upon Lola's attitude toward Grass Valley, although she had succeeded in routing one fault-finder and had won the friendship of another. And previous to these disagreeable events she had been robbed of her chief interest in the mining town, for during the summer the Crabtrees had left. Mary Ann had followed her husband to Rabbit Creek, only to be once more forced to run a boarding house.

With Lotta gone from her life a great change came over Lola. The emptiness of her days without the little red-head made her restless and once more she took to brooding, almost sick with melancholy over her separation from the brilliant child with whom she had shared so many happy hours.

Soon after the incident with the minister she began to ride out into the mountains every day. Early in the morning she would mount her horse and after most of the day had passed without her returning, Periwinkle would become so anxious that she would go over to the Robinsons to ask them if they knew where her mistress had gone. Never, when Lola returned at nightfall, would she say what she had been doing or where she had been. She no longer brought plants home with her, and she did not seem much interested in anything. The next day and the next would follow the same routine, until even Lola's neighbors on the Mill Road and the men in the nearby mines became concerned for her welfare.

One day one of the miners saw Lola sitting beside a creek. She barely acknowledged his greeting and appeared to be moody and depressed. When she came home it was to change into a black dress and tuck artificial red carnations into her hair. But she had nothing to do after eating Maria's dinner, and she again lapsed into melancholy.

Periwinkle brought this sad period to an end because she herself became unhappy. When Lola returned one evening the maid refused to talk and after supper, when Maria and the houseboy had gone to their respective homes, she sat in the kitchen saying nothing. Lola emerged from her despairing mood long enough to notice Periwinkle's abstraction. The maid had told the Robinsons that she wanted to return to New Orleans, although she had not mentioned this to Lola. Now when Lola asked her what was the matter the colored girl said, "I'm in a brown study on a deep subject."

It was then that Lola told Periwinkle that she had learned in India that when a man died his soul inhabited a star. She revealed her belief that Dujarier, her lover of Paris days, was a star and that she could recapture his presence if she sat in the woods and waited for him to come to her.

Periwinkle told Lola that no one should try to live with the dead, and the two women were at that moment so close that for a time Lola was lifted out of her mental confusion. She recovered her spirits and began seeing a lot of Johnny Southwick, a young engineer who held a large interest in the Empire mine. He had been infatuated with the Countess for some time but the exact circumstances of their affair no one has ever learned. There is only a little evidence that such a connection ever existed. Johnny admitted to a friend in later years that he had loved the Countess but had not been able to hold her.

The only other intimate account of the period is contained in Stephen C. Massett's autobiography. He was surprised at Lola's collection of pets and her "picturesque little villa" in Grass Valley, but he was more surprised to be received there by Johnny Southwick as if, Massett said, the engineer considered himself to be the host.

XXVIII

WHENEVER she acquired a new lover everything about Lola seemed to change. She wanted company and gaiety once more and this time there was a constant succession of guests, among them the man who was to turn her life once more into a tragic channel. He was to win from her a reluctant love, as Johnny Southwick had never done, and he was to be responsible for the metamorphosis which changed her completely from a woman who believed only in pleasure. Through her association with this young man, who lacked talents, education, and security, she was in the end to find God. Religion had been peculiarly absent in her life because of the circumstances of her upbringing. She thought of God as a being frightful and terrifying, to whom she had never turned for solace and whose love was unknown to her. Satan was much more real, for she had often been told in her early life that she belonged to him and that this was irremediable. It was the reason she had said, "I desire to live before I die," and so she had, and so she might have gone on doing to the end but for Noel Follin, who now entered her life, and who, like a specter at the feast, was scarcely noticed among the company.

Follin was blond, blue-eyed, with an oval face and well formed features. He was retiring, far from sure of himself, and inclined to be moody.

Two nephews of Victor Hugo, who had been for some time unsuccessfully mining near Grass Valley, had decided to return to France. Their decision became the inspiration for one of Lola's parties, with William Stewart and Stephen Field, the Marysville lawyer who was later to become famous as a Circuit Judge of the Supreme Court, as guests. Sam Brannan also came up from San Francisco. He had shed his wife and was still anxious to court Lola. Also present was the son of the Honorable Preston Brooks, and a Southern congressman, the son of Senator Foote of Mississippi, both of whom had met Lola in New Orleans. Among such a gathering Noel Follin was indeed unimportant, yet his presence and his personality, which seemed so mediocre, was to have more significance in Lola's future life than all the others combined. So out of place was he in Lola's drawing room that a group of Harvard graduates, who were seeing the mining country of California, and who had also been invited, saw Follin's embarrassment and inability to cope with the company and kindly drew him into their group.

During the next few months Lola resumed her soirées. Usually she served champagne with cake and a special pudding made by Maria. William Stewart claimed that he only lived for those evenings of music and song and witty stories at the house of Lola Montez. Stephen Massett spent an evening "with the Countess of Landsfeld and the merry group there and then assembled," and wrote a ballad in her honor. Then Ole Bull, the celebrated violinist whom Lola had met in New York, joined the company for an evening. Lola was urged to perform one of her dances and with a lace fan in her hand and in a Spanish costume she danced to the music of the tall, lean Norwegian.

How Noel Follin even managed to get Lola's attention in this confusion was remarkable. He might not have done so at all if a financial crisis had not occurred at the beginning of 1855, following the late summer when Noel had first been invited to Lola's house.

Noel's father, Charles Follin, had rather a low opinion of his son but the senior Follin himself displayed lack of stability. He had married a wealthy widow and dissipated her fortune within a year or two in New Orleans and when she died soon after he had gone to New York. There he had gone to a house of ill-fame near the Bowery and met its proprietor, Susan Danforth, whose charm and sweet disposition won from him an offer to set her up as his mistress. She bore him a son and daughter. The son was Noel, and daughter Miriam later became the noted Mrs.

Frank Leslie, the publisher of *Leslie's Magazine*. Not only Noel but Susan and Miriam were to play important parts in Lola's future.

When he was twenty-three Noel had come to San Francisco in the Gold Rush and had proved to be one of the unsuccessful seekers of fortune. He had stayed on for five years, always hoping to hit something which would give him an adequate living, although he seemed to be ill-trained for anything in particular. Behind him, in Cincinnati, he had left two children and a wife who refused to follow him, unwilling to accept life in California as so many dauntless women had done. Not only did she scorn his poverty, Noel said, but she seemed to be adept at delivering to her husband, by mail, the most studied insults. Each of these letters tore at Noel's extremely sensitive feelings, yet when the letters ceased altogether he was scarcely any happier.

Noel collected bills for a newspaper in the daytime and spent his lonely evenings working in a theatre boxoffice, which gave him his first contact with the theatre. Charles Follin, then on a trip to New Orleans, wrote to Susan that he hoped their son was doing well in San Francisco. "Noel has a lack of steadiness," wrote his father; "experience may have taught him to practice it."

Noel was sending everything he could home to his wife. "I cannot live one cent cheaper alone and I am tired of *being* alone," he wrote to his mother. That his life was without hope and without cheer until he met Lola Montez there could be no doubt, for a succession of letters to his mother and his sister Miriam, still in school, showed the intensity of his despair: "No hand can ever again make the clock strike the hours that are past." He longed for his home and longed to share in the activities of his children, but their life was withheld from him and even his mother had no knowledge of her grand-children to pass on to him.

When Lola at Grass Valley had been about to resume her soirées Noel was already drawing nearer to her, as he was at Downieville. Having no Periwinkle to share his loneliness and no one to tell him to face the world cheerfully in order to conquer it and make a success of his life, he wrote to his mother, "Hope is dark and to think of the future lonely, desolate and hopeless; it is too much, too much. Lately I have become very melancholy in disposition."

Months later he wrote of the financial crisis in California caused by the drought in the gold country, which made it impossible for the majority of the mines to be worked. Banks suspended payments and people were alarmed, but Noel, who had nothing to lose, was more concerned with Lola Montez: "She lives in Grass Valley, one of the chosen spots of the world, with a pet bear, a dozzen [sic] dogs, birds, a summer house filled with the rarest flowers, all sorts of musical instruments. Oh, what a dinner she gave me, cooked by herself, my mouth waters at the recollection, there is all the remnants of a lovely woman about her, her nose appears chisseled [sic] out of marble and her conversational powers are fascinating to a degree. I talked with her in English, French and Spanish."

In March of 1855 Lola suddenly abandoned her soirées and grew restless. The truth of the matter was that she had spent too much money entertaining. One of the mines which was one of her main sources of income was in trouble and other periodic revenues disappeared after the business recession of February. When Noel talked of the great success Miss Davenport had had in playing *Camille*, and related stories of current activities in San Francisco theatres, Lola began to think that she might return to the stage again.

Noel Follin planted the seed and returned to San Francisco, where he tried to arrange a tour for Lola which he could take to her as a positive offer. He was only an amateur as a theatrical agent and it took him three months even to get a hearing on the possibility of booking the Countess, because no one quite believed that he could obtain her.

During the intervening time Lola found strange companions in a renewed rebellion against convention. It amused her to be eccentric and to accept an invitation to go to Rough and Ready to spend the evening with Jennie-on-the-Green, from whom she had purchased her house. Upon her arrival there Lola said to Jennie, "I am bored with a life of retirement and long for the gaiety of the theatre."

She had always felt sympathy for Jennie because of the circumstances in which her husband had died and left her to operate the gambling house in Lola's present home. Frank Moore had quarrelled with a man named McClanahan, who had insulted her at a ball held at the Grass Valley Hotel. Moore was considered to be a pleasant man but McClanahan was famous for his fiery disposition, and McClanahan departed in fury, declaring that he meant to revenge himself upon Moore. When McClanahan returned, Moore saw that he had an ill-concealed revolver upon his person. Without hesitating Moore drew his pistol and fired. McClanahan reeled and staggered to the porch. There, grabbing one of the supports of the lean-to porch, he gradually sank down and expired. In the subsequent trial there was evidence presented that Frank Moore had once been a bandit, so that, although he had killed McClanahan in self defense, he was sentenced to be hanged.

Jennie had not openly displayed the bitterness which underlay her air of cool remoteness. Two days before her husband was to be executed she visited him and carried into the jail with her a small milking stool upon which to sit when she was admitted to his cell to talk to him. The next morning when the guard went to give Moore his breakfast he found him dead. A doctor who was brought in said the man had died of poison and a search was made of the cell to try to find where he had kept it hidden. Only the milking stool might have somehow contained it, and upon investigating it they found a hole had been bored beneath the seat. Strychnine had been poured into the cavity and covered with candle grease. Jennie denied having had any part in helping her husband to escape his execution and said she had brought the stool at his request, since he was fond of sitting upon it, but to her few intimates she conveyed a vindictive satisfaction in the words "I told you he would never hang."

In going to her house, Lola had no suspicion of the lengths to

249

which Jennie had gone in retaliation against the citizens of Grass Valley over the loss of her husband. In spite of her dignified way of meeting people and her quiet conversation, she had changed into a different person, though until this evening Lola had not suspected it. Whatever his past before she had married him, Moore had reformed and had been defending her honor when he shot McClanahan. Lola suspected that when at the house on the Mill Road, Jennie had not been merely a lady gambler, for many men continued to come to the house long after Jennie had left. But since none of the women of Grass Valley had ever criticized her and there were a number of lady gamblers in the vicinity who were considered very colorful, Jennie-on-the-Green was accepted as one of this same company of "local characters."

After she had sold her house to Lola little more had been heard of Jennie in Grass Valley although the men undoubtedly talked about her among themselves and were certain she had taken Curly Smith as her lover. But it was not the sort of local gossip they passed on to their wives, for men disliked the women they married hearing defamatory talk.

Jennie had made some money; she had sold her house to Lola Montez; she had returned to Rough and Ready. No one in Grass Valley thought about her any more. Had Lola still had Johnny Southwick as her lover and told him of her proposed visit, he might have advised her to stay away. But she was no longer Southwick's mistress and did not know that there were rumors about the house where Jennie lived, situated in a hollow behind the toll house.

Jennie was supposed to live there alone. The curtains were usually drawn, she was seldom seen abroad, and seemed to have little interest in the outside world. But several men had noticed, although only one seems to have written of it, that at times riding horses would be tied in the shed behind Jennie's house. There was something odd about a house that showed no sign of life in the daytime, yet evidenced occasional nocturnal activity, lightless and unaccountable.

When Lola tied up her horse that day, no one was in the house except Jennie herself, but as Lola and Jennie settled down to play cards and the evening advanced, visitors began to arrive. Each visitor was a man and each one on his arrival joined in the game. As Lola afterwards explained to Noel Follin, she finally began to suspect that she was in the hideout of a gang of robbers and that Jennie was the undoubted head of the gang. That night Lola lost quite a sum of money and resolved never to return, although when she got up to leave Jennie tried to urge her into another game. But she did not like the looks of three of the men who had been introduced as Smith, Grant, and Bell, and could not be persuaded.

It was to be more than a year before Lola was confirmed in her suspicions. Smith proved to be "Curly," killed in a China-town brawl at Grass Valley, and Bell was later revealed as a small-time robber of lonely travellers.

A short time after her evening with Jennie, Lola made up her mind to accept an offer which Noel Follin had negotiated, and as soon as she made it known that she was available the contract was signed.

First she took one last trip into the mountains to remember the Sierra Nevada, and with the wife of a miner, Mrs. Randall, set forth in a buckboard wagon for Downieville. At intervals they camped, killing grouse or fishing, and cooking over a camp fire. Afterwards they slept under the pine trees, Lola lying with the bandit's gun within reach of her hand.

Sometimes, Mrs. Randall said, she would find Lola sitting in the woods with tears welling over her cheeks. She admitted to a reluctance to leave her mountain home, but did not add that financial reverses had led her to the decision.

Then Lola returned home and, assisted by her servants, covered the furniture and wrapped the ornaments in newspapers. The gold leaf pieces and mirror which Ludwig had sent her were taken over to the Robinson house for fear they might be ruined by dampness, and while Lola was there superintending the move Mrs. Robinson mentioned that Mrs. Crabtree had left a trunk to be stored with her.

It may have been this which inspired Lola to take a trip the next day to Rabbit Creek, where Mrs. Crabtree was running a second boarding house, and where she had had another child. Her husband, Lola found, had told the local theatre manager that his daughter was a polished dancer, and the manager had consented to see Lotta perform. Her ability amazed him. The child danced with rhythm and grace, and when she sang the full power of her personality was projected. The manager had billed her as "La Petite Lotta," Mrs. Crabtree had hurriedly made her a costume, and Lotta had appeared before the gold miners in a room filled with the smoke from pipes, and on the crudest sort of stage with candles in holders for footlights. She had won the hearts of the miners and gold nuggets began to pile up at her feet.

When she reached Rabbit Creek, Lola discovered that Mrs. Crabtree was about to give up her boarding house and was planning to accompany her daughter on a tour through the mining camps. Lola told Mary Ann that Follin had arranged a tour of Australia for her and that she was forming her own company. She asked to take Lotta with her.

Such an opportunity would have made Lotta famous, but Mrs. Crabtree resisted the temptation. Uncritical as she was of Lola Montez before others, she undoubtedly considered her to be far too notorious and unstable to have charge of her child. But she was disturbed by Lola's bitter disappointment when she said good-bye to Lotta, and equally disconcerted by her child's heartbroken response to the affection of the famous dancer.

Lola had scarcely gone before Mrs. Crabtree set off on the tour with Lotta. Taking her baby son and Lotta in a wagon, together with a violinist, she followed the theatrical manager, who was leading on horseback. Her husband was, as usual, away on one of his luckless and prolonged searches for gold, and she had no idea when he would return. The message she left him simply read: *"Will see you again someday."*

XXIX

In March of 1855 Lola left Grass Valley to spend eight weeks playing at the Metropolitan in San Francisco before departing for Australia.

The mining town regretted her leaving and the newspapers there and in Nevada paid her tributes. Her affairs with the German Baron, Adler, and with the engineer, Southwick, were not, perhaps, as unknown as she might have hoped, for the Grass Valley *Telegraph*, while praising her original mind, yet said: "She is far from being a proper exemplar to be held up as a pattern for others," although they spoke at some length of her sympathy toward her fellow men and her generosity to those in need of help. There was hardly a person who did not feel that something exciting and interesting had disappeared from Grass Valley which could not be replaced. During her final days she had given away all but one of her dogs and all of her birds, and on the last day she was seen leading the bear into the mountains. She returned with his silver chain wrapped about her hand and it was plain that she had been crying as she had turned this beloved pet loose in the hills. People crowded about the stage coach to bid her farewell and one man, said to have been the attorney Stewart, remarked that she would be remembered as having lived there when others, who felt themselves far more important, would be forgotten. And it was true that Grass Valley's greatest distinction even a century later was predicated upon this and the fact that Lola's house was still standing as it does today.

At the Metropolitan with all its elegancies—red velvet upholstery on the seats, gold decorations, a velvet stage curtain, a horseshoe circle of storied boxes, and chandeliers lit by coal gas—Lola played her usual successes such as *Lola Montez in Bavaria* and *The Maid of Saragossa* to packed houses.

Letters written by Noel Follin and Lola at this time bear the hint of a relationship closer than that of agent and actress. Follin the ne'er-do-well should have been triumphant because he was handling an actress and dancer whose success was assured. He should, too, have at least given way to some small indication that he, as no one else had been able to do, had persuaded the famous Lola Montez to return to her profession. He must, too, have been convinced that this had been done solely on his own merits, for his last letter gave no indication of knowing that Lola's resources were at a low ebb.

He may have had moments when he still wished he could see his mother and sister, but a letter written on May 31st of 1855 betrays something else as well. Clearly he is in the toils of a woman about whom he speaks at first with great formality, and then, forgetfully, calls Lola. To follow her is the way out of all his difficulties, the means by which he can liquidate those debts accumulated when he was unable to collect his salary during the business recession. But his hold upon her is precarious and that, instead of triumph, is stressed beneath the words he uses to conceal what is actually uppermost in his heart.

"Dearest Mother and Sister: I hardly have the heart to write. I have tried to do so twenty times during the last week but could not. Now that the moment has arrived *in desperation* I send a few lines; in three days I will leave California. I am going to Honolulu, Sidney, Australia—China—Calcutta—Bombay—Constantinople and England and so on to Paris and New York. I shall be gone two years or more. I go with the Countess Landsfeld, Lola Montez, as agent—if successful I shall make twenty-five thousand dollars. I have nothing to lose and all to gain; things are and have been very dull in California for months.

"Lola pays me $100 per week and 2 percent on receipts. It is a bold move."

To that he added that he could not tell his wife and bade his mother do so for him. Then there was this strange sentence which was as close as he came to revealing his mental turmoil. "I dare, dare not trust myself to say more. I should die if I did. God bless you. I love you. Noel."

Lola and her company, consisting of James Simmons, Mr. Daniels and Mr. Jones, all former members of the Metropolitan theatrical company, Mrs. Feddes, actress and singer, and her two daughters sailed on the *Fanny Major* for Sydney, Australia. When the news of Lola's departure was known it spread all over San Francisco, and there was almost as large a crowd to see her off as had gathered the day of her arrival. The ship sailed from the old Cunningham Wharf and the great mass of people jammed the structure all the way back to the shore. The San Franciscans stood on tip-toe trying to catch sight of her among the passengers who were boarding the ship, until suddenly someone cried out, "There's Lola! That's her with the green parasol!"

Among the crowd were several reporters who had not anticipated that she would board the ship at such an early hour. In the crowd pressed to the edges of the wharf it was impossible for these men to make their way, and as cries were raised of "Hurrah for Lola!" not one of the newspapermen could capture what Lola called out in reply. At the rail of the ship she stood in a pink dress trimmed with ribbon, the green parasol resting upon her shoulder and a long ribbon fluttering from its handle. Her enormous eyes and black curls were framed by a pink bonnet as she threw kisses to friends in the crowd. At five-thirty P.M. the yards were squared and the ship finally left port. Lola did not move away from the rail for some time.

The trip, which lasted thirty-seven days, was broken by a stop at Hawaii, and a letter from Lola sent back to San Francisco described only the taking on of provisions and expressed surprise that live pigs and poultry were also brought aboard, as well as pineapples, yams, breadfruit, and cocoanuts.

But from Hawaii word was also carried back to San Francisco of Lola's erratic behavior aboard the *Fanny Major*. She had taken her remaining dog with her, and when the steward took a dislike to the animal and began to whip him when he got in his way, Lola did not go to the captain to complain but drew a dagger from her purse and threatened to stab the steward if he did not desist. She then said she would not stay in the first class cabin which he served and withdrew to the steerage, where she remained for the rest of the voyage. Neither Noel Follin nor any of the other members of the company could reason with her.

At Sydney they anchored in Jackson Harbor, where more than four hundred vessels were in port, drawn by the enormous trade then flourishing with Australia, where a new gold rush had just begun.

Emigrants to the teeming gold fields were welcomed to Sydney, although the citizens were vague in the extreme as to the whereabouts of the gold diggings. In fact, it was considered one of the peculiarities of Sydneymen that they could not give a direct answer to this question.

Lola soon learned that the Australians, who occupied the tall buildings and houses of dressed stone in this port, had other singular characteristics. Meals consisted of cold beef or mutton roasts, set out together with loaves of bread and a knife and cutting board. With this they took either rum or porter and it was difficult to obtain anything else, even in the best restaurants. The Australians seemed perfectly satisfied with the lack of style and limited variety of the food. In spite of this, gold miners in their working clothes were not permitted to enter restaurants and had to go into the kitchen if they wished to be served.

Walking about in the company of Follin, Lola talked to many Australians and learned from them that over two thirds of the country was unexplored and that there were sections which were inhabited by savages who killed game with a peculiar weapon which they called a boomerang.

At Sydney her first appearance was at the Victoria Theatre on August 23rd, where she played *Lola Montez in Bavaria*. The Sydney residents, crowding the theatre to capacity, were intrigued with the political angle of the play but had bought their tickets principally because of Lola's scandalous past. Meanwhile, according to reports carried to San Francisco, Lola back stage was quarrelsome and difficult, defending herself against a theatre manager who was too familiar with her, and offending the sensitive Noel, who felt it was his duty to protect her.

It was not until September 6th that Lola performed her "Spider Dance" and discovered that she had quite a different audience from the ones she had known in California. Stuffy Victorianism existed in Sydney and although only six ladies had had the courage to be present at her first performance, the number of women increased as the run continued until the night she did her dance. The search for the spiders was to this moral audience suggestive and shocking, a conception shared by a newspaper editor who described the dance as "the most libertinish and indelicate performance that could possibly be given on the public stage."

Lola hurriedly abandoned Sydney and the next performance given was at Melbourne, where another editor pronounced her performance immoral. The familiar horsewhip in hand, Lola went to his home, where he not only refused to see her but had her shoved off his stoop.

Next day, when a Frenchman who had known Lola in Paris called upon the editor and challenged him to a duel, he was subjected to the same treatment a dance-hall bouncer would have given him.

Lola then learned that her old enemy, Miska Hauser, was in Melbourne and that he was a close friend of the vindictive editor. He had obviously inspired the campaign against her, and she could do little about it. But at Adelaide, the center of the gold rush at that period and one of the most important cities in the Australian entertainment field, she was able to avenge herself. Hauser was scheduled to give a concert the night before Lola appeared, and dressed as a man she spent the night tearing down all the posters advertising his concert so that he was almost without an audience when he appeared. Most of the miners, who came to town only occasionally, remained unaware of his presence.

Hauser seems to have felt sufficiently guilty about the untrue newspaper report he had instigated in California to have remarked that he hoped she was not holding it against him, and also said that he was amazed at Lola's youthfulness; she seemed not to have aged a day since he had last seen her, and he now believed her to be thirty-one as she claimed.

At Geelong at the Theatre Royal she made but one appearance, before an audience who thought she displayed too much leg, or "good understanding," and called upon the Mayor to stop further performances. The matter was referred by the Mayor to a magistrate whose decision was that Lola, being a person who was "not of moral character," should be denied the right to continue performing.

The next lap of her tour was at Ballarat, a mining town. Here another editor, named Seekamp, made an attack upon her and Lola, whip in hand, tracked him to the United States Hotel. Seekamp had heard of Lola's impassioned defense of herself in other places and faced the white-faced woman with a like weapon. When she raised her whip he raised his and the two of them stood lashing each other until some miners rushed into the hotel, rescued Lola and berated the editor.

When she appeared on the stage that night, considerably marked in spite of powder used in an attempt to conceal the red welts, her audience of miners stood up in their seats and cheered her.

But the fight was not over. Lola could hate injustice for herself as well as anyone else, and she was willing to fight against it to the bitter end. Seekamp had the upper hand however. He used his newspaper to defend himself and accused Lola of having said disgraceful things about the Ballarat theatre manager, one Crosby. On reading the article, the manager sought Lola out in her hotel suite and picking up her whip, which was lying nearby in her parlor, struck her across the back with it with such force that the whip broke in two.

Lola refused to appear at the theatre again. It had been her intention to go on a tour of India and the Orient but this final incident made her decide to return to San Francisco. She gave one more performance for the benefit of British soldiers who had been wounded at Sebastopol, and so ended the tour on which she had been unrestrainedly acclaimed by audiences and universally attacked by newspapers.

The last threat to her in Australia made Lola retreat to a novel type of self defense. On hearing that she was to be served with papers in a damage suit, she sat in her suite as the ship was about to sail, her door shut but not locked. Through the door she called out that she was undressed. "If you want to take me in this condition," she cried out, "you are welcome!"

During those last weeks in Australia both Lola and Follin had had to face the fact that the tour was a failure. To get her company home would take the last of Lola's resources but she was never a coward and lack of fear was to carry her through to a course of recovery. All her depressed periods had to do with her internal struggles, those periods when she lived in the past, surveying all the strange things that had happened to her. It was not by any means a struggle with her conscience nor a resolve to expiate what others might have called her sins, but rather a consideration of her propensity to become involved in tragedy. There was a letter in which she had expressed this looking inward upon herself: "My career has been one of such vicissitudes and adventure that it almost equals those given in popular works of fiction. I sometimes look back on my life and wonder 'is this true? Have I existed or is it all a dream?' " To her the mystery of why she was besieged by so much tragedy was unfathomable, and she was always haunted by the prediction Alexandre Dumas had made that she would bring ill-luck to those she loved.

Unknown to her, there was a paradox in the letters written about her before and after Dujarier's death. Previous to her meeting with Dujarier and before she became accepted into the company that had frequented George Sand's salon, she had been often described as gay and effervescent. Her beauty "distracted"

259

the women who wrote about her but they also considered her to be flighty, flirtatious, and likely to involve herself in some disgraceful situation because of the way she excited men.

After the death of Dujarier her tragic despair had been commented on when she appeared in court at Rouen. She was never again to be called frivolous and many historians of the period, after she joined Ludwig, credited her with great seriousness. It was certain that she must have developed during this time, and what confused the women who wrote of her in her earlier years was this later flowering of intelligence.

Lola had always had the ability to think and to reason things out for herself, as well as charm, wit and a gift for entertaining people in conversation. Yet her mentality swung like a pendulum, sometimes to great heights of reasoning, sometimes stopping altogether when she became enraged against cruelty or injustice. To the world at large Lola was always a mystery and even to those who managed to get close to her she was more often than not a riddle. Her life moved from happiness to despair: one minute she was gay, witty, surrounded by companions; the next she sat alone in the woods seeking to keep a tryst with a dead lover. Yet it was not enough that she could look toward the heavens and select the star that represented Dujarier. There was always something beyond, an unknowable experience to which she aspired and had only glimpsed through her experiences of love.

Her nature was entirely opposite to that of Noel Follin, whose dejection of spirits constituted a burden which he daily carried. Not even the anticipation of success as a theatrical agent had acted as a spur to the young man's animation, for although he had overcome his financial difficulties, he had loaded his conscience with an adulterous affair with Lola.

Towards the end of her stay at Sydney, Lola had encountered the younger brother of the Duke of Wellington, Charles Wellesley. He was a Major-General in the British army and a married man, and he might only have called on Lola because he must have been acquainted with many of the men who had paid court to her at Half Moon Street. But call on her he did and Noel Follin took offense, claiming that she had flirted with Wellesley.

Undoubtedly Lola had grown weary of Noel's sensitiveness and his incessant carping over the attentions shown to her by other men. There was, too, on the return voyage, a great deal of whining on his part over the financial failure of the tour. Later on Lola told very little of what happened to terminate their relationship beyond stating that as the ship was near Fiji one day, she went to her cabin to bring him a sum of money she held in reserve which she said she was going to urge upon him.

No one was near them to witness what happened when she returned to him on deck, but presently an agonized scream was heard, and when people rushed up in response to her cry they found her lying unconscious and Follin nowhere in sight. Presuming that Follin had fallen overboard, the captain had the ship stopped, and a thorough search was made of the cabins while the crew scanned the waters about the ship. The captain was finally satisfied that Follin could not be found and they continued on their course.

Lola's loss of consciousness was more like a coma than a faint, and extended for an alarming period. When pressed for an explanation of what had happened, she would only say she had gone to her cabin to get the money for Follin and then had discovered that he was nowhere about when she returned on deck. This did not explain her scream but she would never elaborate on the incident for the rest of her life.

XXX

NOEL HAD DISAPPEARED on his twenty-ninth birthday, July 8th of 1856, from the *Jane E. Falkenburg*, on a run which was tragic from the start. Later a member of the crew was also drowned and one of the officers aboard the ship lost his hand when he accidentally discharged a gun. The passengers came into port with a subdued air and on her arrival in San Francisco Lola seemed crushed. Never again was she to be seen with a horse-whip in her hand, trembling with uncontrollable anger, bent on retaliation. Her audacity, her tempestuousness, her untranslatable quirks of character almost disappeared; instead her behavior was exemplary; quiet and thoughtful, she neither caused nor sought excitement.

Spending a social evening among a group of actors shortly after her arrival, she said, "I have been wild and wayward but never wicked." This was her oft-repeated statement and more than once it had appeared in her letters, but to these theatrical people, according to an account written by Laura Keene, Lola now said it as if she had an uneasy conscience, and the sentence seemed to take on an entirely new tone of remorse. At another time she said, "I believe Noel committed suicide." The impression was that Follin had quarrelled with Lola over her receiving the attentions of other men and as Follin threw himself into the ocean she fainted.

On her return, everything conspired to depress her. Johnny Southwick was ill and she heard that he was not expected to live. Allegedly she did not see him but sent him financial aid through a mutual friend.

During her absence in Australia various newspapers in the gold country had kept track of her whereabouts. One wistful item had been confined to Lola's once well-tended garden at Grass Valley, lying uncared for and dying. Only the rose trees, grown ragged and unkempt, still bravely bloomed, and the story went on poetically:

I passed by the garden and saw the wild brier
The thorn and the thistle grew broader and higher.

After a few days in San Francisco Lola went to Grass Valley, but remained there only a short time. Since paying off her company she had little in the way of immediate funds; the income from her mining investments had petered out, and she had only the revenue from Dujarier's estate to live on. The need for money forced her to dispose of all her household possessions except the gold-leaf furniture stored with the Robinsons; but she was still capable of optimism and believed she would again settle down someday in a new home where she could have these remaining possessions about her.

The furniture gone, her house stood empty for only two days before being sold to the postmaster, Frank Bosworth, but during that time some of the people who lived along the Mill Road broke in and carried off souvenirs of the Countess' stay in Grass Valley. Pieces of the well worn, handwoven carpets were cut from the floors. Doorknobs disappeared. The lace curtains, hanging fragile and yellowed, were divided up among eager keepers of mementoes and the upholstery was stripped from three shabby, abandoned chairs.

The Robinsons later gathered together samples of the curtains, the carpet and swatches of the upholstery, to be kept together in their family against a possible day when Lola's home might be restored as a memorial to her, but it was little Lotta Crabtree, as yet only nine years old, who was one day to gather nearly all the furniture that Lola sold or left in Grass Valley and keep these things throughout her long life.

After disposing of her house, Lola went to Nevada, which, on the day when she had returned from Australia, had been destroyed by fire. She wanted to see what remained of the town which she had loved and which had given her so much happiness, and learned on her arrival that the fire had started in a blacksmith's shop and had soon gone out of control. Although an alarm had been sounded at once, a high wind had carried portions of the burning roof of the shop on to a brewery next door and from there the fire swept across the street to engulf the Kidd and Knox stables and the United States Hotel.

All of Nevada's four hundred wooden buildings had been destroyed, and of the twenty-six brick buildings only six still remained standing. Firm in their belief that brick could not catch fire, some of the merchants had remained in the structures they owned, only to die of suffocation.

Saddened at seeing the town in ruins, Lola finally took the stage for Grass Valley for the last time, passing the section known as Lola Montez Hill which had recently been named after her. And when she departed from Grass Valley, it was to leave behind her the only period of security she had ever known and sever the roots she had put down in the mountains of California.

On her return to San Francisco she rented a small house on Telegraph Hill, overlooking Portsmouth Square, and surprised everyone with the collection of birds and dogs she had brought back from Australia. The birds she placed in cages about her rooms, except for a white cockatoo which rode upon her shoulder when she went on her daily walk. Wearing a white-collared, deep blue velvet jacket with jet buttons down the front, and a black silk skirt, her face screened behind the heavy flounces of lace that fell from her black hat, Lola could not have been easily identified had it not been for the cockatoo. For her walks she picked Montgomery Street, the most crowded of the thoroughfares. Coming down from Telegraph Hill, she walked down one side of Montgomery and back up the other, her dogs romping at her heels. In Portsmouth Square people stopped her and made a great fuss over the bird because he could talk, and soon the two became familiar figures.

Lola was undoubtedly trying to create interest in herself, for on August 8th she appeared again at the American Theatre in *Lola Montez in Bavaria,* and later in *A School for Scandal,* playing a varied repertory throughout the rest of August and through September, every performance drawing a full house.

With her income restored she began to entertain, but now she invited only those in the upper stratum of the theatre. Politicians and the socially prominent of the city she ignored.

Among the people who came to see her was Mrs. Crabtree, now living in San Francisco where Lotta was soon to appear, using her full name in the billing instead of "La Petite Lotta," as in the past. In spite of Lola's pleading Mrs. Crabtree would not let her daughter go to visit Lola alone, as she had done in Grass Valley, and her refusal was based on a peculiar objection. She noticed that Lola was given to moodiness and viewed with alarm the actress' claim that she was now able constantly to contact the departed spirit of Dujarier. Mrs. Crabtree told an actress friend of Lola's that she presumed Lola had taken up the current fad for spiritualism, and she undoubtedly felt that a belief in such communications from the dead would not have a desirable influence upon her daughter.

Lola's belief in what other people called "trances" attracted the attention of the *Golden Era.* The paper reported that a man named Underhill had managed to convince Lola that he had had the same sort of experiences in recapturing the presence of a beloved who had passed away. But when she realized that Underhill meant to use her as a means of launching himself as a spiritualist, she ordered him out of her house, calling him a charlatan, and from that time on refrained from further mention of her contacts with Dujarier, unhappy that anything so private had come to the attention of the local newspapers.

Though Mary Ann Crabtree sought to keep her daughter from Lola, the child still loved her as she loved no one else outside her own family, and when Lola descended upon the Crabtree residence and swept Lotta into her arms the child hugged her ecstatically. Every subsequent meeting between them marked a step in the career of Lotta, for she learned from the

Countess the importance of drawing attention to oneself in the theatrical world and was to use this knowledge well, capturing the world's notice for many years. Yet Lotta, young as she was, must also have been aware of the evils a bad reputation could bring, for she kept her life spotless as her mentor had never learned to do.

At Lola's house there was wit, champagne, and "a court of admirers." Lola was spending her money with a lavish hand, giving supper parties and serving the best foods the market provided. She hoped to accumulate savings but in a desire to free herself of what she was gradually to recognize as her obsession with Dujarier, she tried to recapture a life of gaiety.

Like Mary Ann Crabtree, Periwinkle had also tried to keep Lola from talking of Dujarier's spirit, but it had taken the newspaper account to bring her to her senses. Yet there was still another circumstance troubling Periwinkle. Ever since the death of Noel Follin, Lola had became careless of her grooming. She seemed preoccupied with the tragedy of his death. The black curls, always so shining, and the wave in her hair, usually so smooth and glossy, now often went untended. Lola did not care if her stage clothes were unpressed, even allowing herself to be photographed in wrinkled untidiness, and people wrote letters about the change in her appearance, almost all of them believing her to be remorseful over Follin's death, or too much interested in spiritualism to care about her looks.

During a month's successful run, when she had a large income, Lola realized that her way of life would not allow her to help Follin's widow so that his children might be provided for, and she decided to sell her jewels.

They were put up for sale with the auctioneers, Duncan & Company on Montgomery Street, but though they were valued at twenty thousand dollars, she received less than ten thousand. The sale began at ten A.M. and her entire collection of diamond jewelry, diamond-set watches, chains, and so on was sold in a wareroom packed with bidders who paid in cash. One of her necklaces, a diamond cross with seven large diamonds and twenty-eight smaller ones, a pair of pearl earrings, a diamond brooch, and a magnificent pigeon-blood ruby hanging from a chain, brought the highest amounts.

Had Lola been present to deliver each item in person the prices would have sky-rocketed, but although the bidding was spirited her absence took the edge off the enthusiasm. The *Alta California* learned the purpose behind the sale of the jewels and revealed that Lola had ordered the proceeds to be deposited with Davidson & Company for transmission to New York, to be delivered to the heirs of Noel Follin. What the public did not learn was that Noel's wife in Cincinnati refused to accept the draft when it was presented to her and ordered it returned to Lola, spurning the gift because of its source.

It was not known until the day after the auction that Lola had left for Sacramento to appear at the new Forrest Theatre, which had been named after the famous Shakespearean actor, Edwin Forrest. But in spite of a successful run to packed houses, and the obvious enthusiasm of her audiences, who were uncritical because they had come out of curiosity to see her and not to judge her acting or her dancing, she did not make the money she had made three years before in Sacramento. At that time tickets had sold for as much as thirty-five dollars, but ever since the recession of 1855 the best seats sold for a dollar, boxes brought only four dollars a seat, and even those seats were too few to make the receipts amount to a great deal.

There was a serene atmosphere in the house, quite unlike her previous engagement in the Levee City. Many women were present, there was frequent clapping and later observations on the part of the press that Lola had not aged since she first came to California, which seems to indicate that she must have again been taking care of her appearance.

On the evening of the day of the auction in San Francisco, Dr. Robinson and Caroline Chapman had joined forces and appeared in a burlesque of Lola called *A Trip to Australia; or Lola Montez on the Fanny Major*. It was received with hostility. The people of San Francisco were all well aware of the tragedy that had occurred on the return voyage and of Lola's motive in selling her jewels, and the consensus of opinion was that Lola was sincere in her efforts to help others, and that it was offensive to make fun of her in this way. But when she returned, Lola took Dr. Robinson to task not with her blazing temper of the past but with a new and impressive reasonableness, and while Robinson and his company played to almost empty houses, Lola opened a successful run with standees occupying all the available space.

While she was under the management of Junius Booth at the Metropolitan, he had occasion to notice the change in her. When he told Lola she could not smoke in the theatre, she threatened to slap him, and Booth calmly replied that if she did he would slap her back. To his astonishment she obeyed the order without further argument. Evidently she was mellowing in character and losing the rebellious imperiousness she had displayed before the disappearance of Noel Follin at sea.

At the conclusion of her run she was visited by Laura Keene and some of the members of the latter's company, and Mrs. Keene was also impressed with the change that had taken place, reporting that the dancer's dictatorial manner had noticeably lessened.

Toward the end of October Lola gave up her home, presented her birds to the Pacific Museum, and distributed her dogs among friends. Sadly she bade farewell to her friends, including Periwinkle, who had become engaged to a member of her own race and stayed behind to marry in San Francisco, bringing her long and pleasant association with Lola Montez to a close. Perhaps only the colored girl knew Lola's ultimate destination; certainly no one else did as the *Orizaba* left San Francisco for San Juan, Nicaragua, late in the afternoon of October 20th, 1856.

Lola's last performance took place on the 17th and it had been a tremendous success. She left San Francisco as she found it, in a delirium over her, the gentlemen smoking Lola Montez cigars, the ladies reading copies of *Lola Montez, or The Mysteries of the Court of Bavaria,* brought out by the Noisy Carrier's Publishing Hall who had run newspaper advertisements saying: "So tumble on down here, all you admirers of Lola!"

XXXI

HAVING FAILED in her efforts to make Noel's widow accept the money which she had tried to send through a bank, Lola had decided to appeal to Noel's mother to intercede for her, and as soon as she arrived in New York she sent for Susan Danforth Follin. When the older woman entered her hotel room Lola, breaking into heart-rending sobs, sank to the floor and cried, "I killed your son!"

Far from being unapproachable like her daughter-in-law, Susan Follin lifted Lola to her feet and clasped her to her with comforting words. She advised Lola to see Noel's widow in person, and apparently Lola eventually did this. For when Mrs. Follin later expressed a desire to send her daughter, Caroline, to an exclusive school in the East, Caroline was placed in Lola's charge and taken by her to Mrs. Williard's Seminary at Troy, New York. When she had also provided for the education of Noel's son, Lola felt she had done all she could to make restitution for the loss of their father.

Alone and weary, Lola Montez faced a disheartening future until she returned to New York and saw Susan again. But soon Mrs. Follin and her divorced young daughter, Miriam, had become like a family to her, the girl replacing Lotta as her protégée. Miriam had lovely features, light hair and blue eyes, and a charming manner, and soon she was learning dancing with Lola as her teacher. With what was left of her money Lola paid for dramatic lessons for Miriam, and by this time had stripped herself of her property, her jewels, and nearly all of her capital.

Every biographer who wrote of her, every newspaper that kept track of her activities, and her friends, with whom she would ordinarily have corresponded, lost sight of her from the time she said good-bye to Susan and Miriam in New York and sailed for France, until she rejoined them a number of months later in February, 1857.

There were strange rumors of a marriage in secret, and false reports were circulated in an effort to find who was the bridegroom. A letter sent from New York to San Francisco by a newspaperman declared that Lola had married Prince Solkowski, whom she was supposed to have met in earlier years when she was alleged to have been at the court of Frederick William IV of Prussia. At the time Lola returned to New York, Solkowski was living on a farm in the United States, but there was no reason to believe that he accompanied her to France. The other rumor was that she had married Mauclerc, an actor, and that he had committed suicide eight days after the wedding, but since Lola was on the stage in San Francisco on the very date named for the supposed wedding, and since Mauclerc soon turned up very much alive, this must have been another oblique way of trying to uncover Lola's whereabouts.

The only public statement that Lola herself made in after years was an admission that she had married again, but when asked by a newspaperman for the name of this fourth husband she said that she couldn't remember it.

The Polish writer Hildegarde Ebenthal, who was actually Princess Ekaterina Radziwill, a relative of Tsarina Alexandra, wife of Nicholas II, later had access to the records of the royal family of Bavaria, and in the chapel of the Residenz found a record of the morganatic marriage of Ludwig I to Lola, the latter using her legal name. Present at the ceremony were some Polish cousins of Ludwig and several members of the German nobility. After the wedding Ludwig invited these relatives, then visiting him, to accompany himself and Lola to Italy. Also accompanying them was a guard provided by Ludwig's son.

News of the wedding and subsequent trip to Italy was withheld from the press and was never actually published until 1899, when it appeared in the San Francisco *Examiner*.

A descendant of Alexander III of Russia, living today, remembers hearing of that ill-fated honeymoon trip of the ex-King and the dancer. For no matter how lenient a view Ludwig's son, Maximilian II, took of his seventy-two-year-old father's infatuation for Lola, the Wittelsbach relatives could not contain their indignation, and set out to make Lola pay for her audacity in at last accepting the aged ex-King's proposal. They refused to treat her with anything but contempt, and as their insults could not be heard by the deaf Ludwig, Lola had no defender and soon found the constant barrage unendurable.*

According to Princess Radziwill, the stay in Italy became a nightmare, but in the end Lola's reason for leaving Ludwig had nothing to do with the campaign against her by his royal relatives. Caustic wit had gradually replaced her temper as a weapon, and she could have been a match for the royal relatives had she chosen to remain. Ludwig and she would have spent their time alone together, as in the past, enjoying the beauties of Italy or Greece, and their other mutual interests.

It was because Ludwig insisted on consummating the marriage that Lola decided to desert him. The marriage, so long proposed and at last accomplished, now revealed something which Lola had certainly not anticipated. It appeared that Ludwig had suffered for years from a venereal disease. Lola soon contracted it herself and thus began the loss of her beauty. The ex-King possessed an iron constitution which did not deteriorate, but Lola, who had come unmarred through so much unhappiness, was far more susceptible to the inroads of the disease. With revulsion for Ludwig, she fled back to America with new jewels and a magnificent wardrobe, but also in the throes of paying the awful price for what she had thought of as security.

On her return she resumed her theatrical career, setting forth with Miriam Follin on a tour in which Miriam was billed as Lola's younger sister, Minnie Montez. They appeared at Albany to crowded houses in the Green Street Theatre, but there was little financial gain as the best seats sold for a dollar

* Note: Source of material will be sent to researchers on request.

and those in the rest of the house for only fifty cents or a quarter.

On February 7th, 1858, Lola saw a chance to gain much-needed publicity. She and Miriam were playing in Providence on the 8th. The Hudson River, swollen by rains, had risen and submerged many business blocks, homes, and the theatre at Albany. Not to be deterred from leaving Albany, and hoping to gain attention, Lola, instead of going by the longer and less difficult route through Troy, offered some boatmen a hundred dollars if they would take her across the river, which was at that time filled with ice floes. Behind them, as they left Albany, houses were collapsing into the water and animals were being swept away amid the wreckage and drowned. Halfway across the water Lola and Miriam lost the better part of their theatrical wardrobes.

It was a quirk of fate that Miriam, the future wife of Frank Leslie, was ignored by him in the account of the episode written up for his paper in New York, although a drawing of the incident which he published did show Miriam sitting in the boat while Lola remained standing.

"The indomitable Lola Montez," read the article, "who has been playing a theatrical engagement at Albany, desired for some purpose known to herself to cross the river, and nothing daunted at the fearful danger, challenged boatmen to take her across and after a perilous voyage landed safely, being the first person after the storm who accomplished this feat."

The resultant excitement over Lola's venture filled the theatre at Providence and all standing room available was sold for the run.

Miriam was soon judged to be able to carry herself, and she and Lola separated. There may have been other considerations, for Miriam, who had been married under a cloud when a schoolgirl, and whose husband had thereafter disdained her, had been divorced at the time Lola had been in Australia. As soon as she had left Lola, Miriam allowed the President of the Bank of East Tennessee to establish her in a love-nest in New York.

This of itself seems unlikely to have alienated Lola from Miriam, since it occurred after they had severed their joint venture. Something else must have occurred to make Lola's memory something Miriam shunned. Lola had helped Miriam and her mother in their poverty, had given them much of the money Noel's widow had not accepted, and Lola had certainly made Miriam's career possible. But when the so-called Minnie Montez had become the noted Mrs. Frank Leslie, she avoided all mention of Lola when she wrote a book about her trip to California, and although Grass Valley was a tourist Mecca by then, it was the one place Miriam avoided. Whatever the genesis of this strange lack of appreciation, it was evidently something the younger woman wished to forget.

After her brief career with Miriam there were no further engagements on the stage for Lola; theatrical managers had simply lost interest in her. By March of 1858 she was back in London and again involved in a lawsuit. Reports of this case were to spread around the world, for when Lola was called as a witness and asked to say who she was she solved part of the mystery of her past in a number of revealing answers. The case had to do with the insolvency of one William H. Harvey, whose assignee was David W. Jobson. Lola was brought into the case to testify to the character of Jobson and answered that he was a "low London attorney" who had once attempted to extort money from her by blackmail. This was not further explained, but she was subjected to severe cross examination designed to prove that she was not a credible witness. She surprised her hearers when she did not retreat behind any of the enigmas about herself, such as the story that she was the daughter of Lord Byron, or the equally popular fiction that she might be the daughter of the bullfighter, Montes.

Asked what her original name had been she promptly replied, "Eliza Gilbert."

"Where were you born?" she was asked.

"In the beautiful city of Limerick," she replied.

"How old are you?"

"Thirty-three."

"When were you born?"

"That I cannot tell," came the answer, as if this was a question which she, at all costs, must not answer. "I wasn't present when I was born."

"Were you married to Captain James?"

"The ring was put on my finger by a clergyman but my spirit was never united to his."

"What other husbands have you?" continued the relentless questioner.

"Now wait a moment," replied Lola. "I'll have to be sure. I was married to James near Dublin. I was a child of fourteen. He ran away with me—that was my first marriage. He ran away with another lady about a year after I was married. I was living in Mugear, India, then. I came to England. I don't know how long I remained in London after I returned—a few months.

"I was on the stage and practicing under the instruction of a Spaniard named Espa. I was lodging with an old Scotchman and his wife. My father was Adjutant-General of the Army in Bengal."

An audible gasp came from the courtroom but this reference to her father was not resolved until later in the day, when some of the curious had an opportunity to find out just who the Adjutant-General of Bengal had been.

Lola's questioner continued after a noticeable pause, for even he had been thrown off by so much voluntary information on her background and early life.

"Were you living with a man at that time?" he continued.

"I never lived with any man after my husband left me. My husband charged me with intrigue with a man named Captain Lennox, on shipboard, but it was a false accusation made by him, because he was living then with the wife of Captain Lomar, of the 21st Regiment. I went from London to Spain and all over that country. I remained in Spain a few months, learning to dance. I was travelling alone as I travel now. There was a charming little girl, named Dolores, in Spain, whose husband had deserted her."

"For you?" came the insulting and extremely offensive question.

To everyone's suprise Lola remained calm as she replied, "No, I never did any of that sort of thing."

"How many intrigues have you had?" was the next question.

"How many have you?" was the saucy answer. "Well, come listen—none. I resided at the Court of Bavaria two years."

"Who did you know there?" was the taunting question.

"Everybody but yourself," Lola promptly answered. "I knew all of several millions of persons; I knew the King of Bavaria. Mr. Wittelsbach, he was called. That was his name."

"Were you the mistress of the King?"

At this question Lola rapidly rose from her seat, and began to move toward her questioner to slap him for his insolence. Her reply, while she was obviously restraining herself from making a physical assault upon him, was emphatic and convincing. "No, sir, you are a villain, sir."

She then offered to take her oath upon the Bible that she had not been Ludwig's paramour. "He took me before the whole court," she said, "and presented me as his best friend. I was on the stage in Bavaria. It is easier to be a man's mistress than a dancer. I was in Bavaria in 1847 and 1848, in 1849 the revolution occurred, and liberty and I fled. The memoirs that have been written about me are lies."

Continuing then about her career after her stay in Bavaria, she said, "I was living in Piccadilly, London, in 1849 when I saw Jobson. I had come from Switzerland about two months before."

Lola then told the court that she had originally been taken to India when she had been three months old.

The newspapers reported the courtroom as being "in a perfect fever of excitement," on tenter hooks to find out the name of Lola's father. No one quite believed that she was the daughter of an English general, but many retired officers of the East India army and their wives lived in London and from them it was learned that Lola could have been referring only to General Sir Patrick Edmonstone Craigie. This meant that Lady Craigie of Calcutta was Lola's mother. Officers in England remembered that the general had married the eighteen-year-old widow of a Captain Gilbert of the 44th Regiment in India. Gilbert, dying of cholera in 1826, had implored his fellow officer, Craigie, to look after his widow and child. The widow, considered to be the most beautiful woman there, was soon surrounded with admirers, but it was Craigie, then a captain, who led her to the altar.

Then it was remembered that later on Elizabeth Gilbert Craigie had sent out funeral letters to her friends, informing them that her daughter had passed away, and that she had gone into deep mourning. As this coincided with the very period when Lola had left her husband, James, after his disgraceful elopement with a fellow officer's wife, it was now clear to everyone that this daughter had not died. Her proud and ambitious mother, whose husband was by then a general, had declared that Eliza was dead rather than admit that she had been deserted and gone on the stage.

Meanwhile in Dublin a lowly milliner named Miss Oliver declared that she was Lola's aunt and the sister of Lady Craigie, but that her snobbish sister would have nothing to do with her because she cared for nothing but social position.

The family of Lola's first husband, Thomas James, contacted in County Meath, Ireland, now denied that he was dead but was in India, which put Lola in a position of never having been properly married to Pat Hull. Nor could she have been the wife of Ludwig, although at that time the morganatic marriage was not known of.

The purpose of Lola's revelations in court soon became apparent. It was her intention to launch herself as a lecturer and her *Autobiography of Lola Montez*, begun long ago in Paris, was being recast for her by a professional writer. In it—let Lady Craigie deny it—Lola was going to state that her full name was Marie Dolores Eliza Rosanna Gilbert, but that she had always been called Lola. The first and second chapters of her autobiography, which were to serve as material for her lectures, as well as other chapters in the book on various subjects, included all she had revealed in court and added to this many additional facts of interest about her background.

People were delighted to have Lola's secrets revealed and the public in Paris alone was so interested that fifty thousand copies were immediately sold there. Soon not only Parisians but Londoners, New Yorkers, and San Franciscans were poring over the pages of this intriguing book.

They learned that Lola's mother had been related to the Montalvos of Spain, which was already pretty generally known. Next the author revealed that her father had been the son of Lady Gilbert, which revived another old scandal—that Lady Gilbert had had a son who was illegitimate. Gossip was also revived, and possibly stemmed from the milliner sister of Lady Craigie, that Elizabeth Oliver, before her marriage to Captain Gilbert, had been performing in a London music hall. Hardly any one of these rumors was verified, but although the Oliver relationship to the Montalvos of Spain seemed true enough, it was certain that Lady Craigie's claim that her grandfather had resided in a castle in Spain was a fiction created by herself.

The story of Lola's childhood was pitiful enough, even though she did not make a bid for sympathy in writing of it. The reader could not help but draw his own conclusions as to what sort of a woman Lola's mother was, in spite of the way Lola skirted around any criticism of her. Lola had been three months old when she had been taken out to India by her parents, and her father had died a year later. Soon thereafter the widow had married Craigie, and when he was advanced to the rank of major and it seemed as if his accomplishments would carry him beyond this, Lola's mother sent her six-year-old daughter to stay with Craigie's father at Montrose, Scotland. Lola described herself as being peculiar in her dress and manners, having been raised in India, and her stay in the home of her step-father's father, the venerable Craigie, who was Provost of Montrose, came to an abrupt end. Next she was sent to the family of the retired commander-in-chief of the Bengal Forces, Sir Jasper Nichols. Nichols had established a residence in London for his motherless daughters Fanny and Valerie, but the girls were taken to Paris to be educated and in order to be near them Nichols spent more time in France than he did in England. He kindly consented to send Lola to the academy with his daughters.

The majority of the army officers and their wives who lived in India and sent their children to Europe to be educated came back on leave to visit their sons and daughters and spend school holidays with them from time to time, but Lola's mother never came. When the Nichols girls left the academy in Paris and were sent to a finishing school at Bath, Lady Craigie furnished the deserted Lola Gilbert with sufficient funds to maintain her but nothing more. But Lola wished to go to the school at Bath because her only intimate friends, Fanny and Valerie, were there, and finally she was allowed to join them.

Eight years had passed since Elizabeth Craigie had sent her child to England, accompanied only by an Indian servant, but when Lola was ready to leave her finishing school at the age of fourteen, Lady Craigie came to England at last. Her reasons for the trip were anything but altruistic, yet Lola had not a word to say against her mother even when she learned what had brought her to England. As Lola described it, her mother created "a great hubbub of new dresses, and all manner of extravagant, queer-looking apparel, especially for the wardrobe of a young girl of fourteen years," but when Lola finally had enough courage to ask her what it was for, she was told that she was asking "idle questions."

Captain Thomas James, who had travelled home on leave from India on the same ship with her mother, was more informative. He told Lola that her mother had promised her in marriage to "Sir Abraham Lumly, a rich and gouty old rascal of sixty years, and Judge of the Supreme Court in India."

Lola was frightened but determined to resist being sacrificed for wealth and position. Describing herself at that time, Lola wrote, "The little madcap cried and stormed alternately. The mother was determined, so was her child. The mother was inflexible, so was her child, and in the wildest language of defiance she told her that she never would be thus thrown alive into the jaws of death."

Needing an ally, Lola sought the advice of Captain James. She had few friends and did not perceive that James cared for nothing but fast horses and the wives of his fellow officers, whom he took pride in seducing. He was twelve years older than Lola, but these additional years had not added to his maturity, and he could think of nothing but eloping with the young beauty. He promised to take her to his family in Ireland, but instead took her to an inn where she was forced to submit to him.

A few days later when his sister realized what had happened, she took charge of the situation and compelled James to marry the girl. Lola wrote: "The child gained what proved to be only the outside shell of a husband, who had neither a brain which she could respect, nor a heart which it was possible for her to love."

Eight months later they departed for India and eventually her husband eloped to the Neilghery Hills with the wife of another officer. The deserted young Lola had nowhere to turn, and the wives of the other East India officers, after holding a consultation about what was to be done with her, decided to send her back to her mother at Calcutta.

Here General Craigie pleaded that his step-daughter be accepted into the household, but Lady Craigie, who did not wish any competition from her own daughter as the foremost beauty of Calcutta, insisted that she be shipped off to the Craigie relations in Calvinist Scotland. Craigie protested at this decision, saying that it was not only too hard on Lola but unwise.

"Large tears rolled down his cheeks," wrote Lola, when the General put her aboard the vessel bound for England. At the last moment Captain James, possibly afraid of losing his commission because of the scandal in which he had involved himself, boarded the ship in a show of taking his wife back to England, thus bolstering her mother's story that Lola needed medical care after a fall from a horse. And when, on the voyage, Lola had begun her intrigue with Captain Lennox, whom she had previously met, James had grounds for the separation which he later applied for, and provided the basis for Lola's reputation as a woman of scandalous conduct.

XXXII

By the fall of 1858, Lola was back in the United States and on a warm September day was visited in New York by the correspondent of the Sacramento *Union*, Corporal Trim. Trim wrote that Lola had established herself in a snug little wooden cottage on 19th Street, at the corner of Third Avenue. It was, said Trim, "one of those quiet little resting places which are yet visible here and there in the upper wards of the city." To Trim the cottage had all the charm of a country dwelling astray among the noises of the city. Shrubs and late blooming flowers surrounded it. It stood upon a swelling knoll, which gently sloped down in terraces surrounded by a garden wall. The tinkling of horsecar bells could be heard, and when Trim rang at Lola's door canaries were singing within.

Trim had originally met Lola at a theatre in the Bowery and when the maid showed him in he was invited to draw up a chair beside his hostess, who said, "Sit down and talk." He felt, as he later wrote, "the wonderful magnetism with which Lola impresses everything that comes in contact with her."

Trim's purpose in coming was to inform Lola that Pat Hull had died out in California, but the arrival of another guest prevented him from doing so. It was not an auspicious time for telling her of the death of her former husband and he decided that he would call again to impart this news to her. More and more guests assembled and were greeted by Lola before she reseated herself in a large armchair placed in an archway between the parlors.

Trim was struck by Lola's appearance, for she had cut her hair shorter and wore it in crisp curls close to her head. He noticed that she was pale and thin and that her great eyes were sunk in caverns. But she engaged in swift repartee with her guests, her white teeth as flashing and beautiful as ever, although Trim noticed that her dress was elegant it was carelessly put on and wrinkled. As she talked she rolled cigarettes, taking the tobacco from a Russian leather reticule hanging from the arm of her chair.

When more guests had arrived a game of cards was begun, and by eight P.M., when all those invited had assembled, dinner was announced. The dining room was in the front of the basement, a style peculiar to the period. It was hung with cages of birds and lavishly decorated with flowers, and on either side of the room, in the center of which stood a long dining table, were quaint sideboards heavily laden with valuable silver and ornaments.

When all the guests were seated the place of honor at Lola's right was taken by a Captain De Riviere. Corporal Trim was shocked to find this man held in such esteem, for De Riviere was known in New York for a scandal in which he had been embroiled and which had given the leading gossips of the city endless material for discussion. To Lola's left sat a young woman who had made herself obnoxious in political circles with her harangues on socialism. Also at the table were newspapermen, several attorneys, four wealthy and fast young men from Havana with whom Trim was familiar, several gentlemen noted as rather loose Bohemians, together with the nephew of the French General Bosquet, and one other woman whom he could not identify.

During dinner, which lasted until midnight, the company talked of art, of literature, of travel and finally of the latest murder, the Burdell case. De Riviere, a sabre cut showing up whitely in the lamplight on his cheek, exclaimed, "I tell you a woman killed Burdell and I'll show you how she did it." Showing himself to be familiar with Lola's household, he searched her sideboard until he came across a dagger of exquisite craftsmanship and with this in his hand he demonstrated the crime: "A man never struck those blows because a man's blow is downright. So! So!"

Lola was obviously embarrassed to have such a discussion at her table and at Riviere's re-enacting a crime while they were at dessert. "Now," she said, as calmly and gracefully as possible, "let us talk about something else."

As later they sat in the yard to watch the brilliant Donati Comet blazing in the sky, Trim wondered at Lola's choice of company. Perhaps, he was later to say, she could no longer gather about her anything more than social dregs. It was known, said Trim, that Lola suffered from an ailment and that it was making rapid progress against a constitution which was impaired by constant smoking and late hours.

Then in November Trim reported to his newspaper that Lola had suddenly sickened of the company she entertained at her cottage and had abruptly left for Europe. She had sailed for Ireland aboard the *Pacific*, landing at Galway on November 23rd. She appeared at the Round Room in Dublin as a lecturer early in December. From there she went to England, appearing at Manchester, Liverpool, Chester and Bristol, to be heard by packed auditoriums. Only at Bath, where she had attended school for eighteen months as a girl and where her mother had finally come from India to see her, was Lola met with an unfriendly and even hostile audience. There was no particular explanation for this coldness, the press of Bath merely expressing a dislike for their town's having been mentioned in connection with the scandalous case against Lola for her bigamous marriage to Heald.

Letters about Lola's appearance in Bath were written by the local residents and one of them went to a certain Mrs. Buchanan, the wife of a florist in New York. The effect of this letter upon Lola's future was considerable. Mrs. Buchanan's husband Isaac was a calculating man, and his wife was subservient enough to obey his orders, even when they were unscrupulously rapacious.

Twenty years had passed since Lola had been in Bath, and

until her recent revelations about her past in court and in her autobiography, no one there had known that Eliza—called Lola—Gilbert was the notorious Lola Montez. Naturally Bath rocked with the news, but Bath society frowned on such a career, and although many of the leading citizens armed with opera glasses went to look at the famous beauty, they were already quite certain that they did not approve of her. It was from such circles that the letter to Mrs. Buchanan emerged. But in Bath, as elsewhere, the Gilbert edition of the *Lectures and Life of Lola Montez* was selling for eighteen pence and being avidly read.

By the spring of 1859 Lola was lecturing in London, but by summer she was exhausted and forced to abandon this new career.

In Regent's Park one day at this time a correspondent for the New York *Tribune* witnessed an incident which gave him pause as he was strolling through. Two children ran screaming from a shaggy dog that was barking as it chased them. When the dog gave up the pursuit, he ran back to a lady dressed in black who was just entering the park. Indignantly the mothers went up to her to complain.

"My good woman," said the lady, "the dog will not hurt your children. He likes them and so do I." Then, summoning the children, she seated herself on a park bench, called the dog to her and bade the children get acquainted with him.

The women seated themselves beside the owner of "Gyp" and had no sooner done so than the lady in black took a Bible from her bag and began to read to them.

The correspondent of the *Tribune* moved closer, believing the woman must be some sort of religious fanatic. But to his surprise he recognized her as the former dancer, Lola Montez.

"Who I am," Lola was saying, "is no matter. Once I was as ignorant as you and very much more wicked. There was not a wicked thing that I did not do and though I had plenty of money and friends, yet I was never happy until I found out the beautiful truths of this little book."

Having read a line or two to the startled mothers, she rose and said, "I will see you here another day and tell you and read you much more." Then she gave them a few coppers for their children and wandered away.

The *Tribune* reporter hurried after Lola to interview her for his paper, and she told him she had been visiting the poor of London to distribute copies of the Bible to them. The reporter thought her sincerely religious, though a penitent Lola was hard to believe in.

The correspondent next reported that Lola had resolved to retire from the world to consecrate herself to a life of devotion.

She had saved a considerable amount of money from her lecture tours, and with this she leased a furnished house in Park Lane near Hyde Park. It was her intention to open a lodging house in order to secure a quiet living, and she invested four hundred pounds in the enterprise. But her talk of having lived a life of sin and her eagerness to read passages from the Bible to prospective boarders drove them away. Nor could she manage English servants and was soon in debt, beset with lawsuits and creditors. When her lease and furniture had to be sold, she was left with only fifty-six pounds, and so despondent was she at the time of the sale that when she was ordered out of the house she developed brain-fever. For a while it seemed she would die.

Then a kindly couple from Derbyshire who were visiting London heard of her plight. Wealthy and childless, though they had never met her they provided her with medical care and afterwards took her by train to their country home. Here, attended by nurses and servants, she recovered her health.

The summer was at its peak and Lola spent her time in a garden surrounded by a brick wall and a high hedge, which separated the forty acres of the estate from the roadway. When she was able to walk about she strolled in the nearby meadows where a herd of deer grazed. Feeling she might want to be alone, her hosts gave her their gate-keeper's cottage, which faced upon a garden filled with statues grouped about a fish pond where swans floated languidly. Later they also provided her with a horse to ride.

The elderly couple had by this time grown so fond of Lola that they asked her to remain with them to live as their daughter, offering to make her their heir. Lola, however, although grateful for all they had done for her, could talk of nothing but her desire to become a foreign missionary. Friends of the couple who saw her at this time felt that she lacked stability, although they did not doubt her sincerity.

By November of 1859 Lola decided that she would return to America, and when visited by the *Tribune* correspondent he discovered the origin of her interest in religion. She told him that when she had been spending her final days in Grass Valley someone had given her a book to read called *The Principles of Nature, the Divine Revelation and Voice to Mankind*, written "by and through Andrew Jackson Davis."

Said Lola, "The book gave me the curiosity to study the Bible." She said that when she had finally read the Bible she knew she must spend the rest of her life seeking to spread its message.

Instead of becoming a missionary, however, she embarked on another lecture tour—which turned out to be a miserable failure. She had begun to keep a diary and in it she wrote passages filled with self-castigation and bitterness. "What has the world ever given to me?" she asked. "And I have known all the world has to give—all! Nothing but shadows, leaving a wound in the heart hard to heal—a dark discontent."

Her last appearance upon a lecture platform was at the Melodeon in Boston, where a correspondent of the New York *Tribune* went to see her "holding fast to a pair of opera glasses." All over the hall opera glasses were raised as Lola appeared, for the rumor was abroad that the great beauty of Lola Montez was waning. In the soft light which fell upon her hair they could see little except that her features still appeared regular and pleasing. What shocked everyone was Lola's choice of a dress, for she wore a loose white gown, which was draped into folds reminiscent of the styles worn in biblical times. This attempt to hide her wasted form caused so much comment that even the far-away San Francisco *Bulletin* was moved to print an article on her renunciation of fashionable attire.

Her failing health caused her more and more to seek the consolation of religion. The spiritual feeling she had captured so often when she felt the presence of Dujarier began to take on new meaning. It was mystical, difficult to capture, as she had described it to an intimate or two in California, but this translation into the indefinable world of the spirit suddenly became all important. In her friendless groping for consolation she discovered a Divine Being who watched over the world. She told of searching the heavens upon a moonlit night and of finding a brilliant heavenly body fixed in the sky. This, she decided, was the Star of Bethlehem, luminous as it had been that night when Christ was born. She had found God and wrote, "The world cast me out, and He, the pure, the loving, took me in."

She began to attend the Methodist church and although she did not become a regular member of that denomination she admired them for their sincerity and their loyalty to their faith. She tried to put aside her regrets for Grass Valley and the memory of the fatal day when Noel Follin had persuaded her to leave her home and she had foolishly hearkened to his promises of a triumphant tour of Australia. "My calm days at the cottage are gone—gone. But I will not look back."

Accounts of Lola's activities at this time have been saved in letters of that period. Henry Chapman, an agent in New York, wrote that he one day encountered Lola walking in the Bowery and learned that she had been looking for him. Chapman took Lola to Taylor's restaurant, then one of the finest in New York, and they talked over dinner. "She had changed greatly," wrote Chapman with regret, "a change impossible to imagine."

Lola had been seeking him to ask him to manage her as a lecturer, since she had an offer for more engagements. Looking with consternation upon the faded and obviously ill beauty, Chapman evaded her request by saying that he was otherwise engaged. Lola told him that she was living quietly with a family and that she had acquired a belief in the after life.

Some time later she called on him, and he was moved to compassion by her appearance. "She was sick and wasting away. I shall never forget that interview. She said, 'I have atoned for all and am not afraid to die.' " Chapman felt that she knew she had not long to live.

A letter written by another person who met Lola at that time discloses how she occupied herself and where she lived from May to October of 1860. Lola rented two pleasant furnished rooms in a boarding house on Old Clover Road in Brooklyn. A number of the boarders were Methodists and she sometimes accompanied them to the Nathan Bangs Church nearby. Although she was then living under the name of Fanny Gibbons, because she did not wish to be identified with her notorious past, the minister knew who she was and called upon her, and when she returned the call his wife and daughters became very attached to her. On Sunday afternoons the ladies and gentlemen residing at the Clover Road boarding house gathered about an organ in the parlor to sing psalms. Lola showed a particular fondness for "Nearer My God To Thee," and "Rock of Ages." Again, these letters indicate that she often spoke as if she had a premonition that she was soon to die. One afternoon she said that she enjoyed these gatherings in the parlor very much and exclaimed to one of the guests, "Oh, I am so interested in those Methodists; they are so loyal, just like our Catholic people at home."

However, the other boarders, and this letter writer in particular, soon began to regard her with some alarm, for during her five months' residence she grew more and more eccentric and began to arouse the attention of strangers in the street. It was undoubtedly impossible for her to change her nature completely and although she had conquered her blazing temper and her imperiousness, she was still somewhat rebellious against convention and still sought affection by doing things which were unconsciously meant to draw attention to herself. No doubt this had taken the place of the love she had sought in her youth, when her mother had sent her away from home, and it still did.

So, as she walked toward Prospect Park in the evenings, she would stop the young people she encountered and ask each individual if he or she liked books. She carried with her copies of Pope's *Essay on Man* which she would give them, and she would go on distributing them to youngsters until she ran out of copies. When she reached Flatbush she would stop at a dairy for a drink of milk. Though she was clearly harmless, eventually people along this route began to avoid her.

At the beginning of October Lola went walking down Broadway with a sister of Louis Kossuth, the Hungarian patriot, who had been aboard the ship which had first brought her to America. At this point there occurred the first of two incidents which were to bring her life to a melancholy close, for it was now that Mrs. Buchanan, formerly of Bath, encountered her.

In California after Lola's death the alert editor of the Sacramento *Union* distrusted the whole account of Lola's final days given to the press by Mrs. Buchanan. So suspicious was he that he engaged a former Chinese resident of Sacramento, Ching Foo, to make an investigation of the circumstances. Ching Foo was thorough and what he discovered about the rapacity of the Buchanans has been verified by a letter, still in existence,which confirmed the circumstances he uncovered.

Mrs. Buchanan's story was that she had attended the Montrose Seminary at Bath with Lola. One day while out walking with her husband on Broadway she passed a lady she thought she recognized as an old school mate. Her husband, claimed Mrs. Buchanan, persuaded her to retrace her steps and intercept the lady. There were many incredible elements in this story, including the fact that twenty-two years had passed since she had seen Lola, who was then only fourteen, and that the latter was now wasted away, hollow-eyed and sunken cheeked.

Even more incredible was Mrs. Buchanan's claim that she did not know that Eliza Gilbert was Lola Montez. She could scarcely have avoided knowing it, since the newpapers had been full of the story for the past two years and Mrs. Buchanan was in constant correspondence with relatives and friends in Bath who had heard Lola lecture. In fact, even Lola's mother when she read of her daughter's illness in a London newspaper had turned to Mrs. Buchanan's relatives in Bath in order to find out where her daughter was. Mrs. Buchanan, therefore, must have known it was Lola the day she stopped her on the street.

Lola was taken under Mrs. Buchanan's wing, urged to join Mrs. Buchanan's church, and was soon showing every confidence in this friend who had appeared out of nowhere. The Buchanans, however, moved with caution and although they invited Lola to come to live with them, they did not press her to do so.

Lola had given up her rooms in the Clover Road boarding house and she had not yet decided what to do in the future, when once more she went for a walk down Broadway accompanied by the sister of Louis Kossuth.

While Lola had been in England Noel Follin's daughter, Caroline, had left school to marry an officer in the United States Navy. Lola had previously met the officer and when Caroline had written to Lola, asking her if she approved of him, Lola had answered that she was delighted with her choice of husband. Caroline had gone on her honeymoon to a distant place and had just returned on the day when Lola again walked down Broadway.

Seeing Caroline, Lola rushed up to her impulsively and embraced her. The girl drew back coldly. "Madam," she said, "I do not know you."

Lola looked at her in disbelief, repeating, "Not know me? I am Lola—Lola Montez."

The answer was cold: "Madam, I do not know you. I never saw you before and if you persist in speaking to me, I will call a policeman."

Up until the time of her marriage, Lola had supported the girl, given her her clothes and her education. Now the ungrateful Caroline had no further use for the woman who had befriended her, and Lola returned sadly to her companion and went home. That night she was found lying in her hotel room unconscious. Her left side was paralyzed, her face was twisted to one side, and she was unable to speak.

The news of this seizure did not immediately reach the Buchanans and when they heard of it Lola had already been taken out to Astoria, Long Island, by friends who had offered her shelter. The weather was mild and Lola sat out in the garden, surrounded by late blooming flowers. A newspaperman who went to see her wrote sincerely, even if without originality, that it made his heart bleed to see this formerly dashing and beautiful woman so changed. Lola was dressed in a morning robe above which she looked out at the newspaperman from hollow eyes. She made repeated efforts to speak an intelligible word but was unable to do so. From her friends he learned that she was melancholy and depressed.

The news of her stroke was published not only in California and New York but in London. Lady Craigie, unable to learn from the newspaper accounts where her daughter was staying, obtained from Mrs. Buchanan's relatives the information necessary to track down the Buchanans, hoping through them to locate Lola. To the Buchanans of Bath, Lady Craigie revealed her intention to go to America, which information was relayed to Mrs. Buchanan in New York some time before Lola's mother arrived there.

By the time Lady Craigie had sailed from England, in November of 1860, Lola was able to walk and had partially recovered her speech. Her friends in Astoria encouraged her to talk and learned that she abhorred her mother—and with sufficient reason.

From Mary Oliver, the sister Lady Craigie had disowned, Lola had learned that her mother had been a music hall performer who had lived with the East Indian Army officer, Captain Gilbert, and that after being away for some time Gilbert had returned one day to discover that Elizabeth Oliver was about to bear his child. Elizabeth had a furious temper, she did not want the baby, and she was not overly eager to marry anyone as poor as Captain Gilbert. Yet the scorn Lady Gilbert showed toward her son's mistress piqued the beautiful and socially ambitious Elizabeth to give up her ideas of a wealthy marriage and accept this far less desirable arrangement. Lola confessed to her friends (for she was eager to confess these days) that she had not been born to Elizabeth two years after the marriage took place, but only two months later.

Lola was always regarded as a burden by her mother, who soon turned her over to an amah in India, an arrangement which continued even after Gilbert died and Elizabeth had married Craigie. But when at the age of six Lola had begun to be praised for her beauty and her step-father showed that he worshipped his step-child, her mother made plans to get rid of her . . . the plans that, as Lola now saw, had launched her entire tempestuous, star-crossed career.

Miserably unhappy after she was sent to Scotland, subjected to the unbending rigidity of General Craigie's old maid sister, refused re-admission to her rightful home in Calcutta, and thrown on the mercy of Sir Jasper Nichols, Lola had been an unwanted and homeless child until her mother had noticed her existence only long enough to try to marry her off to Sir Abraham Lumly. Failing in this, Lady Craigie had scorned Lola after her marriage to Thomas James. The rest of her career the world knew. And now the mother who had refused to acknowledge that she was alive had decided to come to America.

When Mrs. Buchanan rushed to Astoria to tell her this, Lola became almost hysterical, declaring that she did not wish to see her—that her mother could only be coming because she wanted Lola's jewels and money.

Mrs. Buchanan then urged Lola to come to her house to live. She would hide her in the attic bedroom of their New York home and keep Elizabeth Craigie from finding her, would obtain a nurse and provide her with every comfort. Lola was, however, persuaded to stay on where she was for a time and might have remained there had not the newspapers discovered her whereabouts just as Lady Craigie reached New York.

Before Lola's mother was settled into her hotel, Count Blum, who had known Lola in Paris, went to Astoria to call on her. He had worked out a scheme by which Lola could petition Ludwig of Bavaria for the restoration of her income, and had already drawn up a paper giving himself a large percentage of any money which might be collected. The idea of this cry for help seemed to distress her and she took pen in hand only after much persuasion by Blum. But as she started to sign her name she stopped, and throwing the pen down, exclaimed, "I won't do it!"

A week or two before this Lola had written to a Dr. John Cooper, then practicing in New York, asking that he make a professional call upon her. It was probably difficult for the doctor to make the trip out to Astoria, but when he received a second letter asking him if he made a habit of investigating the moral character of prospective patients before calling upon them, the doctor felt forced to respond.

He found Lola well cared for but in a state of apprehension at her mother's pending visit. She confided to him that her mother had ruined her life because she was jealous of her, and begged the doctor to help her to get to Mrs. Buchanan's house, where her friend would hide her.

At the Buchanan house Lola had a nurse, Mrs. Hamilton, and saw an Episcopal minister, who was much impressed by her return to religion and wrote of visiting her there.

Whether or not Lady Craigie saw Lola has never been made clear. As far as can be determined Lady Craigie did little but ask a few questions of Dr. Cooper as to the nature of Lola's illness, then very shortly she departed for England again, saying that she would soon return. She left a sum equivalent to about ten dollars for Lola and seemed anxious to be done with the whole unpleasant business.

Once in England, she deluged Mrs. Buchanan with letters, however, but received only one letter in reply. It was filled with nothing but lies. Doctor Cooper had been dismissed from the case, and did not therefore know that the patient was no longer in the Buchanan household. Mrs. Buchanan avoided mentioning him when she wrote her totally untrue reply to Lady Craigie, in which she stated: "I should have written to you before this had I anything new to communicate. Your daughter is recovering her health fast. She is now able to walk alone with very little lameness and looks better in health than I have ever seen her. Mrs. Hamilton is very attentive and she appreciates all the comforts she receives from her. Soon after you left I thought it prudent to call in a consulting physician, feeling the great responsibility resting on me. She drives out in a carriage once a week and enjoys it very much."

Lola's rapid recovery rather bewildered Lady Craigie and she wrote to Dr. Cooper, "I hope you will kindly excuse the trouble I am giving you, for from *no one* could I get such reliable information regarding her state of health as from you. I was well satisfied at your *judicious* treatment of her and considered her progressing most favorably. When I left New York, in a conversation I had with you one day you said she had what is called softening of the Brain; is this still your opinion, or has she got over it, and what does she now suffer from?"

This letter seems far more concerned with keeping the true nature of Lola's illness discreetly unrevealed than with anxiety for an only child who may be dying, and certainly is quite pointed in its interest in how long the patient might live. It is not given over to alarm or sorrow. This was a cool analyst looking the situation over and carefully weighing the possibilities. "You will very much oblige by giving me *all* the particulars you can regarding her. My journey to New York, sudden and back so soon, and other things while there upset me very much, and I have been *very far* from well since my return. I was very sorry I did not see you the day before I left, as I expected, and wished; I would have been glad to have a little private conversation with you—I wish this letter to be *private* and *confidential*. I never experienced so severe a winter as this is. I feel the cold very, very much, the mildest winter upsets me."

With this letter Elizabeth Craigie enclosed a copy of the letter Mrs. Buchanan had sent her. Dr. Cooper, when attending Lola at the Buchanan house, had not seen any consultants and he must have been sure that no such rapid recovery as the letter from the florist's wife described could possibly have occurred.

A letter written by Mrs. Cooper confirms the truth of what the investigator for the Sacramento *Union* later discovered. Dr. Cooper learned from Count Blum, with whom he was acquainted, that Lola was in a miserable room, wretchedly cared for, and in much suffering. The doctor may have believed that Lola chose this residence, after leaving the Buchanans, out of a desire to do penance for her past life, for when Cooper saw her, Lola, perhaps from pride, never said why she had left the florist's home and seemed to be concerned more with how her mother had tracked her down, telling him that her mother had been after her money because she reasoned that a woman who had been the favorite of a king would have jewels and wealth.

At the time Lady Craigie wrote Dr. Cooper, her daughter was already slowly sinking to her death. Lola at this precarious point lay quietly watching the heavens for the Star of Bethlehem. A minister of a fashionable parish went to see her and read passages of the Scriptures to her. He later wrote of Lola that in the last week she seemed to draw great comfort from this. If the minister was shocked at the condition of the room in which she lay, he too may have believed that she was practicing a penitent Christianity. He had seen her surrounded with luxuries in the Buchanan home only a few weeks before and, like Dr. Cooper, must have thought her choice of a residence voluntary.

On the 17th of January, 1861, the minister was reading to her and as he paused she said, "Tell me, tell me more of my dear Savior." With these words she placed her hand upon the Bible and in that instant died.

The next day Mrs. Buchanan took charge. She went out to Greenwood Cemetery in Brooklyn during a storm, and selected a grave on a slope overlooking an artificial lake.

Few followed the funeral cortege on the long trip to the grave, but Dr. Cooper, steadfast in friendship, went all the way to the cemetery on that bitterly cold and dark winter day. Dr.

Brown, the rector of Grace Church, more of a social arbiter than a man of religion, conducted the ceremony, and as he hurried through without interest, Dr. Cooper was horrified to hear him whisper in an aside to the sexton, "Hurry up with that dirt, darn you!"

When Lola's estate came to be settled she was found to have nothing left, although a sum of $1,200 was later discovered in a bank and used to pay for her funeral, the cemetery plot, and Dr. Cooper.

It was then that Ching Foo, making the investigation for the Sacramento *Union*, decided that he would go to 194 W. 7th Street to look at the room in which Lola had died, Mrs. Buchanan, upon being interviewed by the newspapers, having told them that Lola had died with every comfort provided for her.

The address proved to be a tenement in the district which was later to become known as Hell's Kitchen. Entering the room from which Lola's body had been removed after her death, Ching Foo found it just as it had been. Over part of the window was nailed an old piece of ragged carpet. There was neither a bed nor a chair in the room and upon the floor, on a filthy mattress, were three old coverlets.

When he questioned the other tenants in the building, Ching Foo was told that Mrs. Buchanan had rented the room and brought Lola there, leaving her in charge of an old woman. Whenever Lola attempted to drag herself painfully out of the room to speak to the other tenants, the old woman rushed out after her, sometimes dragging her back by the hair. This old woman was a filthy hag with an evil disposition, and Mrs. Buchanan had never once returned to see Lola until after her death. She had provided nothing in the way of comforts for the invalid.

Ching Foo then learned that Lola still had had the diamond necklace, worth twenty thousand dollars, which Ludwig had given her, besides a collection of other jewels, worth a like sum, when she had gone to the Buchanans. Lola had trusted Mrs.

Buchanan completely, and in exchange for a promise from Mrs. Buchanan that she would be looked after for the rest of her days, had signed a legal paper giving everything she had left to the wife of the florist. As soon as the paper was signed, Mrs. Buchanan had moved Lola from her house to the tenement on 7th Street.

Thus ended the life of Lola Montez, who had danced before kings and toppled a throne.

Bibliography

Aretz, Gertrude, *The Elegant Woman* (London, 1847)

Aikman, Duncan, *Calamity Jane and the Lady Wildcats* (New York, 1927)

Asseline, Alfred, *Victor Hugo Intime* (Paris, 1885)

Ayres, Col. James J., *Gold and Sunshine* (Boston, 1922)

Barbon, Alfred, *Victor Hugo* (Paris, 1885)

Bell, A. Craig, *Alexandre Dumas* (London, 1950)

Benjamin, Rene, *Balzac* (New York, 1927)

Bolitho, William, *Twelve Against The Gods* (New York, 1941)

Brett, Oliver, *Wellington* (New York, 1929)

Chandler, Peleg W., *The Law Reporter*, August 1846, Vol. IX (Boston, 1847)

Channon, Henry, *The Ludwigs of Bavaria* (New York, 1933)

d'Auvergne, Edmund B., *Lola Montez* (London, 1909)

De Amicis, Edmondo, *Studies of Paris* (New York, 1879)

de Pourtalas, Guy, *Franz Liszt* (New York, 1926)

de Pourtalas, Guy, *The Mad King* (New York, 1928)

Doumic, Rene, *George Sand* (New York and London, 1910)

Ebenthal, Hildegarde, *The Tragedy of a Throne* (New York and London, 1917)

Finch, Henry T., *Wagner and His Works*, Vol. I (New York, 1893)

Flower, Sir Newman, *Just As It Happened* (New York, 1950)

Gagey, Edmond M., *San Francisco Stage: A History* (New York, 1950)

Goldberg, Isaac, *Queen of Hearts* (New York, 1936)

Grant, Elliott, *The Career of Victor Hugo* (Cambridge, 1945)

Gribble, Francis, *Alexandre Dumas, Father and Son* (New York, 1930)

Hall, Sir John, *The Bravo Mystery and Other Cases* (London, 1923)

Harper, George McLean, *Sainte-Beuve* (New York, 1909)

Hornblow, Arthur, *A History of the Theatre in America* (Philadelphia, 1919)

Howe, Marie Jenney, *George Sand: The Search for Love* (New York, 1927)

Jackson, Joseph Henry, *Tintypes in Gold* (New York, 1939)

Josephson, Matthew, *Victor Hugo* (New York, 1942)

Kinyon, Edmund, *The Northern Mines* (Grass Valley, 1949)

Leslie, Mrs. Frank, *A Pleasure Trip from Gotham to the Golden Gate* (London, 1877)

Lewis, Oscar, *Lola Montez* (San Francisco, 1938)

Massett, Stephen C., *What Jeems Pipes of Pipesville Saw and Did* (New York, 1863)

Maurois, Andre, *Byron* (New York, 1930)

Mayne, Ethel Colburn, *Lola Montez* (London, 1909)

McCabe, John H., *McCabe Theatrical Journals and Diary Vol. II* (unpublished)

MacMinn, George, *The Theatre of the Golden Era* (Caldwell, 1941)

Millard, Bailey, *History of the San Francisco Bay Region*, Vol. III (San Francisco, 1924)

Montez, Lola, *Autobiography and Lectures of Lola Montez* (Paris, 1858)

Newman, Ernest, *Wagner as Man and Artist* (New York, 1924)

Odell, George Clinton, *Odell's Annals of the New York Stage*, Vol. 1 (New York, 1927)

Orr, Lyndon, *Famous Affinities of History* (New York and London, 1914)

Poths-Wegner, Friedrich, *Lola Montez, Historischer Roman* (Leipzig, 1916)

Kobbé, Gustav, *The Loves of Great Composers* (New York, 1904)

Rogers, Andy, *A Hundred Years of Rip and Roarin' Rough and Ready* (Rough and Ready, 1952)

Rogers, Cameron, *Gallant Ladies* (New York, 1928)

Rourke, Constance, *Troupers of the Gold Coast* (New York, 1928)

Sainte-Beuve, Charles, *Portraits Littéraires* (Paris, 1829)

Schermerhorn, Elizabeth W., *Seven Strings of the Lyre* (New York, 1927)

Seyd, Felizia, *Romantic Rebel* (New York, 1940)

Sitwell, Edith, *Victoria of England* (Boston, 1936)

Troubat, Jules, *Saint-Beuve, Intime* (Paris, 1903)

Weinstock, Herbert, *Chopin: The Man and His Music* (New York, 1949)

Werner, M. R., *Barnum* (New York, 1922)

Winwar, Frances, *George Sand and Her Times* (New York, 1947)

Wyndham, Horace, *The Magnificent Montez* (New York, 1937)

Zweig, Stefan, *Balzac* (New York, 1946)

Note: Specific references for the material used in this book are on file at the California Room of the California State Library, Sacramento.

Index